Alonzo Hall Quint

The Potomac and the Rapidan

Army Notes from the Failure at Winchester to the Reënforcement of Rosecrans

Alonzo Hall Quint

The Potomac and the Rapidan
Army Notes from the Failure at Winchester to the Reënforcement of Rosecrans

ISBN/EAN: 9783337416959

Printed in Europe, USA, Canada, Australia, Japan

Cover: Foto ©Suzi / pixelio.de

More available books at **www.hansebooks.com**

THE

POTOMAC AND THE RAPIDAN.

ARMY NOTES,

*FROM THE FAILURE AT WINCHESTER TO THE
REËNFORCEMENT OF ROSECRANS.*

1861-3.

BY

ALONZO H. QUINT,

CHAPLAIN OF THE SECOND MASSACHUSETTS INFANTRY.

BOSTON:
CROSBY AND NICHOLS.
NEW YORK: O. S. FELT.
1864.

ELECTROTYPED AT THE

Boston Stereotype Foundry,

No. 4 Spring Lane.

I DEDICATE THIS VOLUME

TO THE

True and Faithful Wife,

WHO HAS NOBLY BORNE, FOR HER COUNTRY'S SAKE, THE PAIN OF LONG

SEPARATION, AND THE CARE OF CHILDREN, AND WHO STILL

PATIENTLY WAITS FOR HER HUSBAND'S RETURN;

ONE OF THE THOUSANDS OF BRAVE WOMEN

WHOSE HEARTS SUFFER IN THIS

SACRED WAR.

PREFACE.

When I had the good fortune, in the spring of the year 1861, to be appointed Chaplain of the Second Massachusetts Infantry, I was asked by the proprietors of the *Congregationalist* to become a correspondent of that paper. I did so; and have written, with tolerable regularity, ever since. The Letters, so furnished, form the basis of the present volume.

This book is, however, far from being a mere reprint. I have omitted much; and I have also added much from private notes, especially of facts, which could not properly be made public at the time of their occurrence. I have revised the whole as carefully as the very limited time at my disposal will allow.

In no sense do these pages assume to be a history. They contain merely the frankest record of impressions received by an eye witness, of places and scenes in our eventful campaigns; while, of my peculiar duties, I have never avoided nor intruded mention. Friends have urged me to believe that these observations may be worth adding, in this more permanent form, to the materials of the future historian.

If any one discovers a change of feeling, from that of political antagonism to the administration (generally obscure, of course), to that of hearty confidence in the ability, honesty, and wisdom of its present head, I am not careful to deny it. Regretting deeply some acts, yet I wonder only that public affairs have been conducted so well, and promise so auspiciously.

A somewhat parallel work, — the Record of the Second Massachusetts Infantry, — though covering the same campaigns, will prove to have an entirely different scope.

I acknowledge my great indebtedness to the scholarly taste and accuracy of my friend, Mr. Samuel Burnham, of Boston, for his assistance in my absence. The index, also, is entirely his work.

CAMP OF THE SECOND MASSACHUSETTS INFANTRY,
ARMY OF THE CUMBERLAND, March, 1864.

CONTENTS.

POTOMAC AND THE RAPIDAN.

CHAPTER I.

THE FAILURE AT WINCHESTER.

NEAR DARNESTOWN, MD., September 6, 1861.

You think it strange that I do not write. But I remember that machinery used to suffer more by standing still a few months, than it would have done from the wear of use; and that, when started, it ran heavily till the dust and dirt worked out and off. The very oil that had lubricated the bearings hardened into a hinderance.

How could you expect, then, my mental machinery to start into smooth running, after a few weeks of such change as that from a quiet village pastorate to the life of a camp, and the total cessation of all writing save the hasty epistles to a few, very few friends, to revered and beloved father and mother, and to the two, mother and child, whose faces are first in thought at morn, and last at night? It used to take time to get into writing order after returning from one's summer vacation; if that so diverted the mind from its usual current, how much greater the effect where *reveille* wakes

(9)

one at morning dawn, where guard-mounting, parade, drill, and scouting are the day's history, and where tattoo and taps are the last sound before sleep — save when hostile shots call for more sentries, or the long roll starts every soldier to arms ; where the very Sabbath morn is the hour for weekly inspection ; where one's congregation is marshalled by the drum-beat, and marches by companies, with soldierly tread, to the grove of worship, to stand or sit in ranks, and where your very choir is detailed by orders, like a picket guard! Nor are you to forget that the comforts of civilization are not always at hand. You sit at a comfortable desk, and have a good pen (provided it is quill), and an inkstand. I seldom see ink, as a fluid. I sit now on a bundle of straw. I hold my paper on my knees. A canvas shields me from the pouring rain. On my door there is no such ingenious catch as guards your sanctum (partly because I have no door), and no man is barred from the chaplain's tent. My time is occupied. We are continually moving. Imagine, therefore, the difficulty of writing.

And now, when I am virtuously determined, what shall I write about? War? I have no engagements to describe. We have been in an enemy's land, it is true, and our sentinels have been fired upon night after night. We took our place in a noble column of twenty thousand men, burning to fight, but, within ten miles of the enemy, our general, like a King of France, —

> " With twice ten thousand men,
> Marched up a hill, and then marched down again, —

and left Johnston to go unchecked to fatal Manassas. But no bloody scenes have we yet experienced, though the bullets are restless in our muskets.

I could write of leaving home ; of a dear church still in

memory ; of the crowd and hurrahs which speeded us ; of the last hand-shake at the railway with as dear a friend as pastor or man ever had ; of a little note received there, now treasured near the heart ; of the curve which hid the eight years' home at last ; of the real ovation in New York ; of a long, wearying journey, night and day, across New Jersey, sweeping through Central Pennsylvania, meeting the fires of the iron furnaces at morning gray, dipping our hands and bathing our faces in the beautiful river of the Lehigh Valley, dashing down the magnificent wheat-fields of the Cumberland Valley, across the lordly Susquehanna at Harrisburg, making no rest till we enter Hagerstown at midnight, there for the first time to meet pacing sentinels, and hear the peremptory " Halt ! " at every corner ; of the marching to the Potomac, camping a night by its waters, of fording at dawn, entering Virginia ; of passing by old skirmish fields and deserted camps of rebellion ; of many a hard and toilsome march ; of camps where every man who slept slept upon his arms. And now we wait in readiness for whatever orders may come ; and when the fray comes, Massachusetts blood will be true.

Of a chaplain's position I will write to-day, though with but a few months' experience. Could the opportunities for good here, and the strange fascinations of this strange life be felt, not a minister in Massachusetts but would long for these scenes. Our government did well to establish this office. Do not believe the burlesque which describes a chaplain's position as useless or uncomfortable. He must meet hardships. Sometimes he may go hungry. Often, perhaps, he must make, with others, the ground his bed, with no covering but the skies. Often will he be wet and tired. But one with a good constitution draws only new life from these things. He is invigorated ; and headaches are unknown ;

and fastidiousness of appetite vanishes; and fear of cold air
ends.   Sunburnt and rough he becomes, but he is the more
a man.   And the more a minister becomes a *man*, the better
he can fulfil his noble mission.

There is every opportunity for usefulness.   Our officers
welcome every effort for the religious good of the regiment.
Our men meet openly and frankly every advance which they
feel comes from the heart.   Every privilege a chaplain asks
for (if he is wise enough to confine himself to his own affairs,
and regard the duties required of the men) is freely granted.
" May I have evening prayer-meetings occasionally? " I
asked of our colonel.   " Certainly," said he, " every night
in the week, if you wish."   The hour or place of public worship is at my own disposal.   I have the freest entrance to
every tent.   I have the privileges of an officer without his
vexations.   I have countersigns, and what is at present an
exceptional case, I can cross the lines at pleasure.   I distribute such books and papers as I please.   With much that
is painful to meet, — pains of body and evils of conduct which
jar upon the nerves, — yet the opportunity for good is abundant.

Then there are special conditions which help usefulness.
While it is impossible to know all the men, yet one is armed
with many a letter from mothers and sisters.   One learns
the circumstances of many young men.   The hospital makes
acquaintance with the sick.   The very care of post-office
helping brings personal knowledge of many home ties.   The
discipline of a regiment, also, is favorable to the encouragement of good habits.   The very rule of obedience to which
all are bound, illustrates obedience to God.   The necessary
trust in commanders is a faint image of needed trust in God.
The punishment of wrong strikes at the root of sickly ideas
as to God's indifference to sin.   And the constant change of

place and of the kind of duty easily illustrates the faith of
one who " went out not knowing whither he went."

But the chief advantage is in the thorough breaking up of
old associations and habits of life. New scenes have dis-
placed the old. The old formality is ended. Intercourse
between minister and soldier is free and familiar — far different from that in the stereotyped localities where the parishioner sleeps in his hired pew. An unknown freshness and
life is the rule. The crust which grows over men at home
is broken. Society is disintegrated ; it crystallizes in new
forms. There is no time to settle into chronic dulness.
Events are too rapid to allow of bondage to form. Men in
proximity to danger are not insensible. Our New England
men are not ashamed to acknowledge their need of God's
help, and many a petition goes up in silence when they start
on some expedition.

It is not strange that one forgets entirely the momentous
question whether Scripture should precede singing, or singing
precede Scripture ; whether the congregation should, during
singing, face the minister or the choir ; whether standing in
prayer is a saving ordinance ; whether it is wicked for a
minister to disuse the razor. All these things are vital,
doubtless, at home ; but here, where men have taken their
lives in their hands at their country's call, such formalities
seem trivial. Pardon me, if I suggest, also, that one forgets
even his denomination, though far from forgetting the dear
friends with whom he has taken sweet counsel. Whether
immersion is better than sprinkling, or bishop than minister,
or predestination than free-will, — all are swallowed up in
the vital questions of life or death, God's favor or his frown,
the broad Fatherhood, and the unity of discipleship. In such
a changed life, written sermons are forgotten, and pulpits

2

are obsolete. The minister and a thousand men stand up face to face and heart to heart, ignorant but that before another day the ranks may be thinned.

DARNESTOWN, MD.   From notes of July 10-20, 1861.

WE joined General Patterson's command on the 12th of July. It was a pleasant afternoon when we entered Martinsburg, and found the road lined with soldiers who seemed to have no special occupation that day.   Doubtless the men were brave men, but their less than three months' service, many of them under poor officers, had failed to give to many regiments a soldierly appearance.   It seemed exactly as if everybody was bent on a holiday excursion.   But the men were in the best spirits, and eager to do something in the fighting line. We camped with the rest, and began to "forage" for information.

We learned that General Patterson's force had assembled at Chambersburg, where he took command about the first of June.   He had advanced to near the Potomac about a fortnight afterward, and on the 16th of June crossed half or more of his force into Virginia by the Williamsport ford, but on the next day, or day after, had returned to the Maryland side.

No further movement had been made until the 2d of July. On that day he recrossed into Virginia, meeting no opposition save from a few skirmishers.   But at Falling Waters, a little stream five or six miles further on, he encountered sufficient force of the enemy to bring on a smart little action, in which he drove the enemy for two miles.   When we passed over the road, ten days afterward, the broken fences and rem-

nants of equipments thrown away in flight showed unmistakably the rout of the rebels. General Patterson stopped pursuit,
but on the next day entered Martinsburg without opposition.

Nine days more had elapsed when our regiment joined the
army at Martinsburg. Wonder was quite freely expressed
that so much delay had taken place, both before leaving
Maryland and after arriving at Martinsburg; but this was
only camp talk. Orders were issued, however, on the 14th,
to be ready to move the next morning; and the hills around
Martinsburg were brilliantly lighted that evening by the fires
where rations were being cooked for the march. It appeared
high time that some movement was made, if the general expected to use his men, as their three months' term was nearly
ended, — our own regiment being, I think, the only three
years' one in his command. The rebel General Johnston was
well known to be between us and Winchester, and everybody
was in excellent humor at the prospect of advance.

We did move on Monday morning. The army was
marched on two parallel roads. Huge wagon trains accompanied us. Our forces were generally reckoned at about
twenty thousand men.

We reached Bunker Hill in the afternoon. If the enemy
had been there, he had left before we reached the dirty hamlet. There were plenty of rumors that he was on a great
variety of sides of us; but if he was, he kept quiet. We
bivouacked. Next day we heard stories of terrible obstructions on the roads. Johnston, men said, was at Winchester,
with forty thousand men, sixty pieces of artillery, savage
earthworks, and miles of rifle-pits. I do not think that anybody believed much of the talk; certainly, everybody wanted
to try the matter.

And on Wednesday morning, we moved. It seemed that

the hopes of the army were to be gratified. A little puzzled
at first we were; for we took a road eastward, while Winchester lay southward. But "we are going to flank them;
we go down on another road, and avoid all the obstructions."
So we went on, crossing a creek to which an old road, just
repaired, led us. When, however, we turned toward Charlestown, and thus away from Winchester, perplexity was felt,
and then displeasure.

The idea generally held had been, that our object was to
whip Johnston. But I had picked up the fact, from what an
officer knew, and what his military experience told him
ought to be, that General Patterson's movements were in
correspondence with those of General McDowell in front of
Washington, and that the recovery of Winchester was of
little importance compared with the need of keeping Johnston
there. I confess I could not see how that was to be done,
but I do not understand strategy.

How angry the men were on finding they were going to
Charlestown! They called it a retreat. From that moment
they lost confidence.

Of proceedings at Charlestown I saw nothing, because
our regiment was sent on the next day to occupy Harper's
Ferry. We did so, and received a flag which the women
had privately prepared to present to the first regiment of
Union troops which should enter the town.

The corps came on to Harper's Ferry on Sunday, the 21st.
Then we learned that Johnston had left Winchester; that
General Patterson had appealed to the troops to remain
beyond their term of service, and march on the enemy; and
that almost all had refused, on the ground that the time for
advance had been thrown away, and they would not serve
under General Patterson. These were camp stories, it is true,
but I think they were correct.

Very soon, General Patterson was relieved. General Banks took command. His first act, I believe, was to cross to the Maryland side. The three months' men rapidly left. Of those still there the general knew the feeling perfectly. Three years' men came rapidly in. Colonel Gordon was continued in charge of the Ferry, and three companies of the Massachusetts Second were left on the Virginia side, under command of Lieutenant-Colonel Andrews. There we lay, with that part of Virginia lost, until, in the latter part of August, the whole Corps moved to their present position.

Many details have come to light, of course, in the nearly two years since the foregoing was noted down. Who was to blame, if blame existed, is a matter for military men to decide. The people were indignant then because their expectations were not fulfilled; so was the Corps, because not led against the enemy. It seems settled that General McDowell would have conquered at Bull Run, but for the few thousand men which, led by General Johnston, reënforced the rebel army. General Patterson, it was alleged, wasted time, both north of the Potomac and at Winchester. I have stated already that the same feeling prevailed in his command. He declared that he waited for transportation, and also for harnesses for the artillery horses, while north of the river, and that at Martinsburg he was actually keeping ·Johnston at Winchester. That he recrossed the Potomac on the 16th of June, he insists, was necessary, because General Scott took away at that time all his regulars and some other troops, and left him without a single piece of artillery, in front of superior forces. His turning off at Charlestown, he says, was only in pursuance of a plan, previously assented to in Washington, to abandon the long Williamsport line of supplies, and secure Harper's Ferry as his base. But that

that was approved as an earlier project, and not as a retreat, seems clear.   He believed in the stories of large forces
at Winchester, which hardly another man probably did.
The truth has appeared that Johnston could never have had
over fifteen thousand men, even if more than twelve.   General Patterson's force, by his own estimate, was eighteen
thousand and two hundred effective men, consisting of seventeen and a half Pennsylvania regiments, five New York, and
one each from New Hampshire, Massachusetts (three years),
Indiana, and Wisconsin, — averaging six hundred and fifty
men each, — with one thousand cavalry and artillery.   On
the day we left Martinsburg, the three months' men had from
four days to nearly a month to serve, two thirds having less
than a fortnight.   Most of these, it is true, were raw troops ;
but so were Johnston's.

When General Patterson left Bunker Hill, on the 17th,
he thought he had accomplished what was expected of him ;
namely, the detaining of Johnston at Winchester until after the
date assigned by General Scott for the advance of McDowell,
the 16th.   A longer experience in the field would perhaps
have forbade his depending on a promised date of a battle
yet to be fought.   Whether, however, he could have detained
Johnston at Winchester, puzzles an ordinary thinker.   How
any " demonstration " could have kept Johnston from leaving
that town any time he chose, is hard to see.   For Winches-·
ter was exactly between the position of General Patterson
and the point of railway Johnston would aim at to go to
Manassas.   The rebels cared nothing for Winchester.   Bull
Run was the important place.   To threaten Winchester
would not keep a rebel army there.   If Patterson approached
Winchester on one side, Johnston could certainly march off
on the other, which was the way to Manassas.

Whether General Patterson should have attacked Winchester at an earlier date, is another question. He thought it a useless attempt. We now know that the forces there were small, and that the defences were contemptible. But he did not believe so then ; and able officers agreed with him. We have no right to judge a commander by data we now have, but which he could not then have.

I have heard able military men say that Patterson's position was wrong from the beginning; that he should have occupied Harper's Ferry early, securing rapid supplies, and have taken position to command the Shenandoah fords. Then, if Johnston moved towards Manassas, he must have exposed himself greatly ; or, General Patterson, if he preferred, could have reached Bull Run as early, at least, as Johnston. But of this matter I am not competent to speak. Certain it is, that on the day when Patterson turned back to Charlestown, Johnston, who appears to have been doing precisely what Patterson was sent to do, — detain his enemy in the valley, — was satisfied that he had succeeded, and immediately started for Bull Run.

NEAR DARNESTOWN, MD., September, 21, 1861.

THREE weeks have passed away since we encamped on this spot, — how many of us I must not tell, though probably the enemy know with sufficient accuracy, from the traitors with which this section abounds. There is no harm in saying, however, that while General McClellan is in command of this whole "Army of the Potomac," the immediate charge of the troops this side of Tennallytown (a few miles north of Georgetown) is divided between General Banks — in whose

division we are — and Brigadier-General Stone, who is
located further up the river. Thus the north bank of the
Potomac is lined with a fine army. As it becomes evident
that the enemy may cross, if cross at all, above Washington.
our position becomes important. On the opposite bank are
rebel troops in plenty, with whom ours exchange various
kinds of courtesies, sometimes with good-natured greetings,
sometimes with crashing shot and bursting shell, or with the
Enfield minies, which leap a mile or so at a jump. In such
a neighborhood, we are by no means indifferent, when there
comes, as it did last night at two o'clock, " Be ready for the
field at a moment's notice." We were ready ; the muskets
of the Massachusetts Second are never out of order ; its cartridge-boxes are full ; its courage is always high ; its order
perfect ; its bearing stalwart, firm, and solid ; its material
active, hardy, and brave, — embracing old soldiers of the
Mexican and of the Florida wars, of the English army, of the
European Continent, of Sebastopol (both Russian and English), and of the noble Havelock in his march to Lucknow ;
its officers able and educated ; its commander a graduate of
West Point, nine years in the army, a soldier in Kansas, in
the Oregon wilds, and through the war which led our victorious troops to the city of Mexico, — still bearing in his
body the Mexican lead. The regiment drills hours every
day, waiting the hoped-for opportunity to show in action
what it can do.

Our regiment is still in the Second Brigade (General
Abercrombie's), with the First Pennsylvania Battery, the
Twelfth and Sixteenth Indiana, and the excellent Twelfth
Massachusetts, which last has just marched (by night) to a
spot still nearer the river. Other brigades are around us.
A system of signals is well organized. The telegraph is

nearly established. Any attempt on the part of rebels to cross the river will precipitate upon them a vigilant and hardy army.

The ordinary routine of campaigning of course goes on. We have few hardships ; the food is good and abundant now ; the climate is delightful ; there is little sickness.

But this routine is sometimes changed. It was to-day. In the midst of active drill, the step ceased, the bugles were silent, the ranks took their iron position. It was when the band of another regiment passed by, pouring out their melancholy wailing for the dead. It was a soldier's funeral, and among the thousands in our camps, there was a reverent silence.

My thoughts went back to the first funeral at which I had officiated. It was at Harper's Ferry, while our regiment occupied that post. There had been brought into our hospital a soldier of the Fifteenth Pennsylvania, — then on its way home at the expiration of its three months' service, — whom that regiment left with us one afternoon as they passed through the place. That evening, as I passed at a late hour through the hospital, I noticed this new face, and on inquiry found the facts. He was sick with typhoid fever, very sick. Little more than a boy in years, he was to me, then, nameless, not one of ours, but he was a suffering soldier, and may God bless every one of such. I did not press him to speak, but he recognized the name of our Saviour, and looked up as if waiting to hear. It was too late to question, too late for human comfort. I dared say little, but I could not but think that some friends, father, mother, perhaps a yet closer one, whom I never saw, and doubtless never shall see, whose very residence I know nothing of, might be glad to know that some of the blessed promises of our Lord were whispered in his ear,

and that a few words of prayer asked for the soul of this
dying man, whose hand I held, the favor of our Father and
our Saviour. That night he died.

He was buried the next evening in the way of soldiers,
which, to one unaccustomed to the sight, is deeply interesting.
A suitable escort (for a private, eight rank and file, properly
commanded) is formed in two ranks opposite to the tent of
the deceased, with shouldered arms and bayonets unfixed ; on
the appearance of the coffin the soldiers present arms.   The
procession then forms, on each side of the coffin being three
bearers, without arms ; immediately preceding are the eight
soldiers, with arms reversed (the musket under the left arm,
barrel downward, and steadied by the right hand behind the
back) ; in front is the music, than whose dirge no sadder
sounds ever fell upon my ear, as they proceed to the place of
burial.   With slow and measured step, and muffled drum,
they move.   At the grave, the coffin is placed upon one side,
the soldiers resting upon their arms, the muzzle upon the foot,
the hands clasped upon the butt, and the head bowed upon
the hands.   The chaplain, who has walked in the rear of the
coffin, conducts the burial service ; " earth to earth, ashes to
ashes, dust to dust."   Three volleys are fired over the grave,
and the last kindness to the comrade is over.   The graveyard
left, immediately the band strike up a cheerful air, and take
their way back to camp and to living duties.

It was thus we buried the stranger soldier.   He had no
friend who knew him there.   No kindred wept by the side
of the grave.   His bed was made alone, in a deserted graveyard, on the bold cliff that overlooks the two rivers united in
the mighty stream which pours its affluence into the Atlantic.
But the soldiers subdued their roughness, and laid him down
tenderly.   The frequent oath was unheard.   The solemn

silence was scarcely broken by the low words of command. When the sharp volleys echoed up and down the valleys, the shadows had already fallen on the lordly rivers, the Potomac and Shenandoah, rolling by, far below us; but the gorgeous evening sunlight was richly clothing the dark green forests of both Maryland and Virginia heights, towering over us. His grave was cut in a hard and rocky soil; but out of that soil the evergreen was thriving and the wild flowers perfumed the air. It was on the very day his regiment was mustered out of service, that we buried him; and turning backward to our fragile homes, we found the order already given, "Ready to march;" and soon we struck our tents, and forded the dark and foaming river which separated the rebel from the loyal state. *He* had forded a darker and rougher river, which, we hoped as we left him, no longer kept him in a world of sin, and out of the land of perfect peace.

And so will throngs be buried, in this sad and mournful war. But out of the great clouds of private sorrow will rise the triumph of our country's glory.

NEAR DARNESTOWN, MD., September 27, 1861.

No movements have yet taken place here, beyond the occasional arrival and departure of regiments, and a now and then change of camp of some regiments. It is whispered that an advance may be made within a few weeks; but that silent man who wields the order of the army of the Potomac gives no sign. Intense activity prevails, however. Drill, drill, drill; and now the battalion drill is performed with knapsacks as if for march, by which the men are becoming prepared for the time when tents and wagons are left behind in camp, and they meet the foe face to face. Officers are hinted to with reference to the propriety of *their* having haversacks also, capacious enough for a few days' rations against the time when board will be scarce. All sorts of rumors fly around, and every new regiment expects to land directly into battle. But a little experience induces a cool distrust in everything except absolute orders to march, especially in a regiment like ours, which is, I believe, the oldest in service here, having had the felicity to form part of " Patterson's Column," which, to new regiments, seems antediluvian.

To-day is a rainy day. It drizzles a while, it pours a while, and then, by way of variety, pours and drizzles. All drill is suspended. Men stay in their tents, — barring the luckless fellows who pace up and down in overcoats, with muskets reversed, — relieved, however, every two hours, for another batch to get wet. Only the necessary duties of camp go on. In their tents some men read ; some write (often affectionate epistles — as their care to keep the sheet hidden shows) ; some mend trousers and such things ; some sing ; some gamble (which is not made an offence by the articles of war), and by which some of our men are stripped of every cent by experienced sharpers — poor moths, who will fly into the candle in spite of all remonstrance, though some have been saved. Some draw great enjoyment from tobacco smoke, their remedy for various ills. The sutler drives a brisk business in gingerbread, lemons, nuts, confectionery, and such like. And so the day wears on, not dismally to them, nor without opportunities of usefulness, to which the rain is no obstacle when one has rubber coat, leggings, cap, and cape.

The *ordinary* routine of the day in camp is this : at twenty minutes past sunrise the *reveille* is beaten, drum echoing to drum, till regiment after regiment is again a hive of busy life.

Roll call immediately follows, every man in company line. At seven o'clock the drum and fife announce breakfast, which cooks permanently detailed for each company have been preparing. At half past seven is sick call, when the surgeon meets all soldiers not able to be out. At eight o'clock is guard mounting, which is quite a display. The band are in position at their ordinary place for dress parade. At their music a detail numbering, at present, one lieutenant, one sergeant, four corporals, and seventy-two privates, marches to the parade. The line is formed, the arms are inspected, and appearance noted. The men are then marched in review, and then one "relief" (there are three) to the post of each sentinel, where, after various useful, but to me mysterious conferences, the old sentinel is relieved, takes his place in the rear, and a new one is stationed ; and so on around the camp. The old guard discharge their pieces, and are dismissed, each one having been, for the twenty-four hours, two hours on guard and four off in every six — a post of honor and of grave responsibility. To sleep on his post hazards the penalty of death.

Then, in decent weather, at nine o'clock the music sounds for company drill, — each company by itself, — when all kinds of queer manœuvres are gone through for an hour and a half. At one o'clock is dinner. At three P. M. is battalion drill, when the regiment drills under a field officer, with a briskness and life probably pleasanter to see than to experience. This lasts an hour and a half. At twenty minutes before five is the first call for evening parade ; twenty minutes are devoted to the minute inspection of arms and equipments ; and at five o'clock is the dress parade, the great show of the day. At six P. M. is supper. At half past eight tattoo is beaten. and the roll called ; at nine o'clock "taps" on the

3

drum signalize "lights out!" And after this only the solitary step of pacing sentinels, with now and then a challenge and response, or perhaps the gallop of an orderly with some despatch to the commander, breaks the stillness of the night. We have no locks on our doors ; but one feels secure enough with eighty sentries around the camp, and a thousand bayonets at hand, with yet other regiments and sentries still circling outside, and with mounted men scouring the land for miles in every direction.

The President's Fast Day, yesterday, was appropriately regarded. An order from General Banks called attention to it, and directed its observance. It was a day of rest from drill, in fact from all work which could be dispensed with. The most noticeable feature of the day was the public service, held in a beautiful field near the little village of Darnestown, whither all the regiments in this immediate locality proceeded in full uniform, and with arms. It was a beautiful sight, when from many different camps the several regiments marched toward the field, some on the open road, some winding through the woods, all with their music. Each was assigned to its place in the most orderly way, until thousands upon thousands stood in a dense mass. A platform held the various chaplains, the commanding general, and many of his officers of rank. The sight from this elevation was beautiful. The green wood skirted the field at a short distance on the right. The little village lay quietly in front. Directly before the platform were the solid ranks of infantry, reaching far right and left and in front, with cavalry on the one flank and artillery on the other. The multitude of banners, the motionless posture of men, the thousands standing in compact array, the glittering of the sunlight on a forest of bayonets, the firm and devout air, with the reflection that in a

few days this mass of soldiery might be hurled upon the
enemy, — many, alas ! in human probability, never more to
return, — could but inspire a beholder with mingled feelings
of delight and sorrow.

The services were these : The President's Proclamation
was read by Chaplain Gaylord, of the Thirteenth Massachusetts ; Chaplain Reed, of the Thirteenth Pennsylvania, offered
the prayer of invocation ; Chaplain Sewall, of the Twenty-
ninth Pennsylvania, read selections of Scripture, and the
hymn, " My country, 'tis of thee," in which the united bands
led the voices of the soldiers ; Chaplain Phillips, of the Ninth
New York, offered prayer, and led in the Lord's Prayer ; the
Chaplain of the Second Massachusetts read the Army Hymn,
— which was sung to " Old Hundred," in a majestic style, —
and he made the address (or sermon, it may be) for the
day ; and Chaplain Lasher, of the Fifth Connecticut, offered
the concluding prayer, and after the doxology, pronounced
the benediction. The topic of the address, after an introduction alluding to our peculiar need of God's help, was,
" The cause in which we are enlisted is a cause on which
we can hopefully ask God's blessing " — the cause of government against anarchy, of government against an unpro-
voked rebellion, of a government forbearing to the last
moment, of a government rebelled against because its instinc-
tive principle is Liberty, by traitors whose sole moving principle is Slavery.

One could hardly realize the change from quiet home worship to the gathering in one service of a whole division of
the army. But when the commanders had sprung to their
saddles, the rattling of sabres had ceased, the rumbling of
artillery wheels had passed out of hearing, the dancing banners had disappeared, — then reveries of home came back,

and faces of parishioners, and laughing eyes of children, and
the mental photograph of tried and faithful friends, whom
may God bless.

————

CAMP NEAR DARNESTOWN, MD., October 5, 1861.

IN the absence of special news, why shall I not recall such
rambling reminiscences as have outlasted our several later
marches, regarding the places where JOHN BROWN acted and
suffered? The movements of our regiment, it happened, led
us to every spot memorable for his transactions; and there
were few whose interests did not lead them to examine these
localities. Why not? It is true that when one remembers
the general disapproval with which the sober judgment of
the North answered that startling raid, it seems strange that
a Northern regiment should march through New York, with
a thousand voices singing that peculiar song, —

"John Brown's gone to join the army of the Lord,"

with the gazing multitudes joining the wild chorus, —

"Glory, glory, hallelujah!"

Nor am I now ready to approve of it; nor will many. But
it was then evident that there existed a latent admiration for
the stern, persistent, self-sacrificing man, perilling and losing
life for a cause he believed to be righteous. Nor is it possible to ignore the fact that now his enemies have made
themselves our enemies; that the system whose outrages
tasked, perhaps overpowered, the strength of his reason, has
insanely raised its sacrilegious hand against our country; and
that if John Brown deserved death, infinitely more does every
rebel now in arms. His crime — if crime it was — is insignifi-
cant beside that of these perjured thieves and traitors. He was

a *man;* what I think of the people here, thus far, I will tell in some future letter.

We entered Charlestown, Va. (I shall take the places as we came to them), late in the evening, after a long and hard day's march. Our regiment had spent the preceding night in bivouac, where we had the pleasure of commencing an out-door experience of no tents, with the ground for bed, and, that night, a projecting root for pillow, — than which no night's need have been better, barring a shower toward morning. At four o'clock in the morning our regiment was in column ; and it had, during the day, an honorable position in the rear guard of an army of twenty-two thousand. It was evening when we approached Charlestown. The running of cars from Winchester — the rebel camp — to Charlestown, heard all the preceding night, had raised an expectation of active duty ; but a few shell from a light battery had scattered the rebel cavalry, who left Charlestown as the head of our column entered. It was a beautiful evening. Light, fleecy clouds occasionally glided before the moon, only to bring out in silvery brilliancy the long column of dancing bayonets, visible in front or rear, as they rose and fell over the rolling ground. The tread of troops and the rumbling of wagons hardly broke the quiet. As we approached the town, the sentence was passed from one to another, " In this town John Brown was hung ; " and probably no thought was so predominant as that, when our tired men sank down upon the ground to sleep.

Late as it was, I had occasion to walk a mile or more, with one or two others, to the village, where our assistant surgeon had to provide accommodations for a sick officer. It was past eleven when we entered the shabby town, and sought the hotel. On our road we met one of the guard,

3 *

who showed us our way, and as we were crossing a stone bridge, he pointed to the right : " In that field," said he, " John Brown was hung."

At the hotel we found the landlord somewhat impracticable. He was secession in feeling, and vexed — as all the Charlestown people were — at the entirely unexpected arrival of our army, and no better natured for the lateness of the hour. He was, in fact, somewhat sullen, until a thought entered my mind to try, at random, the effect of certain signs belonging to an institution which an absurdly humorous writer in the *Congregationalist*, a year or two ago, called " the worship of demons," — to whom I owe thanks for many a hearty laugh these weeks. The signs fortunately struck the right spot, and were responded to. Our sick were attended to, and a hot supper provided for ourselves ; and we were speedily on terms of free chat with the landlord. Talking with him of the crowds then in town, he replied, " We haven't had such a crowd since John Brown was hung." A little encouragement drew out his opinion, as well as a full account of the circumstances. The latter were in all the papers. The former showed the effect which John Brown's manliness had even on a Southern mind. He respected the old man. I particularly recollect the deep impression which John Brown's indignant refusal to avail himself of the plea of insanity, urged by his counsel, had made. The very words were quoted, and it was the evident opinion that but for that the life of the accused would have been saved. The quiet firmness of the death scene, and the apparent honesty throughout, were far from forgotten. The people evidently had felt that Brown was a hero, but in a bad cause.

The next day I visited the jail and the room where he had been confined, and so did many others. It is upon the main

street, and by no means repulsive. The kindness of the jailer
was still commented upon. I visited also the court-room
where the famous trial took place. I saw the spot where he
had reposed. I sat down in the chair of the judge. The
places where the counsel stood were pointed out; and I
summoned up, as well as I could in fancy, the scenes which
in that room had shaken half a continent. I saw also the
field of execution, as did thousands upon thousands. The
place of the gallows was ascertained, — the timbers of which
were preserved in town, — and multitudes eagerly carried
away memorials, even to the soil which pressed against the
posts.

Our regiment was in a few days sent forward to occupy
Harper's Ferry alone. It was an honorable post, and we
were welcomed with joy. To see tears rolling down many
a cheek at the sight of the old flag, was a pleasant sight after
the sullen hate of the other places where we had been. Here
remaining for some weeks, with our own colonel as commandant of the post, even after the bulk of the army had
come, we had opportunities to visit every memorable spot.
The famous Jefferson Rock was there; but few visited it,
while many curiously examined every place famous for John
Brown's footsteps. The massive and beautiful bridge which
he had held, over the Potomac, was in ruins. Southern
vandals had destroyed it. But the place of his guard was
remembered. The spot where he had stopped, and then,
not wisely, released, the railway train; the arsenal held by
him at first; the ruins of the very muskets once at his disposal, now lying in heaps where our own troops afterward
fired the building to keep them from rebel hands; the rock
in the river where one of his men was barbarously shot in
crossing; the mountain woods where another hid till driven

out by hunger,—all these plenty of citizens were ready to
show. But chief in interest was the engine-house where his
final and useless defence took place. I recognized it from
the pictures then published. It has two double doors, each
wide enough for the entrance of a fire-engine, — thick, massive doors. There still remain, unaltered, the several holes
made through the brick walls, to enable the besieged to fire
on their assailants. Former spectators showed where the
few United States soldiers unhesitatingly advanced to batter
in the doors, and where companies of Virginia soldiers had
wisely hid out of danger of the rifles, contenting themselves
with preventing escape till men of some courage should dare
a capture. All the arsenal buildings were worthy of inspection, but the long lines of noble shops were mainly in ghastly
ruins; the very trees of that once beautiful spot, scorched to
death, cast the shadows of their leafless limbs upon the
blackened walls. One of them. still retaining a roof, I shall
always remember as the place where our Northern regiment
met to worship, while the roar of thunder and the flash of
lightning were the accompaniments to the old psalms which
rolled through the long structure. But, by some chance, the
only building of that vast series which still remains uninjured, is the engine-house which John Brown made his
fortress; and over it still wave the green trees, unhurt. Is
it a prophetic emblem?

Our regiment, by and by, crossed the Potomac. It was
by the same ford, unused for many years, till now reopened,
by which the Virginia troops departed for Cambridge in
1775. On the Maryland Heights opposite we bivouacked
for weeks. Yet, by the providence which seemed to follow
us, we were in the fields and snug by the house of the first
man who met John Brown, when, under an assumed name,

he was looking for a farm to occupy, preparatory to his peculiar purpose. From him, whose heart was unlocked by the same key as the Charlestown landlord's, I gathered full accounts of their conversation, and how a farm, mentioned by this man, as he and Brown stood at the gate before us, was taken. Brown had made a favorable impression, as well as his sons; " he never saw anything out of the way in him," though Brown would *never enter his house.* The farm was two or three miles off, and there is nothing peculiar there. The people were mystified by Brown's movements, he said. Some peculiar articles which he had they thought were some kind of *divining* tools. Brown laughed when he heard of it; they were *surveying* implements.

The last spot I saw in this connection was the school-house where the arms were hid. One night, going out with our adjutant, who was taking particular care on that occasion in stationing our picket guard, about three fourths of a mile from our guard we came to the building referred to. It is smaller than any of our country school-houses; like even dwelling-houses here, it is of logs, with a layer of mud of equal thickness alternating with each log, save at the corners. A respectable farmer in New England furnishes better accommodations for his pigs. The roof is now partly destroyed, it having been set on fire. The floor is nearly all gone. Under that floor the arms had been concealed, and there also was hidden one of the men, while his enemies were searching the woods, and even entering the house. It was from this building that Brown dismissed the school one day, to take possession. It is a quiet place, half a mile from the Potomac, with nothing habitable near save the huts of boughs which rebel soldiers had since occupied and abandoned.

If I were asked the impression made upon my mind as to

opinions in these localities, I should say that while John
Brown was and is called a fanatic, he was and is respected.
He was made, by the trial and execution, a hero. The daring exhibited in his attempt, the manliness he showed on his
trial, the calmness with which he met death, made a lasting
and deep impression. The local effect was powerful. On
our march to Charlestown, stopping for a few moments at a
house by the way, I pointed out the path to some soldiers
crowding in for water, that I might appease the needlessly
frightened family. While waiting till all were satisfied,
some conversation took place with some of the inmates, who
were secessionists, in the course of which the mistress of the
house said frankly, " We do not dare direct our servants as
you spoke to those soldiers." I had merely and pleasantly
pointed out a path away from the lawn, and I asked her,
" Why?" " We are afraid of them. We have not dared
order them since old John Brown's affair. The servants
have always said since, ' Well, somebody's coming like old
Brown, yet.' " Such is the general feeling in that vicinity.
Nor did the slaves hesitate to express their delight at our
presence. Shame on the miserable business our army had,
to send back fugitives !

Nor did residents there attach only a local importance to
the transactions of that time. They felt — and I feel with
them — that thence dated this war. The South trembled on
seeing that its pet system had no safe foundation. Its En-
celadus was under the volcano, and the heavings were too
perilous. From that date it began to arm. All over the
slave country military companies were formed. Its Wises
began to plot. Its Floyds began to steal. And therefore,
when the war began, the South was ready, while the unconscious North, which had disapproved the raid, and supposed

it had thereby satisfied the slave power, was totally unprepared. Thank God, it is so no longer. The free North is
pouring down its sons by hundreds of thousands — in no war
to abolish slavery, it is true, but none the less to insure its
doom. Had the South remained loyal, slavery would still
have been protected. It is now *too late*. And if our government be wise, besides its immense armies, in the fear of
the Southern heart John Brown's ghost is worth a hundred
thousand men.

CHAPTER II.

TO CONRAD'S FERRY AND RETURN.

CONRAD'S FERRY, MD., October 24, 1861.

No longer at Darnestown, and no longer writing of a fixed camp, and its routine of little details.

It was on Monday evening last that orders came to the corps, suddenly, to cook two days' rations for haversacks, and three days' more for wagons; it was intended, however, that we should not leave till morning. A few minutes more, and orders came to leave tents and wagons, and as speedily as possible be upon the road. It was then eight o'clock; at half past eight our men were in column, with knapsacks packed and on their backs; at half past three o'clock in the morning our regiment was at Conrad's Ferry, eighteen miles away; and in a few minutes our pickets lined a mile of the Potomac, within musket shot, across the river, of the scene of the mournful, stupid waste of life, which has carried, on the wings of lightning, anguish to a multitude of Massachusetts homes.

Our orders were based upon the passage of the river which had that day taken place here. It was at first supposed that the movement had been successful at Conrad's Ferry, as well as at Edwards's Ferry, four miles below; and General Banks's division was sent on to support the movement into Virginia.

It was true that General Stone had succeeded in throwing over several thousand at the lower crossing. But how disastrous the result was at the upper, you too well know. It was this which hastened our march to the then entirely defenceless spot, commanded by an exultant enemy. Two or three regiments only went to Conrad's Ferry; most of the corps was sent to Edwards's Ferry.

Our men did not know whither they were bound, nor why — except that it was to the enemy's country. Never were they more happy. They took the road with songs, no instrumental music being now allowed on march. The weight of their heavy loads was unfelt. They needed but little pause for rest. The hope of meeting the foe was their life. Our drill, our equipments, our men and officers — too long had it been felt that these were idle, while raw militia had been sent to spots they could never hold against the keen enemy we were to deal with. But our men were doomed to disappointment. Worse — they went only to meet the shattered remnants of broken regiments. Before we had been ordered to start, the battle had ended in defeat.

It was at Poolsville that the first news met us of the defeat. There was the camp of the Fifteenth Massachusetts, and there some of its sentries informed us of the result. All along the road from that point we met fugitives straggling back to their camp. By the road were many men utterly worn down with fatigue, sleeping on the ground; and now and then were groups around a fire hastily built on the roadside, dejected, but still burning with a desire for a new struggle. Many were but half clothed; some without even trousers or shoes; some wrapped only in blankets. We learned from them little more than that the river had been crossed, and that the gallant Fifteenth had been shattered

4 .

almost to atoms. They did not know the circumstances nor extent of the loss.

The morning dawned, but the sun was invisible. With the gray of the early hours came down a steady, drizzling shower, deepening into a pouring rain, which lasted for most of the day. Our quartermaster had moved his train with wonderful ease and despatch, and at about six o'clock it arrived, enabling our men to secure a rude but substantial breakfast; and in the course of the morning we went into camp.

We found everything in mourning. There was no sunshine. Nearly opposite was plainly visible the spot where our gallant fellow-soldiers had been led to slaughter. The howitzers which the enemy had captured were mounted in sight. Between us and the opposite shore was Harrison's Island, over which the advance had been made, and from it were coming the dead and wounded — the results of the battle. In that island hospital strong and true men were dying, and many were suffering agonies. But the hardest feeling to bear was, that these lives had been wickedly thrown away on a useless, foolishly planned, foolishly executed expedition. In a house on the Maryland shore were others dying, — and the dead were buried near, — a house in which the holes still remained, which, at a former day, the enemy's balls had cut, and where their shells had exploded.

Of this affair a multitude of reporters have already gathered probably every incident, and they are spread before you. Of its general character, perhaps I should give some account, as received from men who were in the action.

The expedition toward Leesburg was commanded by Colonel Baker, a United States senator from Oregon, as acting brigadier. He had at the Ferry his own regiment (the First California), the Fifteenth, Nineteenth, and Twentieth Massachusetts, and the Tammany (New York) regiments. A scouting party of the Fifteenth had been sent over the night before. Returning, it reported that there was a small camp of the enemy not far from Leesburg. Before daylight of Monday, Colonel Devens (in command), with four companies of his regiment (the Fifteenth), and one hundred men of the Twentieth Massachusetts (Colonel Lee accompanying), had reached the Virginia shore, sent over by order of General Stone to destroy the reported camp. He had commenced crossing about midnight. The crossing took place over the island, which had been occupied, and somewhat fortified, at an earlier day, and which is about one hundred and twenty-five yards from the Virginia shore, and four hundred and fifty from the Maryland. The only means of transportation to the hostile side of the river consisted of a small boat, which would carry about twenty, and a scow, on which perhaps seventy men could be crowded, but old and leaky, as the final catastrophe most sadly proved. At one time in the afternoon this boat was pulled across by a rope made up from pieces taken from canal boats ; but the service answered only a very brief time.

The Virginia shore is a bluff, said to be (and apparently correctly) about sixty feet high. Up this height our men climbed, and on the bluff remained Colonel Lee, with his men, while Colonel Devens advanced towards Leesburg, which is some four miles distant. The reported camp proved to exist only in imagination ; openings in a row of trees had been mistaken in the night for tents. The force proceeded with care, reconnoitring the ground. At about eight A. M. the enemy were observed, and soon fighting commenced.

After driving the enemy, it seemed best to fall back to the bluff, as the rebels were evidently increasing.

Colonel Devens afterward returned to his former advanced position. Here, about noon or a little later, the enemy attacked. After a short affair, it seemed prudent to return to the bluff, from fear of being cut off.

At about twelve o'clock, Colonel Baker, the acting brigadier in command, had begun to send over reënforcements ; about half past one he crossed himself. The First California went over entire, as rapidly as the poor means of transportation allowed. Three companies of the Tammany (New York) regiment, with Colonel Cogswell, and more of the Twentieth Massachusetts, also crossed.

As the reënforcements reached the gallant Fifteenth, they found them little beyond the river. I have said already that the bank was over sixty feet high. Climbing to the summit, they found a track about seventy feet in width, exceedingly broken, and curved, with rocks, bushes, and logs — impassable, indeed, for a horse. Beyond this was an open place, almost a lawn, about three hundred feet wide by four hundred and fifty yards long, — the length being towards Leesburg. Here the battle was resumed with great energy. At three P. M. the firing was very brisk, and for the next hour it was exceedingly furious on both sides. An order for artillery had been sent immediately after the first reënforcements arrived, — the enemy all the time rapidly increasing. Two howitzers (regulars) were sent over with great difficulty, and about a quarter past four, Lieutenant Bramhall, of a battery attached to the New York Ninth, with a rifled cannon, a six pounder. Those guns had to be carried to the southward of the high bluff and rugged track, to reach the open scene. As the forces were then placed, our troops were on that side of the

open field which was nearest the river, the right and left wing
a little advanced, so as to form a concave front towards the
enemy, but in a corner of the bushes ; a howitzer was at each
extremity, and Lieutenant Bramhall's gun a little in advance
of the centre, on slightly elevated ground.   The enemy were
also under cover of the woods, their sharpshooters in trees
for more deadly aim, and rarely coming into sight for a large
part of the fight.   Our men had skirmishers on both flanks,
in the woods, where much fighting took place.   For several
hours it was severe.   The enemy fired in heavy volleys, as if
a regiment were shooting at once.   "The bullets fell like
hail," says an officer, who, though fighting with the greatest
bravery, strangely escaped uninjured.   The enemy had no
cannon, but their force was not less, it now appears, than
five or six thousand, to which our forces had but about sixteen hundred in opposition.

Our men fought with the utmost bravery, but they were
gradually overpowered by numbers.   About three o'clock
Colonel Baker was killed.   "Had I two more Massachusetts
regiments," said he, a few minutes before he was shot, " I
could beat them yet."   Colonel Cogswell, of the Tammany,
took command.   The fight still continued, but in vain.   It
was at last determined to attempt a movement towards Edwards's Ferry.   The formation of the troops was commenced
with that view, and partially executed, when a dash of the
Tammany companies (drawn out by an officer who suddenly
appeared in front and called them on) into the open space
was met by such a murderous fire as to throw everything into
confusion.   Our troops then descended the bluff, and formed
on the plateau below.   Resistance was still made, but in vain.
Our men took to the water.   Many were drowned.   Many
were shot in the water.   The boats had both been sunk entire,

1 *

with their loads, and no transportation remained. Unfortunately, no officer had been left in charge of the boats. Half of our troops were killed, wounded, or missing.

The policy of the enemy was to worry our men for the day, and then to throw a heavy body of reserve upon our exhausted soldiers ; and it succeeded perfectly. The sadness of the results is equalled only by the stupidity of the plan. The crossing at this bluff — while half a mile distant was an open and level shore, — the criminal neglect to provide proper transportation over and to secure a possible retreat, and the uselessness of the enterprise, deserve rigid examination.

The next day General McClellan came. The troops across at Edwards's Ferry were ordered back. What plans that general has, nobody knows. Whether he directed the recent movement, we have yet to learn. But he expresses his surprise at the method in which it was carried out. His presence, of course, superseded General Banks, as that general superseded General Stone.

Last evening we had an order to move to Edwards's Ferry. " The enemy threaten us in force," was the order ; " send two of your regiments, especially the Second Massachusetts." We marched six miles, and then were sent back, the emergency having passed. And we are still in camp.

Muddy Branch Camp, Md., October 31, 1861.

No more " near Darnestown." No more of that hard-trodden field where our camp lay ; nor that road by its side, with multitude of pedlers. We have been to Harrison Island, and in sight of Ball's Bluff, which rested as quiet and silently as though blood had not dyed its soil. We have

countermarched, and our division is near the Potomac, below
General Stone's command, and near Darnestown as a *fact*, but
not as a *date*. We now are in a quiet, pleasant field, away
from the road, which itself is away from the main road. The
"field and staff" have pitched their tents in the edge of a
wood, and as I sit at the "door of my tent," the shade of oak
and walnut is pleasant, this beautiful "fall" day. A little
fire is burning a few feet before me, and the smoke curls
up lazily in the sunshine. The air has the lovely, dreamy
haze of autumn. The trees are gently shaking off the ripe
leaves. The hum of insects is not yet ended. Near are the
strokes of our woodcutters' axes. Farther off is the murmur
of a rapid and a steep waterfall. The season is

> "Like an emperor triumphing
>   With gorgeous robes of Tyrian dyes —
> Full flush of fragrant blossoming,
>   And glowing purple canopies."

Our men do duty where

> "The wide, clear waters sleeping lie
>   Beneath the evening's wings of gold,
> And on their glassy breast of sky
>   And banks their mingled hues unfold."

It is a "muster day," and drill is omitted, and music silent.
It is a day to dream of home! Home! Thanks for a home,
whither the needle points steadily. And prayers for one sad
man to whom yesterday's letter said his home was broken;
his wife had left this world, and so left her four now mother-
less children, with no relative this side of the Atlantic save
their father, and he bound by his oath to his country.

But to another topic.

I know that my handwriting is usually blind. Friends
insist that it is undoubtedly an imitation of Greek. It was

the father of Dr. Chalmers (was it not?) who saved his son's
letters for the doctor to read at his semi-annual visit.   I have
suffered maledictions from compositors, I know.   Once I
determined to prove that I could write legibly ; and I wrote
an article in the old-fashioned, round Boston hand, which was
a marvel of clearness and beauty.   Compositors were delighted.   Alas! it was like the century plant ; one bloom
exhausted my powers, and I have never written a decent hand
since.

It is not strange, therefore, that I am quoted as saying,
" we have been in *no* enemy's country," when I really said,
" we have been in *an* enemy's country."   Small errors I
pass by ; this I correct because of its involving a mournful
truth.

We have been in *an* enemy's country.   Sent into Central
Virginia, a continuation of the beautiful Cumberland valley,
the central of the three parts into which mountain ranges
divide Virginia, — a medium as to slave population, between
the eastern and western portions, — midway between a loyal
and a rebellious section, — we found it as alien from the
government as, any foreign power, and as hostile as the bitterest war could render it.   I see much in Northern papers
about freeing the Union sentiment, awaking loyalty, and the
like.   But I did not see such sentiment in Central Virginia,
where it ought, above all places on rebel soil, to have been
exhibited.   Nor do I see much of it in Maryland, where it
ought to be predominant.

Confining myself to Central Virginia, I do not believe we
met, outside of Harper's Ferry, half a dozen reliable Union
men.   The people were willing to buy and sell, and they could
teach Yankees lessons in sharpness.   But as to any open,
ingenuous loyalty to the Constitution, it was almost unknown.

At best they were sullenly quiet, but by no means hearty. Sometimes they were outspoken. One good lady expressed to me the hope that every Northern soldier would be killed. At Middleway the stars and stripes were greeted with the ugliest of expressions, and "The Star-spangled Banner" and "Hail, Columbia," with which our band endeavored to edify them, met with disgust. At Charlestown every shop was closed as we entered, save one; and the occupant of that, though displaying a Union flag, proved the meanest rebel of all. Nor has there been a single place where a little stay did not enable us to learn that the bulk of the inhabitants were in favor of the Southern Confederacy, except Harper's Ferry, which, from its industrial pursuits, had a population entirely different from that of slaveholding places generally. There, was a large mechanical population once employed in government workshops. They had earned some money by hard labor and good wages. They had bought of government neat homes at a low price, paying by instalments for the last four years. They had helped build good churches, and had established public and Sabbath schools. In front of most houses is a little piece of ground, and formerly there were a few flowers — a rare sight in this part of the country. Such a population, though not particularly anti-slavery, was, and principally is, for the Union. Now the churches are mainly shut up. The schools are abandoned. The sidewalks and streets are rough and ragged. Many houses are deserted. Property, often their little all, is valueless. Their incomes are destroyed with the destruction of the government shops. Some of the workmen were persuaded to carry their knowledge and experience to Richmond or to North Carolina, and most of the true men are left totally destitute. Government will probably never restore the ruined buildings, and Harper's

Ferry is ruined. Still, many men there are faithful to their country, in spite of all inducements to treason.

There is no mistaking the general feelings of a people. This people regarded us as invaders. Most of them have no loyalty to be awakened. I write this with a little doubt as to the propriety of uprooting this convenient stepping-stone, on which I myself travelled into a clearer path. But that it is the fact, I am persuaded by an observation of nearly four months in localities which must be far in advance of Southern States in loyalty; and I except only occasional places.

That there will be *apparent* loyalty as our armies advance, is doubtless true; but it will be based on self-interest, not love, nor to be trusted as anything else than a convenient instrument. This state of things arises from two facts:—

First, there *is* an " irrepressible conflict" between freedom and slavery. Free labor and slave *cannot* flourish together. Where industry is considered menial, it loses its vitality. Whites despise it, and become, if poor, meaner than the meanest of negroes; " poor white trash" is their legitimate title. Between, therefore, the two kinds of labor, the sympathy of those who have the power is entirely with the South. Not because slave labor here is profitable; it is not profitable; there are not slaves enough, nor the kind of work, to make it pay, while there are just enough to make their masters lazy. And from the latter fact is their liking for Southern institutions. While, further, there is the deeper feeling that the North despises and dislikes slavery on conscientious principles, which principles the owner of one slave feels the burden of as well as the owner of a thousand — a small slaveholder in Virginia as well as the plantation owner in South Carolina. Out of such companionship as that of freedom-loving Northerners, these people are anxious to get.

The second fact is, that the Southern feeling is, and always has been, that of scorn for " Yankees," as they call all Northerners. Most Southerners have carried with them the manners of the plantation, and have always looked down upon the industrious North. They are afraid of Northern thrift and enterprise, while they assume to be a superior race. They dislike its democracy, and prefer the aristocracy of the South — to be tyrannical, if of the favored class ; to fawn, if they are inferiors. All really slaveholding States must gravitate towards the South.

That the rebels must be " conquered," " subjugated," or whatever you please to call it, admits of no question. Our country's coasts, its rivers, its mines, its roads, its telegraphs, demand that it be one. The success of self-government requires it. But how to succeed is the question. That our armies will eventually triumph, is sure, in the fact that Southerners never dare meet an equal force of Northerners in the field. When we have *officers*, we shall conquer. But what to do then? . Is any compromise possible to satisfy them. *None.* To restore the South to its old status, would only restore the old conflicts, more embittered than ever, to our public halls, with the old braggarts, the old liars and thieves, for more haughty boasting, more impudent lies, more successful thefts. Nothing is settled till it is settled right.

But when the South is conquered, it must be held. And that will require a social revolution at the South. Not a mere emancipation of slaves, but a change in the ownership of property. The property holders will always be the dominant class in reality. Introduce a loyal race of property holders, and loyal men of industry, and the problem is worked out. While you are discussing the Fremont proclamation, you forget that the simplest way of proceeding is for the Congress soon to assemble, to pass a confiscation act, by which every man committing a single overt act of rebellion shall forfeit his property. For this the army aches. They see rebels protected, their houses guarded, their property sentinelled. They see disloyal men " conciliated," even though soldiers should suffer. What think you of taking particular pains to restore slaves claimed specially on the ground that, as the whites of the family were all absent, the blacks were indispensable for gathering the crops, while those very whites were officers in the rebel army at Manassas? That was what we did at Harper's Ferry. Or of restoring houses taken for public use, and receipted for, on the same plea of crops, while the proceeds of those crops were to help support Southern soldiers? That we did in the Shenandoah. What think you of Union men being left without work, while notorious secessionists were hired in rebuilding bridges and the like? Just that was done at the Potomac. Where the policy originated, I do not know ; but such things happened in the column of the famous general now returned to private life, until the spirit seemed to be that of the " reward and forgetfulness act" of Charles II., which he carried out by forgetting his friends and rewarding his enemies.

Such a policy will never succeed. It conciliates no rebels ; it disgusts friends. Yet, if " general emancipation" were now made the object of this war, I fully believe that our armies would melt away. Our men are fighting for the flag, not for the abolition of slavery. So far as the army feels, slavery is not a prominent theme or thought. The supremacy of law, and the honor of the stars and stripes — these are the soldier's principles. General emancipation would add untold horrors to what already has horrors enough — WAR ;

such horrors as the nobility of a true and gallant soldier has no desire to witness ; and would violate constitutional principles, beyond which our armies would be palsied. At the same time, if there is any work which our soldiers loathe, it is the returning of fugitive slaves. They despise it, and they are despised for it by the chuckling scoundrels who claim the " guarantees " of the constitution which they have deliberately thrown off. But they are not fighting for " abolition." *

But if you confiscate the property of rebels, you have the means to pour in a new population. At the end of this war there will be hundreds of thousands of young men ready to take and hold, with an arm used to the rifle, such properties. There are plenty of stalwart mechanics who could and would redeem this Southern soil from the blight with which Southern shiftlessness has cursed it. Of its Harper's Ferries, with magnificent water powers, with their vicinity to the land of cotton, with all needed avenues to the sea, Northern skill would make new Lowells and Lawrences. These houses of half log, half mud, would give place to New England villages. The church and the school-house would renovate the character of the population, and the iron hand of Northern power would rule with a strength against which Southern impetuousness would struggle in vain, as Southerners have always been powerless, the world over, against Northern steel. Slavery itself would vanish before such a resistless power as free labor, enlightened by a free conscience ; and the blacks, thus freed, would become supporters to a system of national industry. The now dominant class, once poor,

---

* I was right *then*, but I should not be right to use the same language *now*. The feelings of the army have gradually and totally changed. Few soldiers of any rank now but detest slavery, and mean to fight it.

5

would lose their pride with their power, and a new race of
men would come into being.

Strike, then, for a Confiscation Act; and do not divide the
North and weaken our armies by impracticable propositions
of unconstitutional measures.

———

NEAR SENECA, MD., November 15, 1861.

THE news which delights our minds is doubtless the same
as with you — the successful attack at Port Royal. We are
far more tranquil than you are in regard to news; less ex-
citable, less worried. We are away from the sensation despatches appearing hour after hour on the bulletin-boards,
where one statement is contradicted by the next. A newspaper, with us, is a precious article. A Baltimore daily,
which I succeeded in picking up yesterday, passed through a
multitude of hands, until pretty thoroughly used up. It rejoiced our hearts with the official account of the success on
South Carolina soil.

By the way, what a ridiculous mass of blunders are heaped
up in the columns of various dailies! The errors which a
mere lack of care allows are sometimes inexcusable. Thus
Harper's Weekly points a moral from the defeat at "Edwards's
Ferry," whereas at that place there was no battle. "Right
wing" and "left wing" are huddled up in inextricable confusion. You should note that Colonel Baker's force was the
"right wing" of the entire movement, covering the extremities
of three miles; while Colonel Baker's force had itself a right
and left, covering but a few hundred feet. One Boston daily
rightly takes somebody to task for calling General McClellan "Commander-in-Chief," and then announces that his

true title is " Lieutenant-General," — which is, really, a grade created by special act of Congress for General Scott, and, by that very act, will cease to exist when General Scott ceases to bear the title. But some of the pictorials are the richest in ability. The places they portray are frequently beyond recognition. A picture of the burning of the arsenals at Harper's Ferry, which I chanced to take up a few days ago, amused me somewhat, from the fact that the only two buildings which it represents as burning, are the only two there which bear no mark of fire !

There have been no marked changes in this vicinity since the Ball's Bluff affair, and the consequent immediate move-ment of troops. Between Washington and Muddy Branch, there are few troops this side of the river, but the Virginia side is occupied. General Banks's division lies at Muddy Branch and Seneca, on the Maryland side. General Stone is next above, covering the river nearly to a point opposite Leesburg; and various parts of these divisions are stationed at the Point of Rocks, Sandy Hook, and Williamsport.

Our own regiment has moved its camp a fourth of a mile, to secure a healthier location. The former site was a clayey soil, hard to dry after a rain. In fact, the ground was never really dry after the first day or two of our camping, and the result has been seen in the poorer condition of a generally healthy regiment. The few days which have elapsed since our change show, already, a marked improvement. Our present camp is on high ground, and overlooks the Potomac, visible less than half a mile distant. The health of most of the regiments in this division is good, but reports of visitors to some regiments on the Alexandria side of the Potomac represent an unfortunate state of things. It is impossible to keep health good on low ground near this beautiful but

deadly river. The miasma is terrible. Old residents shun
it as much as possible, and those who cannot do so are a
lank, sickly, cadaverous race ; and, so far as I can judge,
the character of most of them answers to their looks.

The matter of health has always been attended to in our
regiment. In reading an article in the Atlantic for November, I noticed that every valuable suggestion therein made,
has always been observed in the Second Massachusetts. The
" Sanitary Commission " was an organization of supereroga-
tion for us — a proof of the value of having experienced
army officers in charge of affairs. Nor can too much attention be devoted to the health of soldiers. A sickly army
cannot fight well ; nor is it fair to men who have left their
homes for their country's welfare, that they should be needlessly exposed to disease.

The measures taken against disease are of two kinds,
namely, — the hygienic arrangements of camp, and the
medical means of cure of sickness. The first are of the
greatest importance. In selecting a site for a camp, one is
sought for which is dry in its character, — elevated, but not
too bleak, — gently sloping, to prevent stagnant water from
rains, — open to the sun, and airy, but shielded somewhat
from winds and storms, if possible. The first work, after
the places for our tents is selected is to sweep and otherwise
clean the ground thoroughly. The whole camp ground is
carefully swept every day by a force specially detailed, till
not even a chip remains. No impurities are allowed near
the camp. At the kitchen fires, in front of the company
tents, deep holes are dug, in which the offal from cooking is
thrown, and every day a layer of earth is thrown in. The
tents themselves are struck not infrequently in warm,
sunny days (if the camping remains long in one spot), and

the sites are dried.   If there is straw in the tents, it is required to be thoroughly dried at frequent intervals.   The
Sibley tents, which our men use, are well ventilated at the
top, by a hole coverable at pleasure.   Regulations allow
unwholesome food to be condemned, and new and good demanded.   To insure the care of the camp in regard to order
and cleanliness, an " officer of police" is daily appointed.

The arrangements for the sick are under the direction of
the surgeon, who has also an assistant, both regularly educated physicians.   Every morning, any man taken sick reports to the first sergeant of his company, who enrolls his
name in a company book kept for the purpose.   Shortly after
breakfast, the drum and fife give the " sick call," when those
of the sick who are able, go to the surgeon, who prescribes
as needed.   If but little indisposed, the sick man returns to
his tent, excused from duty, — the medicine allowed being
furnished in the course of the morning by the " hospital
steward," who attends to the preparation of prescriptions.
If too ill to render it prudent for the patient to remain " in
quarters," he is sent by the surgeon to the hospital of the
regiment.   If one newly reported sick is not able to attend
the " sick call," the surgeon or assistant visits him at his
tent, and directs his removal if necessary.   Our hospital consists of two tents of thick canvas, each about twenty-five by
fourteen feet in size.   Each will accommodate easily ten
patients, and is supplied with bedsteads, straw beds, &c.
The " hospital steward " has general charge of the hospital,
and specially attends to the preparations and administering of
medicines, &c.   A " ward master " has charge of beds, bedding, cleanliness, food, &c., and has several " nurses," — of
which the allowance is one to ten patients.   Two cooks prepare the necessary food.   Other assistants attend to transpor-

5 *

tation and the like. If a man is likely to be long sick, as when a broken limb is to be healed, or he has some chronic disease, he is sent to a " general hospital," — ours being at Baltimore, in the old " National House ; " as the necessity of movements by a regiment render it undesirable to have men in its local hospital, to whom a movement might be disastrous. When men shall be discharged from hospital is under the control of the surgeon, — as, indeed, are *all* matters relative to disease. There is but one head, — which makes the excellence of army discipline. Medicines and instruments are furnished by government, freely and according to the experience of years.

The above are the arrangements in camp. For the sad effects of battle-fields, ambulances and stretchers are ready, and attendants detailed, — that none of our brave men shall suffer more than is indispensable.

I write of this topic because so many hearts at home are anxious, and such details may interest them ; and to assure them that, while nothing is a substitute for *home*, with its warm hearts and gentle hands, yet everything is done which can be done to lighten the burden of disease. Our surgeons spare no labor, night or day ; and our colonel is a frequent visitor among the sick ; our hospital steward is a most skilful worker in medicine ; our ward master is kind-hearted and unwearied ; our hospital cooks are experienced. Yet, in spite of all human skill and care, death cannot be excluded here, but will enter our canvas doors, as he glides into the houses of wood and stone at home, at will, or rather at our Father's will — before which who of us has not been made to weep? Two of our number here have lately died, both stricken with disease in great severity, and both delirious from the hour of their entrance into the hospital — so delirious that

neither could converse. What preparation they had made
for the future *must* have been made before they lay on a sick
bed. We committed them to God, who is rich in mercy, for
the great love wherewith he loved us.

.

NEAR FREDERICK, MD., December 19, 1861.

I WROTE you of our march from Seneca, or " near Darnestown." But I cannot leave Darnestown without a parting
salutation. There our regiment spent more than two months,
varied only by a location in three different places, and by a
hasty march to the mournful Conrad's Ferry. There we
made acquaintances, and, what interested me more, I had
some clerical duties to perform not usually falling to the lot
of chaplains in marching regiments, viz. : I married one couple,
and I baptized two children. The bridegroom was one of
our own men. The children were in two families at Seneca.
Both kinds of service were performed with great satisfaction
— especially the latter ; the latter especially (call it not selfish)
that it was a luxury to see a helpless little babe. To hear
one *cry*, even, is a comfort to one deprived of the privilege he
had at home. I wonder I was ever impatient at it. I mourn
over former hard-heartedness. I warn every father against
recklessness in this particular. I beg my ministerial brethren
especially to guard against any possible fretfulness on this
account, even though it be Saturday evening, and to-morrow's
sermon yet remains a " skeleton." Do not say to faithful
mother or careful nurse, " Why *don't* you hush that baby ?"
Soberly now : thank God there is one to hush. Take it in
your arms, and let its head rest trustingly on your shoulder,
O strong man, and so learn yourself how to rest as confidingly

on God's strong arm and loving heart. " For as a father
pitieth his children, so the Lord pitieth them that put their
trust in him." If that little one leave you, you will be sad
for many a year, believe me, over every impatient and stern
word, though those words were only the ripples on the surface
of your tide of love.

But about leaving Darnestown.

First of all, spell it with an *e*. Mr. Darne, whose father's
name and residence gave title to the place, spells it with an *e*.
In ingenuity of nomenclature, they seldom rise, in these parts,
above attaching some termination to the name of a prominent
resident. Thus came Harper's Ferry, Clarks-burg, Hyattstown, Pools-ville, Buckey-town. Darnestown itself is a little
village on the road from Washington to Poolsville, which
runs almost as parallel with the Potomac as the crooked character of that river allows, and about twenty-five miles from
Washington. Most of its houses are of the log-and-mud style.
It boasts no hotel, though some hospitable people would afford
entertainment for man and beast. It had three " country "
stores, where hardware, dry goods, groceries, boots and shoes,
quack medicines, and whiskey were sold in rather small
quantities — barring the whiskey as to the *small*. There was
a blacksmith's shop, but no shoemaker's. A post-office was
in one of the stores, and before our advent a stage-coach
passed up through one day and down through the next. The
few houses of more than usual pretension would hardly pass
muster in a New England village, and the poorer ones were
sadly dilapidated. " These buildings seem out of repair," it
was said one day to a native. " Wal, yes," was the reply.
" Why don't the people repair them ? " " Wal, we kinder
take things easy, and when they tumble down we build up
new ones " — a work which several gave indications of soon

needing. Two or three houses were enclosed with fences,
and had a few flowers in front ; but as a whole, the village of
one street was of the Rip Van Winkle order, where you would,
and will, see black women cutting fire-wood before the door,
while a white man sits on the door-step smoking his pipe, and
the pigs enjoying the free use of the road, too lazy to move
out of the way of the infrequent traveller.

But Darnestown woke up one day. A division of the
army grouped itself on either side. The pigs and the wood-
cutting went on the same, but sentries at the doors of the
shops interfered sadly with the sale of whiskey. Along the
street was run a telegraph wire, and up a rickety staircase
was a telegraph office. Coaches ran every day. Soldiers
lounged about. Regiments moved up and down. Orderlies
cantered up and down at all hours. Trade inflated. The
at first bewildered traders increased their stock of goods.
Pedlers came. Daguerreotype artists extemporized small
buildings. From a gimlet to a pair of boots (marked Claf-
lin, Boston), whatever you wanted was of Yankee make, save
the execrable pies which flooded the country — unmistakably
Darnestown. Darnestown went to making money with
more than Yankee shrewdness, and Darnestown was
Union — when the army came.

Of schools : there was one little building, but the frightened schoolma'am vanished, and the school-house became a
pedler's shop. The principal school was at Rockville, ten
miles off. I asked one man, a magistrate a mile away,
what a little building in his yard was erected for. "The
front room for a store, the back for a school-room." Then
he and a neighbor discussed the several teachers. One, in
particular, they agreed upon as an excellent teacher, a thorough teacher. They paid him three dollars and a half

per quarter for each scholar. "But we had to give him up," said the owner : "he got the children along as far as he could go, but he had never learned the *higher* branches, such as grammar and geography, and we had to let him go." In one house of a family of pretension only four books were discernible — a Bible, a Prayer-book, a catalogue of some school. and some work of fiction whose name I now forget.

There are two churches at Darnestown, at opposite extremities of the village ; or rather one is a little out of the village. One is Old School Presbyterian ; the other, Baptist. The meeting-house of the latter is log-and-mud, and open to the roof. It has, of course, a negro gallery, entirely separating the black from the white Christians, and reached by a staircase built outside. It is very comforting to know that, by this arrangement, there is no possible danger of contamination. The Presbyterian church is quite a handsome building, framed, boarded, and painted a neutral tint. *Its* gallery is reached by a staircase *inside;* and the basement has, I think, been sometimes used as a school-room. Neither church had preaching every Sabbath. The Baptist was open about once a month ; the Presbyterian, once in two weeks. Neither of the preachers was a resident, I believe, and they divided their time between this place and Rockville, which is a much larger town. The Baptist church became a station for pickets, and on Mondays for a chaplains' meeting, and, subsequently, was turned into a hospital. When I saw it last, a battery was exercising by its side. The Presbyterians, with an attendance largely increased by soldiers, came to have public worship every Sabbath.

As our services were then in the afternoon, I have had occasional opportunity to worship mornings with other congregations. I did so there, at a distance from camp of several miles each way. The first time I attended the Presbyterian church, at the hour appointed for public worship, a prayer-meeting was in progress. Some resident brother conducted the services, and " deaconed off" the hymns, which, though an old New England custom, was new to me. The same brother led the singing, which I should have enjoyed, had he not invariably pronounced the first syllable of each line as " nah." Chaplains were the principal supporters of the meeting. This meeting ended, the minister entered the pulpit, and, assisted by a Presbyterian chaplain, held divine service. The text of his sermon was, " Israel doth not know, my people do not consider," which he applied to the impenitent. Barring the misapplication of the text, he made a forcible and truthful exhibition of a different topic. The sermon was well written, and thoroughly Calvinistic. His tone was severe, Presbyterianly severe, in which he evidently did injustice to his nature. From his general style, I judged him to be liberally educated, but not remarkably patriotic. His whole sermon was directed by eye and gesture to a small boy in a far corner of the church. I pitied that boy.

The soldiers listened with attention and respect. Here officers and men met on a level. Here all arms of the service were blended. The sober army blue of our Massachusetts men contrasted with the gayer trappings of New York. The light-blue stripe of infantry sat by the scarlet of artillery and the yellow stripe and spurs of cavalry. Here the plain dress of private mingled with the chevrons of the corporal and sergeant, nor was repelled by the epaulets or shoulder-straps of captains or colonels. And occasionally might be seen the buff sash, and the two stars glistening in silence on the shoulder of the firmly-knit, keen-eyed, resolute major-general. The rank was outside. Beneath were men, each under the same law, invited by the same gospel. Beneath, too, were Christians. In witnessing a division review, I have thought how infantry, artillery, cavalry, engineers, though distinct in dress, and arms, and drill, are yet animated by one principle : the infantry may have the Enfield rifle or the Springfield, the smooth bore or the altered lock, and yet do service in harmony ; even every regiment has its two flags, one its State banner, with its own name thereon, the other, loftier, the stars and stripes ; and yet all form one army, whose great centre of fealty is the flag. So all Christians, though equipped differently, mayhap, and marching to a special flag of their own, yet bear above that the banner of the cross, and form a great unit, acknowledging allegiance to the one great Captain, Jesus Christ. How paltry are all quarrelings among Christians as to what arm of the service one belongs, or what dress he wears. The Banner, the Great Banner ! The Captain, the Great Captain !

In the rear of this church is a burial-ground, the one most used. Not many graves were there till we came ; but there used to grow larger every week a row of single graves placed side by side. They are the graves of soldiers. And here, on many a day, the village people used to stroll along as the muffled drum passed by, and curiously, yet sympathizingly, see the burial, and hear the three volleys over the open grave, and wonder where his home had been, and whether he had a mother. And they were often kind to our poor sick soldiers, for which the blessing of our Lord be upon them !

There were good Christians there, too. I made some friendships, though they were not with any of the high in their own estimation, but with the more humble. Those of self-importance were generally secessionists. In some families were many religious books ; and I respect one good man, who came to our regiment with tracts, only to find more there than he probably ever saw before. The family where I baptized the one child was Union. I hope to see yet, in future years, that little one, who knew, or seemed to know, when my hand held her, and always smiled when I took her. That family was sorry that we must leave. They said that with other regiments near them before, they had been in constant fear, and constantly suffering loss. But the SECOND MASSACHUSETTS had been orderly, courteous, and kind, and had been a protection. The reason was, we have Men, and we have Officers. Many other regiments have *one*, but not *both*.

The other child I shall never see on earth. He has already gone.

> " And we know — for God hath told us this —
>   That he is now at rest,
> Where other blessed children are,
>   On the Saviour's loving breast."

6 *

CHAPTER III.

LIFE NEAR FREDERICK TOWN.

CAMP HICKS, NEAR FREDERICK, MD., December 13, 1861.

THE change in our situation since I wrote last is delightful. Moving hither from "Seneca Creek," or "Muddy Branch," or "Near Darnestown," we came out of the malaria of the Potomac into pure country air; out of a shelterless, dismal field, into a pleasant grove, gently sloping to the south, where the warm sun lies beautifully down; and out of barbarism into civilization. We hear, by night, the hours struck. We hear the whistle of the locomotive near us, and think how, though five hundred miles from home, that power would take us there in twenty-four hours. We hear, on the Sabbath, the "church-going bell." How pleasantly its music rolls over the intervening three miles and a half, after our nearly six months' deprival of such a sound!

We had had rumors of removal for several weeks; but nobody paid any regard to them, until orders came to send away the sick men of the division by canal. This was as certain a precursor of marching as though the orders were published.

It was on Saturday that the first departure of the sick took place, near two weeks ago. They were to go to hospital at Alexandria, some twenty-five miles off. So our own sick men were sent down to the canal-lock, about a mile from us, there to join with those of other regiments. Special duty led me there, and we were at the lock about half an hour before noon. We had sent over twenty men, and from all the regiments there were between thirty and forty ambulance loads, carrying nearly two hundred. It was a bitterly cold day. The wind swept down the river valley bitingly. As the best to be done, we wheeled the ambulances round against the wind ; and waited — waited, till we were disgusted. It was shameless shiftlessness which forced these men to suffer.

While awaiting the boat, we built a rousing good fire under the shelter of an abutment. When I was a boy I always was particular about the first use of a new *knife*, and I had frequent occasions to try new ones, inasmuch as I lost so many that my indulgent father used to joke me with the statement, that if knives would sprout, our yard would be full of jack-knife trees. Well, I shall always entertain great regard for *this* knife (a capital one, just sent me by that same good father) from the fact that its christening took place in whittling shavings to kindle that fire. For one side of that fire was a rock ; on the other we drove a crotched stick ; and across we put another stick, on which we hung a borrowed kettle, and in that kettle we boiled water, of which our hospital attendants made tea for the sick men, followed by good beef tea as food. Two things are to be noted about the fire, for the benefit of future laborers ; first, it takes one man extra, with a dipper, to put out the fire on the cross stick, lest the kettle tumble into the fire ; and, secondly, it is not discreet to ask where the wood comes from ; the men's sickness must overrule — curiosity. But I confess that a rascally sutler objected to the sudden departure of pie-boxes, until I told the attendants to throw him into the canal if he did not hold his tongue.

We tried to keep up the men's spirits, and they did act nobly. The boat came, but entirely insufficient. Its floor was still wet, for the water had but just been pumped out. There could be no fire, and there was no shelter ; and these men were to go down the canal in that cold night. Straw had been promised, but no straw came. So we took the stacks of corn stalks from a neighboring field, until sentries drove the men off from this property of noted rebels. The boat was loaded at last, too full. I was the last out, and found the advantage of a pair of stout arms, with which to pull myself up six or seven feet. The boat started with its precious freight, and many hand-pressures and " God bless yous."

There was not room for all, and quite a number remained for another day or so. Of those left behind, several were placed in the two houses snug by. Our surgeon and assistant surgeon took care of our own men and of some others ; found beds for them ; appointed nurses ; secured sentries ; provided food, and furnished necessaries. One poor fellow of another regiment excited my pity. He was sitting alone on a bench in a kind of entry, and leaning in the corner of the room. I spoke with him. He told me his regiment. He had been brought down there, placed in the corner, and, by some accident, left. The boat had gone without him. His knapsack had gone aboard. The persons in charge of him had gone back to camp. He had no food. He was convalescent from typhoid fever, but was entirely helpless from disease in the hip. Our assistant surgeon needed only the sight of him to provide for him, and the warm-hearted men of the Second were ready to take care of him. So they did of others, one of whom was too sick — a cavalry man — to be moved farther.

On Monday the remainder were to go — by canal — up to the Point of Rocks on the Baltimore and Ohio Railroad, and thence to Frederick. So, Sunday evening I accompanied the assistant surgeon and ward master to the houses occupied by the sick. It was dark, and we picked our way by the light of a lantern, down through the ploughed fields, and over little brooks. At one house a sutler's establishment was open for trade ; but we were not in that line. Our sick men were doing well. In one room lay several of them, comfortably provided for — a low room, in a mean locality, and with beds upon the floor, but still very comfortable, thanks to our medical and hospital men. And poor as was the place, and dim as its one candle left it, it was a spot where our Lord stood with us, and where the hearts of the sick soldiers were refreshed. Even there were words of praise from spirits which had " peace and joy in believing " But the sick cavalry man had lost his senses.

On Monday the second party from the division went. This time *our* assistant surgeon * had charge. The boat was ready at the time. The ambulance drivers reported to him, and he saw to the embarkation. He saw that nurses did their duty. It was by night they went ; but when morning came, he roused up the attendants, and had warm relishing food provided. He drove away the whiskey-dealers at Point of Rocks, and though they had to wait there a while, the train came at last, and carried them safely to a good hospital in Frederick. But one of our men (a mere boy rather) taken out of a hospital at Darnestown, died the next day, and Wisconsin men fired the volleys over his grave as they buried him. All the sick, save a few to go with the regiments, were

---

* It was Lincoln R. Stone, now surgeon of volunteers.

6 *

thus carried away. Not *all* thus. When the last party started, the cavalry soldier was dead.

On Tuesday our brigade started. The march was like all others, save that both days were very cold. The first day we went to Barnesville, a Maryland village of the genuine kind. Feeling *figurative*, I counted the number of houses; twenty-six, unless I mistook barns for houses, or houses for barns, in several intricate cases. We camped in a beautiful wood. It is strange how dreary a wood or field looks in a cold day, as your regiment enters it, and how cheerful it becomes as tough arms raise the city of tents, and build huge roaring fires. So it was here. The next morning reveille beat at a quarter past four. It was cold work to toss aside our blankets and leave our heaps of straw for the raw air. Great fires again thawed out the chill. Hunger vanished soon. You never appreciate coffee till you try it before daylight in camps of a cold morning, — after having attended to a moderate toilet by the light of a candle, for which a two-bladed knife furnishes a candlestick, one blade horizontal in a tree, and a smaller pointing up at right angles, with the candle stuck upon it. Probably you never yet have learned how good a dish is made of hard biscuit fried with salt pork; though the flavor depends somewhat upon a hard march the day before, a raw morning, and before sunrise.

Between six and seven we were moving again. Down came the tents as the final roll of the " general " beat; into wagons went tents and baggage. The line is formed among the trees. " Forward ! " And just as dawn was disclosing " Old Sugar Loaf," — the Kearsarge or Ascutney of this region, — the regiment plunged down into the valley mists which wrapped its base.

The road was beautiful; only with cold fingers and feet it

is hard to appreciate scenery. In summer it must be delightful: winding around the base of Sugar Loaf, over a spur of it, along by tossing brooks, fording shallow streams, — it reminded one of New England mountain scenery. The reminder was not in customs nor idioms. Calling at a small house whose joint proprietors were doing a brisk business in coffee and pies, and where I made acquaintance with four or five broad-faced, good-natured children, I was amused to hear the father tell one to " go hunt the branch." I ventured to inquire the meaning, and learned that " the branch " was the *brook*, and " hunting " it meant to wash his face in it. I was equally interested in learning that the title of " Koot," which one little girl bore, was intended as " the short " for " Margaret Adelaide," as the mother informed me, after asking the father what the child's name was. But the poor family — none of whose children go to school — is the first family on any road in Maryland, rich or poor, which I have known to decline receiving pay for a cup of coffee or other little luxury. Of course I felt obliged to leave a little token with " Koot."

That day brought us to " near Frederick." That day? Four hours and a quarter took our regiment *fifteen miles*, the field officers marching on foot with their men the whole distance. Then, in a bleak field, and in a cold wind, we stood three hours and a half waiting for orders where to camp. The responsible commander was then discovered in front of a coal fire at a hotel. We were finally sent to a spot near the Monocacy bridge, and pitched our tents, and spread our straw, and built our fires.

Next morning we were sent to this beautiful camp ground. Our camp is always famous for its neatness. And here, underbrush has been cut up by the roots, every leaf swept

off, and trees trimmed of low branches. We have the right
of the line, the Sixteenth Indiana is next to us, the Thirtieth
Pennsylvania a little in the rear, and the good Twelfth Massachusetts on the left.

Our regiment acted admirably in this moving. They
never marched better. They behaved well. There was
little drinking, and no disorder. Nor can it be said of
many regiments, anywhere, that one marched fifteen miles
in four hours and a half, with forty pounds of load per man,
and came in entire, and in marching order. It could not be
said of us, as one officer said of another regiment (his own)
on the road, " The —— had a gay old drunk last night, officers and men." Our officers did not, as did multitudes,
rush into Frederick for comfortable beds and coal fires at
hotels ; for our commander is too old a soldier to leave his
men under canvas in cold weather, and take to luxurious
shelter himself; and he has too good officers to expect
worse of them. In fact, if any of us had asked for leave to
join a small swarm of officers (none Massachusetts) at hotels
in Frederick, he would have found something else on his colonel's face than the kind look he is in the habit of seeing.

Though I have, perhaps, taken too much room already,
you must let me say a word on the recent orders as to chaplains, concerning dress, &c. It is said, in some papers, that
many chaplains are dissatisfied. This may be true at
Washington, but it is not so in this division. It is, perhaps, pleasing to me that the simple dress now prescribed
is the precise one stated as proper by our commander, when
I was leaving home, and which, of course, I procured. The
shoulder-straps, gilt buttons, and swords, on some chaplains,
have always excited the ridicule of army officers. The less
a chaplain assumes to be a military man, the better. His

influence is that of a *Christian minister.* Men expect that, but they do not expect a mere preaching officer. As to rank, due respect, &c., a chaplain needs no military rank, nor exacted salutations. As General Scott informed a committee, a chaplain will secure that position his qualities entitle him to occupy; that is, when officers are gentlemen. Some regiments — many — have officers not what they should be ; and there the best of chaplains find trouble. But the reverse is sometimes true. In this division, we are glad of the new regulation. We believe that a chaplain's position is too noble for him to need gilt and tinsel. General Jackson once told a minister applying for office, " You have a higher office than is in my power to bestow." So has a chaplain ; but it is not a military office ; it is that of friend, adviser, and helper, to both officer and private alike. With such material as ours a chaplain feels no lack of rank or show.

CAMP HICKS, NEAR FREDERICK, MD., December 28, 1861.

WE have supposed that the division was to be put into winter quarters here ; but it seems not. The men have been allowed to make themselves comfortable in log huts, or by board floors ; but it is understood that the general-in-chief has decidedly informed the general of this division that winter quarters are not contemplated. The effect of this will not be great as to comfort, inasmuch as Yankee ingenuity can devise ways and means of keeping warm, unless too much care is taken to conciliate secession owners of wood lots. Did I write you, by the way, of a specimen of this regard for rebels — that certain straw stacks were held sacred at Darnestown, guarded by our soldiers, against the

directions of the medical director to procure straw therefrom,
at government expense, for our sick soldiers on the canal
boat? The question very naturally asked is, What man
owned straw too sacred for government use for sick men?
A man in Fort Lafayette on charge of open treason!

But this statement as to winter quarters is somewhat significant in regard to the prosecution of the war. If it is anything more than a sagacious deference to congressional impatience, it implies an active campaign, regardless of winter.
This division is admirably located for quick service. Its
supplies are easily furnished by rail. It is in a rich country.
If wanted at Baltimore or Washington, a few hours would
carry it to either. If any regiments are wanted for Southern service, Annapolis is direct by railroad. If the Upper
Potomac is to be crossed, it is less than an hour's ride to the
Point of Rocks, by the Baltimore and Ohio Railroad, and
hardly more than that to Harper's Ferry, where opens the
valley of the Shenandoah, in which are Winchester, Charlestown, and Martinsburg, now being approached from Western Virginia — all of which must be cleared out. If communication is to be opened with the West by the same
railroad, miles of which have been rendered useless by
rebels, we are on the line. So that Frederick seems to have
been chosen as a great point to start *from*.

Frederick itself is a rather pretty town, squarely laid
out, and with some fine churches and handsome private
houses. The most of the wealth (not all) is secesh. Many
rebel sympathizers have long since left; and even before we
came, the Union sentiment was numerically strongly predominant. People privately still drink the health of Jefferson Davis unmolested, and publicly look daggers at Northern soldiers, though not very dangerous daggers. The

condition of society is sad, by reason of these troubles. Friends are alienated, relations separated, and even churches divided. To me it is of very little importance that Union men will not trade with secesh, and *vice versa;* but it is a mournful spectacle to see divided churches and wasting Sabbath schools.

The principal churches here are the Lutheran, German Reformed, Presbyterian, Episcopalian, Methodist, and Catholic. The *status* of each Protestant minister is well understood. So far as I can learn, the Lutheran minister* is decidedly and unconditionally a Union man, a Pennsylvanian by birth; his large congregation is mostly Union, though there are quite a number of " peace " men; the clergyman evidently pursues a judicious course, but he has lost several parishioners. The pastor of the German Reformed has an equally large society, and has been here a good many years. He, at one time, omitted the prayer (required in their liturgy) for the President of the United States, and, I have no doubt, did it with comfort; but, being a " prudent " man, attended to the significant hints of several strong Union men of too much importance to be overlooked, and forthwith gave his valuable prayer to our chief magistrate's welfare. Some few secessionists forthwith left, on the ground that, if the pastor was a Union man, they, of course, *could* not attend his church; and if, Southern in sympathies, as they felt him to be, he yet prayed Northern, they certainly *would* not. The Presbyterian minister, somehow Southern in his connections, is also, in sentiment, undisguisedly Southern. To a Presbyterian chaplain, who called on him by way of courtesy, he said, " I should be glad to invite you to preach in my pulpit, but on the condition that no allusion shall be made to the

* Rev. George Diehl, D. D.

course of the North." " I would *not* preach in your pulpit, sir," was the reply to the insult ; " if I did, it should be unmistakably loyal. Good morning." The Union men in that congregation make no trouble, of course ; only rebels are turbulent. The Methodists are sadly weakened ; their minister is boldly loyal, and many Southern sympathizers have left. His Sunday school, even, these eminently Christian men have abandoned. The Episcopalian clergyman is nobly national. Of course he has not made his pulpit an arena of attack on others, but he is known to be plainly and uncompromisingly loyal. Secessionists who leave other churches, find no comfort from him. Still, a large portion of his people dislike his Unionism, as well as his faithful, devoted attention to the sick soldiers in our general hospital. And I cannot help seeing that his position is not pleasant, either now or prospectively, and he ought, with his abilities, education, culture, and piety, to be called to some Northern church. This suggestion, if it meet the eye of any Episcopalian, I beg leave to say is without his knowledge, and I know not but he would dislike it.*

I have had opportunity to be in Frederick two Sabbath afternoons. On the first, my intimate friend, the chaplain of the Twelfth Massachusetts, and myself, found ourselves in the Episcopal church. The pastor himself preached a very well digested and forcibly prepared sermon, on the " necessity of a revelation," as to the being and nature of God. I was greatly interested in it, especially with its practical, sensible application. There were many shoulder-straps in the congregation, and a very sober and reverent attention. The church itself is a beautiful one, severely Gothic, built by

---

* Rev. Charles Seymour, now of Massachusetts.

Upjohn, the special beauty of whose work is, there is never
any *sham* about it; no mastic imitations of stone outside —
that abominable humbug; no blocked off plaster inside — that
transparent lie. I confess I liked so much of the liturgy as
enables the people to have some visible share in public worship; and the habit they had of actually kneeling in prayer,
instead of the bolt-upright stubbornness which many of our
New England congregations cling to so devoutly. Nor was
I any the less pleased with hearing even the voices of children mingling with those of mature age in the Lord's
Prayer. Nor was the congregation guilty of the gross irrev-
erence of wheeling round, backs toward the pulpit, to stare
at the choir. I do not *think* there is any heresy here; if
there is, have a brotherly regard to my reputation, and sup-
press it.

In the evening, we looked around for a prayer meeting.
By chance, we got to the door of the Methodist church; but
learning that a certain tract agent was to hold forth, we got
no farther. That particular agent I had heard once, and I
knew *his* stripe on the great sins of the nation too well to
want to hear him again. It is too late now to bolster up the
"peculiar institution," and I am for the gospel, wherever it
hits. A Christian literature which ignores slavery, while
professing to teach sound morality, is poor stuff. At home,
I attended to what my congregation needed — personal religion. Here, I would do the same — urge personal religion;
but circumstances alter cases, and personal religion here
meets the obstacle of the sin of slaveholding.

So we went on, and came to the Lutheran church. There
was no prayer meeting, however, the second service being
held in the evening. The pastor preached in a devotional
way. The singing, which was congregational, was most

hearty. They have here a very interesting habit of passing around the contribution box at every service.

Last Sabbath afternoon I was again in Frederick, and went to the Lutheran Sabbath school. What a pleasure it was, after near six months' abstinence from such luxuries! The school numbered four hundred, separated into two rooms. In one of them was the infant school, which had that day nearly a hundred and fifty little pupils, from scholars almost ready to pass into the next room down to timid little ones, majestically shielded under the arm of some patronizing brother or sister a year or two older. This department was admirably managed. The singing was delightful, and the very same hymns as are sung at home affected me very deeply. I count it a remarkable instance of self-denial that I declined talking to them. In addition to this large school, they have a mission school of about sixty pupils, a mile away.

At the close of the school, I was a listener at a special service in the church, of, to me, a novel kind. There are two congregations in this church, English and German, and once in two weeks the pastor preaches to the latter. I heard him that day. That is to say, I heard his voice. As I sat there, never did I so realize the force of the Apostle's argument, when he says, "If I know not the meaning of the voice, I shall be unto him that speaketh a barbarian; and he that speaketh shall be a barbarian unto me." Here and there I recognized a word, but, as a whole, it was to me a mass of gutturals — saving the Lord's Prayer, which I was, of course, able to follow by the help of one King James. For further particulars, see 1st Corinthians, 14th chapter.

In the evening, I fulfilled an engagement to be present. How strange it seemed to speak in a church! The absence of uniforms, the want of words of command, the lack of trees, seemed odd. Carpets, and pews, and pulpit, and organ, and walls, it really took a while to get used to them. I rather longed for open air again, and my own ten companies, though I began to feel before closing that I had once been civilized, and, possibly, in suitable circumstances, should be again. But I shall never again be reconciled to the board fence known as " pulpit."

On Christmas, also, I attended the Lutheran church. It was a beautiful morning for the saddle. The ground had been covered by just snow enough to make it white, not enough to leave the least mud in melting — which is all the snow we have had yet. Not even had the slow Monocacy " skimmed over " with ice. The weather was delightful, as it is almost all the time. For the first fortnight of our stay here not an overcoat was needed. At the church, Rev. Mr. Phillips, chaplain of the New York Ninth, preached a very excellent and appropriate sermon. At the same hour, the pastor preached to the German audience in the lecture-room. I was not there to hear; if I had been, I doubt the profit. But I could not help regarding it as rather enlivening, reverently feeling, nevertheless, that I was selected to help administer the sacrament, in a Lutheran form, to a body of German communicants, in the German language ! I concluded to decline. Nevertheless, feeling ashamed of my ignorance, consider me as learning German !

CANTONMENT HICKS, NEAR FREDERICK, MD., January 6, 1861.

CANTONMENT, not camp, by order of brigadier-general. " Camp," say the Army Regulations, is the place where

troops are established in tents, in huts, or in bivouac. Can-
tonments are the inhabited places which troops occupy when
not put in barracks. Then the brigade is in "inhabited
places"? Not at all; but several regiments have built log-
houses, and so wanted a better sounding name than "camp."
As the brigade order says "cantonment," "cantonment" it
is. It reminds one of the mince-pies a boy was calling for
sale. "Hot mince-pies!" "Hot mince-pies!" shouted the
boy. "But why do you call them *hot?*" said a disappointed
purchaser; "they are as cold as a stone!" "O, that's the
name of them," replied the boy.

Several regiments have erected excellent log-houses. The
Twelfth Massachusetts, in particular, has built a small city, in
manner and quality very creditable. Our own regiment,
having Sibley tents, with floors, and stoves, and straw beds,
as yet find no difficulty in keeping comfortable. The general-
in-chief at Washington says that Sibley tents are sufficient
for this climate. *Ergo,* this division is not in winter
quarters.

It is a little interesting that the very day when the order
went into operation re-christening our temporary home, whereby some idea of permanence was intended, there came a
sudden order to the whole division to cook two days' rations,
and be ready to march at a moment's notice. That was
yesterday. Rumor said that somebody had been attacked by
some rebel somebody with a force of 17,000 men at Hancock,
where is an advanced portion of the Western Virginia force,
a place a little west of north from Martinsburg, and on the
Potomac; and that the whole division would go there. But
we had received so many orders to cook two days' rations,
&c., that we pretty generally believed it would result only in
an accumulation of cold victuals. And so it proves. But I

am satisfied that the chances are against our remaining here long. There is no great obstacle to winter campaigning in this section when the ground is frozen as it now is. When the plan of the proper leader is developed in the several directions which look plausible, General Banks will not be condemned to inaction. Raw troops are sent off in the expeditions. Why are the drilled and disciplined regiments left, except to see hard service? The men were delighted
• yesterday at the prospect of marching and fighting. They were merry as larks, and packed knapsacks with songs and jollity. But *impatience* is the great danger again at home. Do let the general's plans work. If anybody wants to urge an immediate advance on Manassas, let him expect, if he were gratified, such a mourning over the slaughtered as would fill the North with dismay. Do people reflect what it is to make a direct attack on an able enemy, on his own ground, in a place admirably arranged by Nature to be defended — where months have been used to fortify every point — where engineers have selected sites for every battery — where a multitude of the heaviest guns command every avenue — where the range of every piece has been calculated — and where an immense and well-disciplined army covers the ground? Ought not people to reflect that they *cannot* understand the art of war like generals who have made it the study of a lifetime? They would not interfere with the blacksmith who shoes their horses; shall they teach an experienced general how to fight?

It is curious to see the queer notions which prevail in some minds. In the matter of promotions, for instance. I saw, a few days ago, the recommendation of a particular person for the rank of brigadier-general; it had four points, and not one of them said " he has the requisite qualifications " ! A

7 *

member of Congress was urging the appointment of another person. " But he does not know how to manage a brigade," it was said. " Well, he can learn, can't he?" was the wise reply. If you were going to have your watch cleaned, would you take it to a man who " could learn"? And you would commit the lives and honor of four thousand men to a man who " could learn," instead of appointing experienced soldiers !

The great want of our army still is *officers*. And the next is discipline. It is very pretty to tell what a patriotic militia* can do; but even the superficial reader of history knows better. In our revolutionary war — often alluded to — it is forgotten that the early troops had multitudes of " old French war " soldiers; and that as the war progressed, the constant entreaties of Washington were for a regular army, and time for drill and discipline. It was not until such troops were made that our country became successful on a regular field of battle. Nor, from our peaceful habits, is there that previous experience which can extemporize an army. Our country will never attain its true power until it has an army — a large standing army ; and perhaps not until every man is obliged, as in some European countries, to serve from one to three years ; nor until a great many more young men have a military education, which, from considerable observation, I am satisfied is, in many respects, the best that *any* young man can have, as preparatory to any profession.

We are having, just now, a little touch of winter. The snow is two inches deep. The cold is by no means troublesome, and our men are sweeping the camp-ground clean. It has a New England look, and makes soldiers from Massachusetts better contented. Woodcutters, too, resume their occupation, and there is a lively appearance in every direction. In Frederick, the season might be called "gay." A

quiet old place, rather Dutchy from its origin,—the entrance
of such a number of soldiers is a comfort to many. Epaulets, sashes, and swords are as attractive to a certain class
of a delicate and tender age as they always have been the
world over. Visiting, driving, and party-ing, are rife. On
New Year's, many families kept open house, and dispensed
hospitalities. Mrs. Banks's reception was particularly
thronged, of course, to a great extent by military, but with
sprinklings of citizens of both sexes. It is not indelicate, I
hope, to say that this lady is very popular, and deserves it.
As an instance of kindness,—the mother of one of our
sick soldiers was on her way from Massachusetts to her son's
bedside. She chanced to be in the same car with the wife
of the general, and in some manner Mrs. B. learned her
story, and, on arriving at Frederick, at a late hour, she took
the mother directly to her own home, at headquarters, where
she was welcomed to the tea-table ; and, as the son was at
some private house, she knew not where, the general immediately despatched a mounted orderly to learn, who returned
with the requisite knowledge. The mother reached her son
that night, some distance in the country ; and two or three
days after, the thoughtful general and his wife appeared, to
visit the sick, and sympathize with the mother. This considerate kindness to a stranger, and regard to the sick (who
was not an officer), tempers the severities of such a wander-
ing life. I have myself heard, at the general hospital, the
praises of this same lady's kindness.

Nor ought I, while on this topic, to neglect to mention the
Christian kindness of many women of Frederick to the sick.
If I mistake not, there is the nucleus of an organization,
which acts systematically. And in that, and in addition
thereto, the women here are earnest and faithful in their

kindness. Many a little comfort finds its way to the hospital ; many a delicate article of food is carried there. And the very presence of these ladies, as they daily pass through the wards, with a kind smile and word, is often equal, at least, to all other means of recovery. It makes the heavy walls look homelike. And yet there are those here in Frederick who discourage such attentions to the sick. They are rebel sympathizers, of course ; and it illustrates what I have so often observed, that I believe it to be nearly universal, that the rebels have lost, in their act of rebellion, almost all Christian virtues, as well as the sense of honor. It is a strange phenomenon, but it is true, that from an active rebel you need not expect, in general, honor, truth, or principle. The public stealings which characterized the Floyds, the Rhetts, and the Benjamins, were the indications of rebel character. Southern chivalry is a myth. Southern honor is a theory of the past. Throwing off their allegiance, forswearing their oaths, plotting and conspiring, they are corrupted through and through.

The Third Brigade, General Williams, has actually gone.

Cantonment Hicks, near Frederick, Md., January 20, 1862.

The brush at Hancock amounted to little. Of course the rebels destroyed, with impunity, a part of the line of the Baltimore and Ohio Railroad, as we had but a small force guarding it. A piece of road of this length it would take fifty thousand men to guard, as each part must be secure against any sudden and concentrated attack of the enemy, who occupy the country on the other side of it. The faint attempt to guard such part of the road as is now in our possession, and the entire

neglect to open the whole, indicate that the general-in-chief
regards the avenue as of slight consequence in his whole
comprehensive plan. A general success would open the road
of itself. With a broad scheme in mind, such incidental
matters can well be postponed.

Last night there came orders to the division to be ready to
move "at a moment's notice." This old stereotyped phrase
has rather lost its force ; but this time we think a little more
of it, as it came from the general-in-chief. There were also
sent orders to grant no leaves of absence, which looks as if
something was meant. It somewhat disappoints the longing
looks of some towards a day or two at home, but nobody
would care to be absent if there is anything to be done beyond
taking scrupulous care of the secessionist's wood-lot where
we are in camp. And that matters are rapidly ripening to a
crisis, nobody doubts. If Congress will provide " ways and
means," and leave the conducting of armies to soldiers, success seems certain. Many persons seem forcibly to think
that victory can be legislated, or that legislation or popular
preference can make a general. It takes a year to make a
good soldier ; how much more to understand, not only particulars, but the art of war?

The soldier's life here has been varied a little by vicinity
to a city. Not that *our* officers have been on "sprees " in
Frederick, or that discipline has been loose. But a certain
number of men daily have been granted permits to visit the
city, and have seen the sights — one of the chief of which is
a grog-shop every few doors on various streets, where sentries seem almost useless. Frederick is a great place for
liquor. And some soldiers will drink to excess. The sum-
mary method of dealing with these places would be best ;
such as our commanding officer took, when, a few days ago,

it was discovered that some loose literature had got into camp among a class that way affected ; — he instantly seized all to be found, and had it committed to the flames, when it speedily became *very* " light" literature indeed. The evil was not general, as we have many sterling men in this regiment ; and it was summarily disposed of. The morals of camp will, I believe, compare favorably with communities at home.

There have been various " parties," and the like, at Frederick. One musical entertainment has also been given — a military concert by our band. The house was crowded ; general, brigadiers, colonels, were there, with plenty of citizens. The music was superb, and received the warmest applause.

My own work, the past week, has been in a different direction — at the general hospital. It was found, some weeks since, that while regimental chaplains visited to some extent their own men there, yet there was no adequate religious care as a system. There is, as yet, no law authorizing the appointment of chaplains to hospitals, but, on representation to General Banks, he heartily approved a plan to have the chaplains of the regiments officiate there in turn, visit the sick, and bury the dead. The past week was my turn.

The general hospital is one, established in some convenient place, to which the regimental surgeons send men likely to be sick for some length of time, or to have severe disease. It is established in buildings, and well systematized. The division hospital is in the " barracks," so called, two buildings of stone, erected in the time of General Braddock, and in that war used for army quarters. You will remember that Braddock's army passed through Frederick, on its disastrous advance ; and, personally, I have felt an interest in the fact that my own great-grandfather was in that army, and once

encamped by a spring near here ; and that no member of
the family has been here since, until Providence attached me
to this division in a holier war. There the buildings have
stood for more than a hundred years, still strong and firm.
The original plan was to build a quadrangle, but only one
side, and a little turning of the two angles, were ever erected.
Nor is the one side continuous ; there is a break, and in that
is now a low building used for kitchen and dining-room. On
the inner side of the building, east of the two stories, is attached a covered walk, from which you gain entrance into
the dozen rooms or "wards" into which each building is
divided. Old-fashioned chimneys offer great hearths for
roaring fires, cheerful, and capital for ventilation. Hideous,
destructive stoves are unknown. One room is kept for office,
one for surgery, and one for the soldiers' knapsacks.

A "medical director" has the entire oversight. The present one is Dr. Stone, our own excellent assistant surgeon,
whose administration warrants the important confidence
placed in him. He has three assistant surgeons, a general
steward, and a nurse to each room, besides two female
nurses, who exercise a general and beneficial care of the
neatness and comforts of the wards, and whose kind hands
often arrange the pillow, or smooth the hair of the poor fellows, with a humanizing touch of home. Of course there
are clerks, cooks, &c., in plenty. And there are good beds
and excellent bedding.

Here there were, the day I went semi-officially (I knew
the place before, for we had men there), one hundred and
fifty-five patients. Most of them were able to sit up, but
some were low. One was very sick, an Indiana man. I
saw him that day, but he was almost steadily delirious. He
was thinking of other scenes ; " mother," and " sister " —

such were his often repeated calls. He seemed to think he saw them; poor fellow! never more in this world. They will wait in vain. A little change in the lines, —

> "For men must fight, though women may weep,
> And the sooner 'tis o'er, the sooner we sleep."

He died that night. And next day we buried him, far from home, mother, sister, — with only six bearers, the eight muskets, and the three volleys at his grave, — but with Christian service and reverence.

In one room, a small one, with four beds, I said to the nurse, "When I was in this room last there were four very sick men from an Indiana regiment." "Yes," said he, "and they are all dead." They were all nearly hopeless cases when brought there. And I remembered that all four were delirious. Many, however, very severely sick, are recovered; as many, perhaps, as at home in the same number. The care is good, the medical advice excellent. But it is a sad thought that almost every one I have visited, in a fatal sickness, has not had his senses in his last days.

It was sad, too, to see a few cases of consumption. It was easy to know that no skill could save them. And yet, every one "had only a cough," and perhaps "a pain in his side." That flattering disease had here its usual characteristics, "soon to be better." Army life had developed the seeds of the disease brought from home; while, on the other hand, it is often the case that apparent tendency to lung disease has disappeared in this open way of living. Some, indeed, who were delicately sheltered, and who formerly sought a warm climate in winters, are now hardened into robust health by this exposure.

But it was not all sad. I will forbear "anecdote." But

never have I seen men more open to religious friendship. Many are Christians, and all seemed ready and eager to listen. They know the feeling of a warm hand-shake, and believe in any manly sympathy extended to them. They had some reading, religious and secular, left them by kind visitors, but there were few, very few Bibles, and such were well worn. This latter want is already attended to, and speedily every room will be amply supplied. It would have done you good to see how happy some of our own men were when I took from my pockets their letters, which I had brought from camp. Be sick away from home, in a soldiers' hospital, and you would learn the comfort of words from home. And none the less would it have excited your Christian sympathy; to see how quiet the groups around the fires would become when the Bible was read, and how reverently they would listen ; and how many of them kneeled in prayer, and how hearty was their " Amen " at its close. In my ministry I have seen many sick. I have witnessed the supporting power of Christian faith, in its most favorable aspects, at home ; in fact, I can look back on no departed one of my congregation to whom our Lord had not given a firm hope in him. But the experience of a sick man among strangers, or at best, fellow-soldiers, is peculiar. And Christ is sufficient for them. These men, whether Christians or not, were not afraid to speak of religion — not merely very sick men, but those nearly restored to health. They " hunger and thirst ; " and the sooner Congress can find time to provide chaplains for hospitals, the sooner it will be doing some good.

8

CANTONMENT HICKS, NEAR FREDERICK, MD., February 10, 1862.

MY application for leave of absence, after passing through
the hands of various military dignitaries for ten days, was
granted, and so, receiving it in the evening, I was next morning on the way home.   Home, so remote, and yet so near ;
nigh five hundred miles in distance, less than twenty-four
hours in time.   The sixth State off, territorially, but snug in
the heart always.

First, the camp disappeared.   Then the soldier-lined streets
of Frederick were left behind.   And from Havre-de-Grace,
picket and patrol were things of the past.   The cars never,
I thought, went so slowly before on civilized railroad ; but
Baltimore, Philadelphia, New York, Boston, all came in
season.   It was with strange sensations I entered home, after
five months of absence.   To sleep in a real house ; to sit at
one's family table ; to be partially choked every morning
by the *reveille* of a three-year-old's chubby fingers ; to be
slowly recognized in the street ; to shake hands with a whole
congregation ; to preach in one's own pulpit ; to feel refreshed
now and then at seeing a blue uniform of some soldier on
furlough ; to pass one night under the roof of father and
mother, — altogether, it took several days to get over the
" bewilderment."   But when a " realizing sense " of the
behavior needed in Massachusetts was obtained, the change
was decidedly comfortable.   I am free to confess that, notwithstanding the great advantages of tents as places of residence, there is much to be said in support of the popular
prejudice in favor of houses.   I detest furnaces, however,
and stoves as much as ever.

If you think such a visit is rest, I wish you could try it.
Such a quantity of errands to be fulfilled ; such numbers of

mothers, sisters, wives, and sweethearts to be talked with
about our soldiers; such a multitude of inquiries to be
answered; such a variety of "letters, or *very* small parcels,"
which I innocently told the public I would take back, and
for which I had to buy a trunk! besides four sermons, all
new; but what are four, or forty sermons, when one has got
something to say? Indeed, I am satisfied that the principal
difficulty in preaching (*don't* say "sermonizing" any more)
is in having something to say! When I had the honor of
being a high officer in an "engine company," we found no
trouble in keeping up a steady stream, even with the "blun-
derbuss" on the leading-hose, if there was water enough
in the cistern; when she "drew mud" was the trouble,
brother minister!

I am glad I went home, besides the reason that it was
home. I did not know how many friends I had, nor how
glad they would be to see me. I did not know how intense
was the interest in our soldiery, both as to their bodily and
spiritual welfare. I did not conceive of the generosity which
said, so many times, "What can we do or give to help the
men of the Second?" Thanks, friends. Our men shall
know your warmth of love better, and their hearts will be
stouter and happier, for your care. And we will never dis-
honor your trust, nor the name of the good old State, when
the time shall come for fiery bullets and cold steel. "The
soldiers are always called 'boys,' are they not?" I was asked.
"Not in the SECOND," said I; "our soldiers are *men*."
They are, many of them, sturdy, noble *men;* they know
they are on a manly errand, and they mean to do it in a
manly way.

It seems dream-like now, that visit. I knew I had to
leave, being a man "under authority," literally. There

was the new parting from the tender but brave heart, which
bears hard separation and unusual responsibility, for her
country's sake ; the unloosing of the little arms, which plead
so earnestly, " Please, papa, *don't* go to the war again ; "
from the church, which waits so patiently and so generously
for a pastor absent in their and his country's cause. When
at the Boston station, I remember seeing a woman parting
from a soldier, just leaving by the same train, and weeping
so bitterly, — both were strangers to me, — while he was trying to comfort her, and her friends were saying, " Never
mind, he will come back again." *Will* he?

Never did I so realize the sacrifices this war exacts.
Truly, not the hardships of a soldier's life, nor even his
peril, nor the taxes to be paid, are the cost of this contest.
That is in the tears of many a wife and child, the anxieties
of many a father and mother, told to God in the daily
prayers of many a thousand households. Never did I so
feel sympathy with our brave men, separated from their
homes, perhaps forever. It will be over by and by. Many
will return. But many? But last evening, — it was the
Sabbath, — as I was sitting in my tent, I heard from many
lips, in a volume of sound which overpowered all hum of
camp, —

> " O, that will be joyful, joyful, joyful ;
> O, that will be joyful,
>   When we meet to part no more.
> 'Tis there we meet at Jesus' feet,
>   When we meet to part no more."

" Even so, Lord Jesus." And soon after I heard old
" Coronation," its last two lines rolling upward, seemingly
from a multitude of voices, -

> " Bring forth the royal diadem,
>   And crown him Lord of all ! "

That shall we do. "We give thee thanks, O Lord God Almighty, which art, and wast, and art to come; because thou hast taken to thee thy great power, and hast reigned."

A night and a day brought me back. Need I say I was somewhat restless to see our officers and men? That I used to wonder how our sick men were? The dead body of one of our faithful soldiers had gone home with me: would there be any dead in my absence? Yes; one had died. Delirious, yet the day before I left, when I saw him in Frederick, he knew me readily; and my good brother of the Wisconsin Third had promised to see him often. And two others were near death, and have since gone. Of the one who died in my absence, his comrades had, with soldierly generosity, sent home the body, and in addition thereto, had added a liberal, very liberal, sum from their hard earnings, to help his family. Our Lord will surely bless them. No others are dangerously, or even severely sick. And some had recovered, and have left the hospital.

Are there any signs of movement? I can see none. One look at the mud would satisfy anybody. Everywhere is mud, mud, mud. It is not like New England mud. It is more like mortar, and deep beyond your imagination. Off from the turnpike roads, it is almost impassable for any respectable load. It rains often, and that deepens the mud. It snows an inch or two, and that becomes mud. The comic picture of a wagoner sitting on a fence, and gazing intently downwards, in search of his wagon and horses which have settled there, is rather an exaggeration, it is true; but it *suggests* a solemn truth. In fact, the embargo on legislation in Congress is hardly more fixed than that on the army of the Potomac. In the mean time rejoice in the successes in Kentucky and Tennessee. Rejoice at the

8 *

recent shelling of Harper's Ferry, whereby a lot of mean old
buildings, which we knew mainly as grog-shops, were burned,
together with the hotel of as pestilent a secessionist as ever
trod.   I shall not shed tears if Charlestown, in Virginia,
where they threw water on our soldiers, shares the same
fate.   In fact, many a Southern town would be improved by
a share of the same course of discipline.   The rascality of
the rebel soldiers at Harper's Ferry, in concealing themselves while a flag of truce was displayed, and firing on the
flag coming in return, is Southern chivalry.   The running of
the gallant Mississippians, at Mill Spring, before a bayonet
charge, is Southern valor.   Two to one is their ratio of
equal forces.

But while I found, on returning, an embargo on movement, I found none on the liquor business.   I wrote you
before of the briskness of that trade in Frederick.   On the
day of my return I found the road spotted with drunken
men.   It seems as though liquor dealers held carnival.   It
is hard to believe that it could not be stopped.   Some Maryland law protects the dealers, I believe; but the power
which sends men to Fort Lafayette by mere executive war-
rant, one would think need not hesitate to pour into the
street the stock which, in defiance of orders, is sold to soldiers, and to turn out of doors the fellows who are getting
men intoxicated by hundreds.   As it is, our own regiment is
kept from it as much as possible.   It is not good for a trader
to be found near our lines in such an occupation.   "Your
officer," complained a liquor-selling Dutchman, "come to
my house, and did speel all my leetel peer."   "Served you
right," was his comfort.   It was fun to see him then
dressed in a barrel overcoat, and marched round the camp
to the tune of the "Rogue's March."   Do you want to know

how to make that kind of overcoat? Take a barrel, leave one head in, cut in that head a hole just large enough to let the affair slip down over *his* head, and rest on his shoulders; no sleeves are necessary.

CANTONMENT HICKS, NEAR FREDERICK, MD., February 21, 1862.

" WHY should I write?" I have asked myself. Who will want to hear from the army, whose share in the news column has, for so long a time, been " all quiet on the Potomac," while a series of splendid victories at Roanoke, in Tennessee, in Missouri, have crowned their armies with glory? But, I think to myself, our turn will come soon. Armies on either side, of five times the size of either Western force, will yet have something to do and to tell. And, in the mean time, multitudes of families are still as earnest as ever in love for their sons in this section of the broad field, by whom everything will yet be read.

It is true we are still quiet. A skirmish above us, by General Lander's force, is the only noticeable incident. You saw, of course, the order of thanks to that general, and he deserves it. But the implied comparisons in that order are strange. He is complimented for " showing how much may be done in the worst weather, and worst roads, by a spirited officer at the head of a small force of brave men, unwilling to waste life in camp when the enemies of their country are in reach." Who would suppose from this that the other divisions, though chafing with impatience to meet the enemy, are kept in their present places by positive orders from the central authority? But such is the fact. And if anybody supposes that any general or division hereabouts *is*

" willing to waste life in camp when the enemies of their country are within reach," just let him get leave from proper authority to move, instead of keeping us tied to a telegraph wire.

We have been reading of the enthusiasm with which Boston was alive at the tidings of victory. There was no less joy here. When the information came from headquarters (reliable accounts are regularly telegraphed to the general, and thence communicated through the brigadiers to the colonels), our commander instantly informed the captains, and they their companies. Such an uproar of enthusiasm! Out poured the men from their tents, and cheered by companies right lustily. Out came the band with Star-spangled Banner and Yankee Doodle, amidst the shouts of the whole regiment gathered round them. You would have thought the staid and sober Second had gone wild. Then the next regiment in line had caught the news, and their music joined in, almost drowned by the shouts of the stout Indianians; and so the next, and the next, until the whole brigade seemed crazy. But who would not shout at such victories over the haughty, lying, thieving rebels? Certainly they would who saw, as ours did, the wounded and dead at Ball's Bluff — for which our Massachusetts men owe yet, and mean to pay, a terrible retribution.

A few days since a few of our men had opportunity for service offered. Orders came to select men from the New England regiments to go West immediately to man the gunboats for the descent of the Mississippi. Only fifteen men were wanted, but scores and scores volunteered. Our fifteen, mainly old sailors, were joined to those from other regiments, and left, with a short and stirring address from our colonel, who has the " art of putting things," and amidst the cheers of the men. The whole from this division are now far on their way, under charge of Captain Cary, of our regiment.

While thus waiting, and impatient at it, our men have gained much in bodily condition, and, so far, inaction is a benefit. Few regiments did as much hard duty as ours on the Potomac, for weeks, without the use of their tents, and it told sadly in our general strength. The rest was needed. Men cannot be transformed in a day into hardy soldiers, and the exposures and toil of a soldier's life are hard to bear at first. Of all our deaths, the proportion was excessive in a body of recruits who came out in the autumn, and entered at once on a service to which the bulk of the regiment had got seasoned. We had a large sick list at Seneca ; but now, only one man of our whole number is sick enough to be in bed, and he not dangerously ill. A few days ago there was not one. There are a few, however, in the hospital, whom it is not thought best to hurry back to their quarters, but all are out of doors at pleasure. It would be hard to find now a healthier regiment than ours. This will save many a man's life in the coming campaign.

Nor do I find that this inaction demoralizes the regiment. I see that some New York paper, to sustain its unscrupulous dislike of General McClellan, speaks of the troops as in worse spirits than two months ago. It is not so here. Our men are in the finest spirits, and eager for work. Discipline was never better, nor more kindly submitted to. Arms and equipments are in the best order. The usual routine of camp duties is not at all relaxed. Comparative idleness, of course, has some evil results. There is, and always will be, more or less vice in a camp of a thousand men ; but there is no marked increase. Indeed, I am more and more impressed with the fact, that in addition to the excellence of our officers, we have a great proportion of upright men, who came into the service from motives of the heartiest patriotism.

Among other devices for this vacation period, we have a small regimental library. While at home, I found that such a help was easily procurable, and soon after my return a good heavy box of standard and readable books came on. I : we public thanks for this, especially to Mr. M. H. Sargent, who interested himself most generously and heartily in obtaining and forwarding the books — the nest-egg of which was a kind donation from Rev. Mr. Tolman's church, at Wilmington. (A few more donations in money would suit me exactly.) If the donors could see the eagerness with which the books are read, they would feel still happier in doing good. Although none but private notice was given to the men, the demand for good and profitable books was and is great. Among those most read (I take from the book where I charge the volumes, to show the taste), are the charming life of Deacon Safford, Winthrop's John Brent, Dickens's Christmas Stories, Abbott's Practical Christianity, Dexter's Street Thoughts, the Lives of Washington, Jackson, Fremont, Franklin, and Boone, Palissy the Potter, Annals of the Poor. I wish I had a hundred more good books immediately.

But I suppose before many weeks our library will be packed up and deposited in the government storehouse, to await a further quiet. That is, when we start for Virginia. People must not think, in their present enthusiasm, that the war is over. Great successes have been ours, but far greater toils await us. The rebels have formidable armies, able generals, large amounts of the munitions of war, an immense territory, and the desperation of leaders who fight in sight of the gallows. There is much fighting yet necessary ; much blood to be shed ; much suffering to be endured. There is no less need of patience, persistence, and energy. The spring campaign will be no holiday. Nor can we hope for uninterrupted successes everywhere. Do not call me a prophet of evil ; I am only warning against too great security, though without the slightest doubt of the final result. I am cautioning against alternations of exultation and depression. The Southern scoundrels, who deify stealing and lying, have too much at stake to submit, even though they ruin their whole territory. Moreover, slaveholding has trained them to be despots, and despots they will be to the end. It makes men thieves, and they will steal as long as they can. It makes them braggarts, and they will brag on the very brink of destruction. When the South is overwhelmed, there will be only an apparent peace ; for I have learned, even so far north as Virginia and Maryland, mingling with all classes, that as society is now constituted, we are two peoples. Men may cry " peace," but until the removal of slavery is plainly, quietly, constitutionally provided for, whether instant or remote is a small question, there is no peace. Slavery is the root of our troubles, because slavery makes men tyrants, and tyrants thwarted are rebels. On such a question I have no ability to show the method. I only fear two things : one, that in the desire for peace, the government will let traitors go finally unhung, and the cause of their treason guaranteed a new life ; the other, lest in trying to remove the evil, we should, as in Hawthorne's exquisite story of the Birth-mark, destroy the life in rash reform.

In our idleness we read the papers. Heaps of Baltimore and New York dailies are sold in camp at the moderate profit of two hundred and fifty per cent. We read with great interest of the doings in Congress, for, though temporary absentees, we are still constituents, and will cast a heavy vote when we get home again. If members of Congress could serve a mod-

erate apprenticeship in the army, it might give them light on
a few topics. One is, sutlerships. Senator Wilson deserves
credit for his attacks on this monstrous monopoly. A sutler
has the exclusive right to sell in camp. A council of administration may fix prices, but it is of little avail. Vast amounts
of trash are disposed of at exorbitant rates. One great evil
is, that many purchasing unhealthy eatables lose relish for
the wholesome food which government provides. While we
were at Seneca, and many men were sick of dysenteries, and
similar diseases, I knew of the sale, in one regiment, of *six
hundred and fifty* full size, unhealthy, New York pies, in one
forenoon.

Another matter, where Congress would do well to pause, is
the discharge of regimental bands. Those who advocate this
cannot have an idea of their value among soldiers. I do not
know anything particular of the science or practice of music
(in fact, I leave that to an amply qualified partner at home,
who attends admirably to that department, with the assistance
of a small specimen, whom I found on a recent visit thoroughly
communicative on the fact that " John Brown's body lies a-
mouldering in the grave ") ; but I see the effects of a good
band, like ours, continually. It scatters the dismal part of
camp life ; gives new spirit to men jaded by or on a march ;
wakes up their enthusiasm. Could you see our men, when,
of an evening, our band comes out and plays its sweet stirring
music, you would say, if retrenchment must come, let it be
somewhere else. Let Congress lay an income tax of ten per
cent., if it will, on officers, while men at home pay but three
— as a reward for patriotic sacrifices ; but let the men have
their music.

Then you have read, with us, the account of a magnificent
party, whose refreshments cost " many thousands." I can

tell you an expenditure far greater. There are many sick soldiers in hospitals. They are provided with none of the delicacies of home. In this town there is a poor woman who supports herself by hard labor; very poor and very hard working; so much so, that she has to weigh *every cent* carefully before spending it. But this poor woman deprives herself of comforts to buy milk and eggs, that she may make some delicacies for the stranger-soldiers in their illness and their exile. That woman, carrying her few custards to the sick men, is, to me, a noble being. It recalls another scene, where "Jesus sat over against the treasury. . . . And there came a certain poor widow, and she threw in two mites."

The public prints do not chronicle this poor woman's deed; but there is One who says, " Inasmuch as ye did it unto one of the least of these, ye did it unto me."

9

CHAPTER IV.

IN THE VALLEY.

CHARLESTOWN, VA., March 3, 1862.

I WILL never prophesy again. A little time since, I wrote that any movement was impossible; while, suddenly, here we are, thirty odd miles off from my last place of date, in the midst of the enemy's country, and quartered, so far as *our* field and staff are concerned, in the hotel of a certain landlord, by an unlucky allusion to whom in one of my letters I came near being involved in a controversy as to the merits of an old and honored institution. The landlord's rooms are unfortunately bare of furniture, as he had sold off.

How came we here? Well, soon after celebrating Washington's birthday we saw symptoms of movement. On that birthday, by the way, our whole brigade marched into Frederick, and there met the Michigan cavalry and the Maryland Second, and listened to the Farewell Address, read from a balcony. We also took off our caps, as a mark of respect to the Being invoked in prayer, but not with any respect for the sleek individual who read the prayer. That officiating clergyman was known early in these troubles as a sympathizer with the South. He it was whom I told you of as omitting prayer for the President from his liturgy, and restoring it, on a gentle hint that he had better do so. His prayer, so far as I could see, was a tame generalization, recognizing the existence of no treason, no war, no army; an insult to his country, to Washington, to the soldiers, and to God; it excited the profoundest disgust. Why could not he have been a *man*, and if he could not pray outright for his country, say so to those inviting him? Some other ministers in Frederick are plainly Union; the Reverend Doctor will be, when the tide sets that way strong enough.

A week ago yesterday we had hints to pack up. On Monday, orders to cook. Then we heard that General McClellan himself was at Harper's Ferry. Then we waited impatiently, until, on Thursday morning, reveille beat at four o'clock, and before daylight we began our march in the mud and mist. At Frederick we took the cars; at evening reached Sandy Hook; crossed on the pontoon bridge, and occupied the empty houses in that desolated place. We did not sleep on feather beds that night; our wagons were in Maryland, and in our " mess" you would have laughed at the scanty supply of crockery, the unmatchable cups, the broken knives, and the solitary fork and single spoon, which we took turns in using.

Early Friday morning, our Second, the Wisconsin Third, five squadrons of the Michigan cavalry, and two sections of artillery, were chosen to make a reconnoissance towards or to Charlestown, as might seem best, under command of our own Colonel Gordon. Speedily we were on the road, the skirmishers in advance, flankers on either side, and pressed forward. The cavalry, with Colonel Gordon at the head, drove on the rebel cavalry pickets, and as the former dashed into and through Charlestown, at full speed, the rebels barely made their escape, leaving arms in their hurried

flight. Artillery had been posted, and infantry stationed
with the batteries just outside of Charlestown, when General
McClellan himself came, and after hasty examination, turned
our reconnoissance into occupation. It was the first time I
had seen the general, and all I could notice in the brief
moments was, that his pictures fail to show what he is, and
that he has an eagle glance, sees everything at once, and has
the air of one born to command, and able to do it. The
next day on came other troops, of whose numbers I will tell
you (privately), that there are a good many infantry, quite a
number of cavalry, and considerable artillery.

So here we are in Charlestown again. Most of the men
are away to the war, on the rebel side. What are left look
as sour as they did last July. They were very anxious, as
they had been told we were going to burn the town. The
negroes had been informed by the masters that we were
going to sell them off to Cuba or elsewhere. And leaders
had urged the people to burn the houses and retire. But
they were considerate. Like the discarded suitor, who did
not throw himself out of a three-story window, because he
reflected that

> " A lover forsaken,
>   A new love may get ;
> But a neck that 's once broken,
>   Can never be set," —

so they thought that their property once burned up was gone.
This twaddle about their burning their towns is supremely
silly. Suppose they do ; *we* don't want to live in their
shabby villages. The few traders left have little stock, but
that little they are perfectly ready to sell to us, as we give
them what is a rare sight here, silver ! Their eyes glisten at
it. Ridiculous shinplasters, of five cents, ten, twelve and a

half, twenty-five, and fifty, are their currency, and dirty stuff
it is, too.* Salt is thirty dollars a sack; shoes, ten to fifteen
dollars a pair; coffee, none; and everything but wheat
scarce and high. Supplies will now come in, and trade
revive. Our soldiers had not been in Harper's Ferry twenty
hours before new signs were out — "military equipments,"
" salt fish, groceries, rum, and whiskey." And in a few days
the bogus currency here will not be worth two cents a peck.

John Brown's memory is still the centre of attraction.
Our men came in singing the " Glory, Hallelujah," and our
soldiers sing it everywhere. Strange as that medley is,
" his soul's marching on " does have a marvellous fascination
to our army. The daring and manliness of that old man
eclipses his fault, and he has become a hero. Again the
soldiers visit the room in the jail where he was confined, the
court-house, and the place of his execution. The room where
Cook was imprisoned is now tenanted by secessionists, and
the court-house by the Second Massachusetts. The papers
relating to his trial are here, guarded with the other public
records, and they excite great interest. Various handbills,
ballots, and such like papers, are obtainable, and are treasured as mementoes. A few of them which citizens have, I
shall send the Historical Society.

Yesterday we had public service. It was a great comfort,
after quite a long deprivation. The men were attentive and
reverent, and the singing capital. But the place made it
memorable. Where I officiated was the court-room, where
John Brown was tried, convicted, and sentenced. There
seven companies of Massachusetts soldiers filled the room.
There was the spot where John Brown had lain upon his

* Shinplasters are ridiculous. I cannot take it back.

9 *

litter. There, in front of the judge's platform, were the
jurors' seats. The chair which the judge had occupied was
tenanted by a Massachusetts chaplain, and Massachusetts
sentinels were on guard at the door and gate. There, the
first time for many a month in this town, did prayer go up
for the President of the United States, the restoration of
peace, the supremacy of law, and the freedom of our country
from its sins. Such are Time's changes. Who could forget
the events of that spot? Let us hope that, as Massachusetts
men occupied that place, so Massachusetts honor, freedom,
and chivalry may yet imbue this whole section with principles which will recognize public morality.

Whether we go immediately to Winchester, no man knows
but one, who keeps his own secrets. I have perfect confidence that we shall, if it is for the best. Our present
position opens that valuable artery, the Baltimore and Ohio
Railway, our communications are easy, and we are in
position to do service. The whole army of the Potomac has,
indeed, done its part. It has not fought, but military men
say it has done as much. The line of our armies reaches
from Fortress Monroe to Kansas. The army of the Potomac
is the left wing. It having the most disciplined soldiers, has
held, as " in a vice," the rebel army of the Potomac with
their best soldiers, and thus enabled the right wing to win its
victories in the West. Their line is now turned. And
now their Virginia stronghold is isolated. The general plan
of operations, as now carried out in the West, was made
known to some entitled to receive it, as long ago as November — the plan of the senior general. He will yet have the
credit for plans which others, in their proper place, have so
brilliantly executed.

Our troops have captured large supplies of food. The

rebels have evidently kept this fertile section as a late resort, and have collected and stored large quantities of provisions, which are falling into our hands. But there is more yet to be done than this. It will be strange, I am satisfied, it this section is not the base of most important operations.

March 8. — There are no changes since I wrote, at least of any consequence. The rebels are now cleaned out of the territory above Winchester; but that town is strongly fortified, or rather the hills two miles south of the town, and a brisk fight is expected there.

Workmen are as busy as bees on the Baltimore and Ohio Railway, which will soon be open. Large quantities of the iron rails stolen from that road are piled up on the Winchester road, and have fallen into our hands.

WINCHESTER, VA., March 13, 1862.

YES, Winchester at last. We started for this place on the 8th day of July, 1861, from Boston, and have just arrived, contemporaneously with the occupation of Manassas by the centre of the army of the Potomac.

Two weeks ago to-day we left Frederick. That evening we were in Harper's Ferry. The next morning Colonel Gordon led a reconnoissance to Charlestown, .and we remained there, and General Banks, with most of the division, came on the next day, as I wrote before. On Saturday last General Sedgwick (successor to General Stone) brought up his several brigades.

Little happened at Charlestown except what I wrote — and one other expedition of our regiment. We had left our

quarters in the town, and gone into camp just outside, on
Wednesday, March 5. Our camp was located in the extensive grounds of somebody's residence — that is, a wooded
field ; but the family, purporting to be Union, and not want-
ing Union soldiers very near, our stay there was limited to
one night, and we had to move in the morning to a new
field.

It was really novel to go into mere tents again. We had
become attached to our board floors and few feet of side protection, though I did not part with mine with such feelings
as I left Seneca, for there I venerated my stone fireplace, as
being built of the same material as the Smithsonian Institute.
We questioned a little whether we should feel the cold ; but
we find no trouble. Again we gather of an evening about
the brilliant camp fires, and enjoy the simplicity of camp
life.

I mentioned the fact that we had one expedition. It was
on Thursday night, a week ago. News came suddenly to
General Banks that the enemy had attacked Colonel Maulsby's Maryland regiment, in force, and that the said regiment
was " cut to pieces." So the general ordered Colonel Gordon to hasten with his regiment thitherward, adding to his
command some other infantry and plenty of artillery. It
was half past two o'clock, and in due time the force had
traversed the six miles to Kabletown. Of course Colonel
Maulsby's regiment was in safety ; the whole trouble had
arisen from the blunder of somebody, by which a cavalry
patrol and Colonel Maulsby's pickets had fired into each
other. Nothing was left but to kindle huge bivouac fires,
and wait till morn.

Our forces threatened Winchester by four roads. The
most eastern was by way of Berryville, in which our regi-

ment was placed. Next, at Smithfield was a brigade. Next, from Bunker Hill; and still farther west, General Shields's division (late under the lamented Lander). And still nearer to Washington was Colonel Geary, who had occupied Lees-burg, and could easily advance through gaps in the Blue Ridge towards Winchester. Towards and into Berryville General Gorman moved, last Monday, with one brigade; but before reaching that place sent back for additional forces. Our own brigade, General Abercrombie's, hastened onward, and reached Berryville towards sundown. I have heard of but one exploit of the brigade first moving. Seeing a body of rebels on a hill, a couple of shell dispersed them with ease. Possibly the apparent danger of the enterprise may be modi-fied by the fact that the rebel force subsequently appeared to have been a farmer on horseback superintending a few labor-ers at work with a *threshing machine.*

Moving in haste, we left tents standing; nor did our wagons reach us until the next day. So we tried our old habit of bivouac. For the definition of that word, look in the Dictionary, being sure to " Get the Best ! " Then imagine the place of bivouac a rough piece of land, sparsely wooded ; huge piles of straw soon accumulated ; great fires along company and officers' lines ; here and there a half-shelter, hastily planned, and built of the rails no longer in fences ; groups eating the rations from their haversacks, and merrily drinking coffee made in the kettles brought each by two men ; and then smoking their pipes, humble clay, and more elegant brier-wood, or pretentious meerschaum ; and by and by, as the tattoo was about to beat, I saw here and there some kneeling, reverently, undisturbed, both Protestant and Catholic, and I knew why. And then the deepening clouds grew blacker. Then the wet drops pattered on the

ground. Then the rain poured down, and the wind whirled
the dead leaves about, and the men lay stretched on the
straw piles, buried under blanket and rubber blanket. Then,
after a few hours, the clouds cleared away, but a cold,
hard wind blew until many roused themselves and built
up the decaying fires, and sat in their warm circle till daylight. The sun rose warm, and the birds went to singing, and the trouble of the wet and cold bivouac night was
forgotten.

Our wagons came on. But after one night in tents we
moved again. Tidings came that Winchester was occupied.
Then, at "retreat," came hasty orders to move immediately,
the messenger saying that the rebel General Jackson had
skilfully marched to the rear of our force at Winchester,
captured General Shields and seven thousand men, and that
General Hamilton was still engaged. It was a ridiculous false-
hood, for which no explanation is yet made, but it was believed.
The messenger afterwards said it was a *joke*. Our men received orders with a universal cheer. In twenty-five minutes our regiment, with packed knapsacks and partly-filled
haversacks, were in column on the road. As regiment after
regiment received orders, and with shouts joined the line, the
scene was intensely interesting. You would have thought it
was a gigantic pleasure party. Day was shading into night
as we moved on. We passed regiments and whole brigades,
ready formed, and waiting the word "forward." "What
regiment is that?" was the regular salutation. Cheers followed, and when Massachusetts troops thus met, the shouts
were tremendous. Mile after mile was passed over. "I
wish I was in Dixie," or "I'm bound for the land of Ca-
naan," or "John Brown's body," enlivened the march. But
as hours wore away, all sank into comparative silence. The

foolish tale which called us on being contradicted, at midnight the brigadier ordered a halt, a few miles from Winchester. We turned into a grove, tangled and rough. Again in every direction were roaring fires. Pine branches made beautiful beds, and the regiments went to sleep in the still and calm moonlight.

When morning came we waited impatiently for orders. It was noon before they came — a tantalizing delay. It began to rain before we were bid to camp, only a few rods off. Our wagons were on hand, and we were a city again.

Jackson had evacuated Winchester. He had done it with as great deliberation as he pleased ; removed all his stores, guns, and munitions of war ; carried off such private property as he fancied ; and left naked the small defences, in which, with five thousand men, he had deluded a whole division. " Strategy " is a great thing ; but driving rebels at the point of the bayonet is the only lesson the South will ever appreciate.

It is a curious truth that, while our papers could not publish the movement of General Banks, it had been known at Richmond on the first of the three days occupied in crossing. Our advance seemed sudden by the Boston papers, but only because they were allowed no intelligence. Really, it has taken a fortnight to get here from Frederick, while no enemy has been met except their retreating pickets.

WINCHESTER, VA., March 22, 1862.

OUR regiment remains located as when I last wrote, though transferred to another brigade. In the new arrangements of corps, Brigadier-General Hamilton is transferred to

the late command of General Heintzelman. Our regiment
has been removed to General Hamilton's late brigade (two
others being taken out of that), and Colonel Gordon commands the brigade. So admirably fitted as he is for the permanent position of brigadier, it is the country's loss that in-
competent men have been bolstered into such places by
political manœuvres, while local spite has operated against
a man who has been repeatedly the resource of our major-
general in dangerous and delicate operations.

Winchester is in "the Valley." Everywhere you see the
cognomen. There is the "Bank of the Valley" — just now
removed; the "Valley Agricultural Society" — office closed
at present; "Valley" this, and "Valley" that. Adver-
tisers have the most complete assortment, of whatever goods
they deal in, "to be found in the Valley." The Valley is
rich, agriculturally. The scenery of the Valley is beautiful.
But the town of the Valley, Winchester, is dirty and shiftless.
Laid out, they tell me, by Lord Fairfax, its streets are
straight, and paved with rough rocks. There are exceptional houses of good appearance, but the bulk of the town
is mean. It has a medical school, or had ; a young ladies'
institute, price $200 a year; several hotels, at the principal
one of which, Taylor's, a dark and gloomy affair, you can
get as mean board as you wish at $2.50 per day; five or six
churches, — Methodist, Lutheran, Episcopal, Presbyterian,
&c. Winchester's population is mixed. It has much of
what I have seen so often that I think it must be genuine
"Valley Virginian," — rather under-sized, slight built, thin
face, black hair, dark eyes, quick-motioned, regular features,
rather sullen in look, passionate, easily prejudiced, without
marks of mental vigor, and sharp in trade as Yankees are
reputed to be.

Then there is the "colored" population in great numbers, — thick as grasshoppers in hay time. And it is wonderful to see the effect of *climate* on complexion. There are very-few blacks here. But from mulatto to Virginia white, there is abundance. A very large number of these unfortunates would pass, but for certain traces of African features, for white persons; showing that, in the course of several generations, the climate of Virginia has nearly bleached the African race. Indeed, among hundreds of this people, I have seen but *one* negro of the genuine color.

Winchester is further remarkable as the residence — when the individual is at home — of ex-Senator Mason. His house stands a little out of town, westerly, — a large, square, old-fashioned, white house, on a sharp knoll, with moderate grounds in front, a sharp flight of steps ascending to the door, over which door is a portico, and over which portico now floats the American flag. The family, library, &c., left town about ten days ago; the contents of his law office departed also. Our friend is not popular in his own town. I was told by an old and trustworthy citizen, that Mason could not secure an election as delegate from Winchester, and that he was considered as not more than a second or third-rate lawyer. "Beef and liquor is all he is fit for," said the citizen. Doubtless his slave-driving manners, intensified in Congress, have some effect on his popularity.

Quite a number of Northern persons are also living in Winchester. Some years ago a joint-stock boot and shoe manufactory was established here, and workmen were imported from New England. Some came from Milford, Mass. Quite a number of Northern-born people also reside in Berryville, about ten miles easterly, where they have been these twenty years. These latter are bitter secessionists, and the

former consider it prudent, even the best of them, to be, at
least, very quiet. When the outrageous oppression exercised
towards Union men is considered, I do not wonder that real
Union men keep still. Of course it is a mean loyalty which
succumbs to threats; but few persons have the manliness to
do right against public sentiment, or when it requires real
sacrifices. The " conciliating " policy also has its effect.
" If you don't take the Southern side," says the rebel government to a man, " we'll confiscate your property and imprison
you." " If you *do* take the Southern side," our government
practically says, " we will not harm you."

Yet, no doubt, as soon as our government shows that it
can and will hold the country, the majority will swing around.
Virginia is a mean State at the best. You remember its
double-dealing last year, when it pretended to be neutral, only
to gain time to plunder fortresses and arsenals; and how,
after it had passed the ordinance of secession, it kept the fact
secret, and continued to delude our government. Captain
Baylor is a fair specimen of Virginia chivalry. At Harper's
Ferry a few weeks ago, to get into his reach a Mr. Rohr,
a loyal Virginian ferryman, he made his servant hoist a white
flag. Rohr started to come on, as before, with another flag.
As he approached the shore, Baylor, with some of his men,
hidden in an archway, deliberately shot Rohr dead. When
at the ferry, I inquired into the facts, and learned that Baylor had publicly declared his intention of killing Rohr in this
way, and that the black who raised the flag was forced to it
by threats. And yet this scoundrel was a Union man up to
the latest moment! If this villain should be caught, would
he be hung? No. " Conciliate." " Conciliate." And this
Baylor is a fair specimen of Virginians. South Carolina was
bold and open; Virginia, mean and sneaking. I respect the
former; I despise the latter.

You see accounts of Southern brutality occasionally.   I have never believed much of that — knowing some noble Southerners. But I am satisfied. A clergyman of this county, I will not give his name, a man who only from compulsion became silent as to the guilt of secession, assures me on his honor, that "Yankee skulls" were hawked about his town after the Bull Run battle at ten dollars a piece. Spurs, also, were made of jaw-bones, to his personal knowledge.* A member of his own church, who was at Bull Run, told him that hundreds of bodies were left headless for such purposes. But I am not at all surprised. I have ceased to feel any wonder at the brutalities of a slaveholding people.

Notwithstanding the occupation of Winchester by the " Northern vandals," shops are open as usual, and last Sabbath the churches were occupied. I took the opportunity to attend service with the Methodists.

The minister of that church was known as a Union man; indeed, a printed sermon of his before the "Young Men's Christian Association" of Winchester, attacked secession without gloves, and it forced him subsequently to hide. I chose his church because, although the Presbyterian would have hit my doctrinal notions a little better, *that* is rank "secesh," and I will have nothing to do with "secesh" religion, not even in those eminently Christian evangelicals of England who have so meanly lent their influence against us in our time of trial. So I went to the Methodist church. The building is a very substantial and quite well-proportioned edifice, of brick, with " circular" pews, an elegant marble pulpit, and galleries ; and it will be quite cheerful and pleasant when they

* I afterwards saw some of these articles; and rings worn by women, who boasted they were made of Yankee bones.

rub off the lying pillars and recesses evidently colored in imitation of each shade of dirt in the valley. The house was well filled, hundreds of soldiers being added to the congregation of citizens. There was no organ, or other musical instrument, but a choir of perhaps twenty singers excellently led the congregation. I wondered, on entering, for what dignitaries the alternate tiers of pews were reserved; but they were soon occupied by women. Men and women sit in separate pews. I had never seen this silly custom before.

Rev. Mr. McReading, formerly in Boston, now chaplain of an Illinois regiment, offered prayer. It was a *good* prayer. The pastor preached from these texts : " We preach Christ crucified." " God forbid that I should glory," &c. " I determined not to know anything," &c. His theme, as announced, was " Christ crucified, the centre of the Christian system." The discourse, which was extempore, had in it a great deal of good thought, put forth in very rash language, and mixed up in a heterogeneous manner. It would do him a world of good to be put under our revered and beloved professor of pastoral theology at Andover for a year. The preacher's evident sincerity was impressive. I could endure his pronouncing *soi-disant* " sawy-dizzen," for he did not call *guard* " gorrd," *here* " yur," as people here generally do. I could even be willing that he should suddenly wheel around and address the minister in his pulpit. But one thing spoiled the sermon for me. He told four falsehoods.

These : with a plan which could not be decently developed in less than an hour and a half, he said he was going to address us " a few brief remarks : " he *knew* better ; he knew he lied. Farther on he said, " but I promised brevity, and will come to an end : " he was only one third through ! Still farther on, he begged our " attention to this remark, with which he would conclude : " but after the remark was attended to he began on a new set of exhortations. By and by, " one word more, which is all I have to say." " One word !" he talked on to the amount of at least five pages of sermon paper, and had an application after that. I presume that this preacher is an estimable citizen, and in private life, honest. It is truly to be regretted that he, or any other preacher, should thus utter falsehoods while presenting the most solemn truths. " One word more !" What a mean lie !

Of course, the gospel hereabouts is set in a pro-slavery frame. Ministers occasionally own their fellow-beings. I used to think that I would admit a brother minister into my pulpit careless of the question whether he were a slave-holder or not. I would not do it now. I will not say that there are not many slave-owners who are Christians ; I know some whom I do respect and love ; some who labor and pray for the conversion of their slaves, as those for whom they must give an account at the day of judgment. But a slave-holding minister — I could not endure that. I am no fanatic. I never even voted a " Republican " ticket. But this eight months' campaign on slave soil, in localities where slavery assumes its mildest type, has made me feel — and I do assure my conservative ministerial brethren that the whole system is infamous. " The sins of slavery !" There are none ; it is slaveholding *itself* that is the sin. Its effect on the masters is one of its greatest evils ; it perverts the conscience, warps the intellect, brutalizes the heart. Believe no such nonsense as that " the slaves are contented." They, with no noticeable exception, *long* to be free. Nor is there any difficulty in settling the slave question so far as our armies go. The property is thenceforth good for nothing. Crowds of blacks

10 *

forsake their masters at the first opportunity. In this very
place, over and over again, do they say, " I have worked so
many years for my master, now I want to work for myself."
They are docile, peaceable, and industrious. They say,
" only *hire* us and *try* us." *Can* it be that government means
to remand these now happy fugitives again to their oppressors? As an army, we have nothing to do with slavery. We
neither entice, nor drive back. The blacks take care of
themselves. I was amused with one case at Charlestown.
A master refused to sell any chickens, even, " because," said
he, " I must feed my poor servants, who will never leave
me ; " and he wanted a guard over his property. In a few
days his " poor servants " were all gone, and this aristocratic
son of one of the " first families of Virginia" was himself
taking care of his solitary cow and pig.

STRASBURG, VA., March 28, 1862.

ACROSS the main street in Winchester, in front of the
court-house, on Monday last, was suspended the sentence
" Theatrical performances here every evening." But within
the court-house, in every available spot, lay the wounded, the
dying, and the dead. On Tuesday was suspended a notice,
" No performance this evening." But within, surgeons were
using the knife and the saw, nurses were dressing ghastly
wounds, and, in spite of all care, scores were passing into
eternity.

This was but one of four hospitals.

It was at sundown, on Friday, when our brigade returned
to Winchester, after a fifteen-mile march, called back by the
battle, and I went immediately to the hospitals. It was our

great misfortune not to be near the contest. Had our brigade been there, with its good fighting blood and the military abilities of its officers, there is every reason to believe that General Jackson's force would have been cut to pieces, instead of retiring in very tolerable order. It is a great disappointment to us; but we had gone where ordered.

The battle was fought about three miles below Winchester, on the Strasburg pike. General Jackson's policy had been to keep this whole corps in the Winchester valley; and with constant annoyance by Ashby's cavalry, and the skilful use of his other forces, he succeeded. We had entered Winchester after very slow approaches, without opposition, Jackson retiring to a safe distance with his inferior numbers. Whether a different plan would not have captured, or at least broken up, his force, it is for others to say, if they would. Jackson made a great mistake when he risked the battle. He was led to suppose, by information from the secessionists there, that Winchester had been evacuated by all our forces excepting a provost guard, while in reality the whole of General Shields's division lay sheltered by hills. The information went mainly from secession women, whose bitter zeal led to the melancholy slaughter of many of their own relatives.

So, on Saturday, a portion of his cavalry drove in our pickets. It was not supposed that it was more than Ashby's lively troops, with a couple of pieces of artillery. Some little fighting took place on Saturday afternoon, in which General Shields's arm was broken by a shell. Desultory shots were exchanged all Sunday, and it was not until the afternoon that it was found that Jackson was present in force. Our troops then, at about four o'clock, were sent out to the amount of eight regiments, with several batteries.

Colonel Kimball, of Indiana, commanded. Jackson's force, as it appeared from rolls captured, comprised twelve small regiments, five hundred cavalry, and twenty-seven pieces of artillery, of which latter, two thirds appeared to be kept in reserve. As you go out of Winchester, about three miles, the enemy had posted some artillery on the left side of the road, supported by infantry, but the bulk of his force was stationed on a commanding wooded ridge, running at an angle with the road, which is low. Our troops were formed a short distance towards Winchester, in a corresponding curve, our artillery principally on a ridge, unfortunately a little lower than theirs, and our infantry somewhat sheltered behind it. Our troops drove them back at first, but they regained and strengthened their position on the wooded ridge, whence they poured a destructive fire. It was necessary to end this artillery engagement, and at the end of one or two hours' hard fighting our infantry were ordered to turn their left flank. It appears that Jackson had similarly ordered an attempt to turn our right. Our infantry, therefore, encountered theirs, and with hard fighting drove them back. Theirs was sheltered by a stone wall, and did great damage. Their battery there was making havoc, and two regiments charged upon it, and, with much loss, captured it. A charge was made upon the centre, the enemy broke, and the field was ours. But Jackson retired in very tolerable order. He has since kept so. The pursuit commenced the next day, has never, I believe, encountered anything more than his rear guard, skilfully fighting and then retiring. He is now doubtless safely encamped some dozen miles from our advanced force. I read in the papers of the 26th the following : —

" 'The loss of the rebels must have been enormous. They have abandoned their wagons along the road, filled with dead and wounded, and the houses on the route are found crowded with their wounded and dying.

" The dwellings in the town, adjacent to the battle-field of Sunday, are also found filled with the wounded.

" The inhabitants aided the rebel soldiers in carrying off their wounded during the day, and burying them quickly as soon as dead.

" Our artillery makes terrible havoc among the enemy in their flight, and the rout bids fair to be one of the most dreadful of the war."

Two thirds of this is pure invention. The rebels suffered, and worse than we did. Success remains with us, and the enemy have retreated. And that is all.

Not all. The battle-field is there. I visited it for a few minutes on Tuesday morning. Whatever excitement there is in the time of action, the next day's look excites only melancholy. It was a raw and chilly morning, and there lay, soon to be buried, more than two hundred corpses. Most of them were as they had fallen, in every position, but most with their faces upturned. Here were men shot in the head ; there a limb shattered ; there a slight hole in the breast ; and again, a shell had shattered every feature. In one spot was a pile of over twenty, mainly from the accurate bursting of a shell in their midst. In another place, their concentrated infantry had suffered terribly from our musketry. A few soldiers were guarding the spot from all depredation. Women were there searching for dead friends and relatives. It was hard to realize, in that calm and silent air, that a few hours before, the scene had been terrific with con-

flict, and full of slaughter.   But the silent and mangled dead
bore witness, and I wished that Jefferson Davis could have
been brought face to face with every corpse, and it be said to
him, " *Your* infernal ambition killed this man."

The hospitals remain also.   Four places were thus occupied, — the court-house, the Union Hotel, and two smaller
buildings.   I was able to visit three of the four on Monday
evening, and until we moved on at six o'clock on Tuesday.
As you entered the court-house, the outer room was occupied
with dead laid side by side, and reverently covered, and
each, so far as could be, with a little slip of paper bearing his
name and that of his regiment.   Passing in, every spot,
save room for the attendants to pass, was occupied by the
wounded, and now and then one was carried to the dead-
room.   Owing to some strange management, for twenty-four
hours neither hay nor straw was procured, and the wounded
men lay upon the floor.   When our brigade came, our surgeons immediately volunteered their services.   They were declined !   The surgeons of General Shields's division " needed
no help," when I saw soldier after soldier waiting impatiently
for necessary care.   The spirit seemed that of some third-
rate physicians in small towns, who are afraid somebody is
trying to get away their practice.   It was only until a most
formal application was made Tuesday morning, by our
brigade surgeon, that the services of ours were reluctantly
accepted.   Nevertheless, with or without formalities, our
surgeons made themselves useful.   The two of our own regiment proved of the greatest service.   Our senior surgeon
remained all night and all day in the court-house, reduced
things to order, and proved himself most admirably qualified
for his post.   Our assistant surgeon did similar work at the
Union Hotel.   Our hospital steward, with his medicines and

apparatus, was there, and of the greatest use. Our nurses were indefatigable. Our litters did most of the work of moving the injured from place to place. However much disappointment was felt at having no share in the fight, our hospital officials did noble service in relieving the unfortunate sufferers.

It was pleasant to see the gentleness and activity of the attendants. Hardy men seemed like women in the care of children. By and by delicacies came from the people. Monday evening many people were called upon for beds. To the eternal infamy of this rebel town, it was hard to procure even a few. One man, living in a fine house, had " no beds for damned Yankee soldiers ; let them lie on the ground." Women, on Tuesday morning, brought luxuries " for *Southern* soldiers," while with us there was no friend, no foe, only wounded men lying there indiscriminately, equally cared for. Women came there to abuse and insult us, with ultra rebel attacks, in the hearing of our wounded men ; but they were speedily sent off. I think the kind treatment of their own wounded shamed them into decency ; or, perhaps, a refusal to receive anything for one class exclusively. By and by they came with supplies, without specifying for which men. The inhuman feelings of these people are painful. They are full of lies, too, and they have made many believe them. One confederate soldier was asked, " Do you have kind treatment here ? " " Yes," he answered, as if wondering at it. " Why, didn't you expect it ? " " No ; I thought you would kill us." " What made you think so ? " " We were told so." Such is Southern honor.

I had the privilege of speaking with many, many soldiers. Many were terribly injured. Many were soon to die. Some died but a few minutes after. There were various feelings.

Some few were hardened, but most were glad to see a
Christian minister. Many more than I expected had a good
Christian hope, and some, who knew they were soon to die,
were happy. One man, from a Western regiment, was *very*
happy, though fatally shot in the neck. He asked me who I
was. " A chaplain." " Of what denomination ? " " Congregationalist." " Ah, I don't like them much." " Why ? "
" Well, I've met some I didn't think much of. I'm a Methodist ; been a church member this long while." " But *I* love
the Lord Jesus Christ." " Well, then, I guess you are all
right ; now pray with me."

One poor fellow of sixteen, from the South, wanted to take
the oath of allegiance. He knew he must die, but he felt he
had been in a wrong cause, — his mother had made him go,
— and if he could take the oath, he should feel better and
die happier. He took the oath, and died.

Others hoped to get well and go home. They would never
engage in the Southern service again.

One man I can never forget. He was a Southerner. One
deed had struck him with remorse. He kept his face covered.
He would answer no inquiries. But I got his story at last.
A few days before, he had gone out with a white flag, enticed
one of our soldiers near, and then deliberately shot him.
Wounded now, his mind dwelt only on that. He felt that it was
murder. He would not have his wounds dressed. Horror-
struck, he was determined to die. He would admit no hope of
pardon. But there was an opportunity for forgiveness. " The
blood of Jesus Christ his Son cleanseth us from *all* sin."

Then there were poor fellows whose thoughts were all of
home. One mere boy, from Texas, talked of his sister ; and
he wanted her informed, and sent his dying love. One man,
a rebel officer, wanted his wife — in Southern Virginia — to

know he died happy, and his blessing to go to his little children. And one had longings for his mother. And so on, on, through the long rows and many rooms.

Strange to say, I felt not the least shrinking in looking on the most terrible wounds. Others tell me they felt the same. But, more to the purpose, I never felt so strongly the value of the way of life which offers forgiveness to sinners in reliance on the sacrifice of Christ our Lord. What else could one have to say in such circumstances? Tell them to amend their lives? Many would end their lives in a few hours. Tell them that sin would not be punished? Their own dread falsified that. But the simple words, " Repent, and believe on the Lord Jesus Christ," meets all times and all circumstances. He who said to the dying criminal " This night shalt thou be with me in paradise," is able " to save unto the uttermost all those who put their trust in Him."

<hr />

EDINBURGH, VA., Friday, April 4, 1862.

I BEGAN to write of our sudden movement to Strasburg ; how gayly, at evening, March 25, our band led off with " I wish I was in Dixie ;" how cold the night became ; how we bivouacked by the roadside about one o'clock, five miles above Strasburg ; how, the next day, we forded Cedar Creek, a rapid and beautiful stream, where the villains had destroyed a fine bridge, and were placed just outside of Strasburg, in a rough and delightful pine wood ; how, the following day, a " scare " sent us forward four or five miles below Strasburg, where we camped again. But I did not finish it, because I thought something on " outpost duty " would be preferable.

So I began to write about "twenty-four hours on outpost;" how, last Saturday afternoon, our regiment relieved another as outpost; how we reached the spot about sundown; how the reserve, the grand guards, the pickets, and the sentries, were stationed; how a patrol went out at daybreak, and a larger one in the forenoon; how the rebels spitefully threw a couple of shells at our pickets; how it rained all night and was wet all day, and how we "hutted" the best we could with boughs and rails; how it was the strangest Sunday I ever spent, barring the preceding, when we watched, at Snicker's Ferry, the repairs making on a bridge, built by an army engineer, which had broken down, from defects a New England carpenter, earning a dollar and a half a day, would have been ashamed of, — by which breakage our regiment was kept back, and its subsequent direction changed. But we moved so suddenly, that I got beyond the topic, as we did the outpost.

We moved thither last Tuesday, April 1. Early in the morning came orders to go without tents or baggage. The whole corps was to move — each division. Everybody knows that General Jackson's headquarters are at Mount Jackson, seven or eight miles below here, where they have been all along, and whence he has made his sudden forays. But a very skilful rear guard — Ashby's cavalry, with some artillery and infantry — have been close up to General Banks's lines. This was all that was to be encountered. As the advance of our corps, Colonel Gordon's brigade was selected, and the whole was under his management, — Captain Corthren's fine New York battery being added, with some cavalry. The next brigade was a mile behind.

Two miles from our camp we halted. The rebel scouts and guns were in plain sight on an opposite ridge, sheltered

in a wood.   A couple of our Parrott guns were put in position with great rapidity ; two or three shells were fired, and
the rebels suddenly left.

From that point, the advance was made in regular order.
Skirmishers and flankers were thrown out, a reserve following, a section of artillery next, and then the next regiments
of our brigade.   It was new to me in certain particulars, as,
although two or three of our companies had exchanged lively
shots with the enemy, our regiment, as a whole, had never
encountered the fellows.   And so it may interest somebody's
mother, or wife, or sister, to see the order of moving, —
which you will read downward.

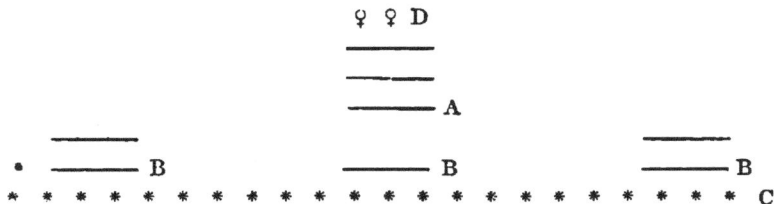

♀ ♀ D
—————
—————
————— A

• ————— B   ————— B   ————— B
∗ C

A,   Three companies, reserve, under Major Dwight. — B B B,   Five
platoons, as represented, with Lieutenant-Colonel Andrews. — C,   Skirmishers, reaching about 200 yards each side of the road, A being in
the road. — D,   Artillery.

In advancing, C is about 130 yards before B, and B about
300 yards before A.   On the skirmishers go, at a cautious
but steady pace, over fences, walls, or brooks, — keeping
their distances, each a few paces from the next man, and
their officers in command, when nearing the enemy ; still they
must press on, though in open sight.   As we moved forward,
the rebels stopped in the woods, scattering as far out as our
skirmishers, hiding behind walls and trees, and getting a shot
as often as possible.   It was the first time our regiment had
been really under fire, but it was beautiful to see how steadily

they moved on, keeping their distances admirably, and firing
at the scoundrels as coolly as though hunting partridges.
Both their bravery and their splendid discipline told admirably; for it was evidently not a pleasant position to be an
open mark for concealed rifles. But not a man flinched, and
a good Providence preserved every life in our regiment;
though blood flowed, not a serious casualty occurred on this
contested march of fifteen miles. The nearest to anything
fatal occurred to a man whose brass plate on his cross-belt
was indented by a ball, which, glancing, tore the belt, pene-
trated three or four thicknesses of clothing, and made a slight
wound. The force of the bullet was severe, but the plate
saved his life. A rebel dragoon was observed taking near
and deliberate aim at one of our officers, but a private seeing
him, emptied the saddle, and so spoiled that shot. In fact,
the bullets evidently buzzed thick enough in the early part
of the march, but the rebels seemed to see quite speedily the
beauty of our Enfields; and in fact, we learned from friends
in a village through which we passed, that the rebels swore
terribly about those " —— long-range Yankee rifles." Of
course we soon met with a bridge torn up, and the beams
partly cut. The Yankees went at it, and in five minutes it
was passable.

At three places they made a stand, each time on a capital
spot. They know every inch of ground here, and it is as
great a country for fighting, as it is beautiful in scenery. The
first was a little outside of Woodstock, which is quite decent
looking for a Southern village. As we came near the town,
the rebels had planted their guns on a height just beyond, and
suddenly opened with whizzing, screaming shells. But it
was no surprise. Colonel Gordon's experienced eye had
seen the capacities of the ridge, and had halted. We open

ranks; down gallops the artillery; up to the near ridge; quick as thought our guns were in position, sighted, fired; "whizz" goes the savage missile, flying through the air; then, in two or three seconds, a sullen sound shows that it has exploded, and the pieces are flying in every direction. Then another, another, and so on, in immense rapidity, and in a few minutes the rebels are driven. We enter Woodstock in quiet, and the alarmed people, over whose heads the shells have been flying, come to the doors relieved. Fragments are lying about in the very streets, and one house shows the long scar which a shell scratched as it fell to the spot where it exploded.

Then the same long line of skirmishers for several miles again. Then we approach the "Narrow Pass" — where the river, suddenly bending, leaves only room for a road. You descend the hollow, cross a swift creek, and then ascend the "Narrow Pass" — completely commanded by a ridge stretching up above. There, again, our commander saw the thing needful. He did not hurry up his artillery, but ordered it back, and hastened our regiment into the valley to the bridge, halting the other regiments behind the ridge we had just passed, and on which he had stationed his guns. It was just in time. The rebel guns had not fired their second shot, when Captain Corthren opened with half a dozen replies, and for a little while the scene was noisy. The Blue Hills echoed back the reports, and the sound rolled up the valley in long thunder. The bridge is on fire, as the rebels left it, and our men go to work to put it out, and succeed. Meantime the storm fell so thick about the rebels, that they were driven from their guns, but the height and the distance prevented any capture. Then the enemy are silent, and finally are running again, and on we march.

11 *

Near Edinburgh we move cautiously. Another stream is there, with high banks and lofty ridges on either side. The bridges, railroad, and common road are on fire, and the enemy have planted their guns again. The bridge must be rebuilt. So the struggle is for position. Again our guns are hurried on through hastily torn fences, over hollows and rocks, and up on the eminence. Soon both sides are at work; the skirmishers are drawn in; the Second advances at " double quick ; " fortunately, for the range of the enemy's guns commands the spot where it had been, and death comes where others loiter. There is a sharp fight now, but the bridge is ours. It is near night, however, and though the opposite height is ours when we want it, it is useless.

Next day was noisy, but that was all. The bridge was rebuilt, while the guns on either side were firing at rapid intervals above. Pennsylvania men did it, and did well. The other brigades came up, but of their number, or place, or destination I must not speak even the very little that I know.

It is a rainy day in camp. Sometimes I used to enjoy rainy days at home, and sometimes I did not.

They were pleasant when one had a heap of odds and ends of work, and a rainy day was so good a time to finish them up. Or, one wanted a clean day for some special object, and had it then, beginning as soon as breakfast was over, hardly stopping for dinner, and not caring whether " the shades of night were falling fast " or slow. But sometimes the rainy days seemed dismal; by reason, doubtless, of a moderate fit of the indigoes, warranted not to fade ; or, possibly, sometimes from some depressing influence of the air. But, on the whole, I used to like rainy days ; not merely for the opportunity for work, but because it was pleasant to make a real visit on one's family, which is rather a rare event. I could both work and have the visit. Some people have an exclusive and forbidden study. I could not. If I locked the door, little feet soon pattered up, and little hands tried the handle. Suppose I said, " Busy now ; " then I heard a good-natured, but self-satisfied and triumphant voice, " Papa, it's ME ! " Who could resist that? ME always came in, and ME and papa had the best time imaginable, to the detriment — no — the decided improvement of writing ; and then ME would sit down quietly to play, and not disturb papa. Children improve sermons. Besides, there are two ways of thinking and writing. Some people think as the horse-cars journey from Jamaica Plain to Boston. From the stables to the office at Eliot Street is the Introduction. At the office is " first." They jog along to Hyde's Corner, and the conductor sings out that name, which means " secondly." At Roxbury is the stopping for " thirdly." " Dover Street " means " fourthly." And from Boylston Street, various halts let out the different parts of the Application, and the office opposite the Tremont House is " To conclude." And all the way along you must keep on the iron ruts. Get off the track, and there is a terrible jolting over the rough pavement before you get on again. Indeed, on the track, every stoppage loses impetus ; and a stop at rising ground is sometimes terrible. That's a good way for those that like it. But I would rather take a seat with some of my people who have fleet horses, as I used to do. You can then start when you please ; you can stop of errands ; you can take the smoothed roads and dodge the pavements ; you can see a little speed on Tremont Road ; and your friend drops you at just such part of the city as you wish. However, different people may have different ways, to advantage. And my way was to have few secluded study hours, but to let all hours be study; and to have the freshness of life illumining the cold rows of books — which books are capital things for a little girl to make houses of. I would as soon think of shutting sun and air out of my study as of keeping out my wife and child. There is a salutary warning in the case of that good minister whose grandchild was always driven from his study. "Mother," said she, "will grandpa be in heaven!" "Why, certainly, my child." "Then it's no use for *me* to go; as soon as he sees me, he'll say, What's that child here for? Go right out of my study!" I fully believe that that divine's accurate "scheme" would have the same resemblance to the real living doctrines of the gospel, as the dry, pressed, squared, and labelled roots and herbs in an apothecary shop do, to the blooming, fragrant, lovely plants out of which they were manufactured.

However, I will go back to the "track" again. Rainy days are *not* pleasant in camp. To-day it snows, it sleets, it hails, it rains. The trees are covered with frozen snow, or half-melted ice, and every now and then they shake off heavy pieces, which rattle down like fragments of shell. The huge tops of the pines, away up above their limbless trunks, frozen into masses, sway heavily to and fro. Drip, drip, from every bough. Pour, pour, in every open spot. The forlorn horses stand with drooping heads, looking ashamed of their condition and disgusted with Virginia — immovable, except when eating their breakfast or dinner. The pet dogs keep inside of tents. The fronts of our canvas houses are drawn outward and open, and great logs support a struggling fire just in front, and live coals are placed in holes within the tent, provided the holes do not speedily fill with water.

Ditches are dug all around the tents, and now and then a ditch runs *through* the tent as a necessary resort. Dripping individuals are solemnly chopping wood. Dismal people go about their duties, hoping to have as few as possible, but of course feeling that, in military service, " to hear is to obey." Rubber coats are in active service, and cap covers and appended capes shelter the head and neck, in the absence of umbrellas, which the government has neglected to furnish. Boots will get wet ; the soft ground yields to every step, and the leather greedily drinks up the moisture. The sentinels, in overcoats, pace up and down, as steady as ever, but wet, very wet, and with arms sheltered as much as possible from the rain. Off on picket somewhere is a company, and we talk over their shelterless, fireless condition. The enemy, with their insulting, but useless artillery practice from the opposite ridge, are doubtless wetter than we are. All soldierly precaution is taken, and officers and orderlies ride away on duties, but with sombre countenances.

" Hard business, sir, this soldiering," says John to my nearest neighbor, the major.

" Yes, John."

" Its aisy for them as sits at home with their good fires, to read of this victory and that, but its hard for them as has to do it, sir."

" Yes, John."

" It would do them good to come out here, and try to warm themselves by a hole in the ground, sir."

" True, John."

The rain, however, does not keep us here, but the plans of authority do. Going forward, we could sweep before us everything of Jackson's command, which probably consists of no more than six or eight thousand. His main camp is said to be at Mount Jackson, a little village about seven miles onward; but he will hardly remain there when we go on, at least no more than to annoy and delay us. A small force, his rear guard, under Colonel Ashby, remains opposite us, but is of no particular account at present. *Why* we wait, of course I do not know. Nevertheless, our men want to do something; their little fighting the other day sharpened up their appetite.

Last Sunday we had public worship again. We had had none, by reason of movements, since we were at Charlestown. But last Sabbath was a most beautiful day. The air was mild and sweet, the sun warm. So in a little hollow near us we met in one of " God's first temples." Sunday in our camp, when we are allowed to remain, is always quiet. I have repeatedly noticed how still and homelike it seems. Our commander never has any work not absolutely necessary; and although there may be as much evil, yet the stillness is always refreshing. Last Sunday even the rebels opposite left off their gunnery Saturday night, and waited till Monday morning, though I do not know why. For whatever reason, not a single piece of artillery was fired on either side, though here and there one could hear the distant sound of a musket.

Sunday afternoon I called upon a presiding elder of the " United Brethren in Christ," who lives in the village a mile away. He had returned only a day or two before from his visits to the churches in his circuit. I was very hospitably entertained by the worthy United Brother, and the excellent United Sister, his wife. This denomination, which was novel to me, seems exactly like the Methodists in doctrine and government,—with bishops, presiding elders, itineracy (less restricted as to time). It is anti-secret society; will not have a freemason in the church. And it is anti-slavery fully. No slaveholder can be admitted to this membership; yet they have about thirty churches in this valley. They are opposed to war, but many of their members were pressed into the rebel service, and some were swept away by the torrent of secession; still we have many friends among them, and the denomination opposed secession to the last. Since the John Brown affair they have met with a great deal of persecution, which is not strange, when they will refuse admission to the master whose slaves they welcome to the church. Their spirit — and I have seen several members — I like exceedingly, as being meek, humble, laborious, devout.

Anti-slavery, and yet spreading here for years, and with thirty churches in this limited locality. Who can say that slavery could have lived if the powerful Presbyterian, Episcopal, Baptist, Methodist, denominations here had resisted it like these poor United Brethren? Who can deny that the Southern churches, therefore, are the bulwark of slavery, and that Northern churches, which silently or actively fraternize with them, are so far forth participants in the giant sin of the age?

You alluded, a few weeks ago, to my " conservative " proclivities. Other papers have done the same, but they erred in supposing I ever believed slavery to be right. I only objected to " agitation," as meddling with what was neither politically nor religiously our business. Therein did I err, both politically and religiously. And still that very error, the very going so far in defending what seemed the constitutional rights of the South, has made swarms of old democrats now the bitterest foes of the oligarchy which dared lay its hands on that constitution, in defending whose apparent guarantees they had been left in a hopeless minority, been censured and reproached, and been placed even in a false position as to their real sentiments. Religiously, we have no right to ignore the claims of suffering millions ; we never had. Politically, the existence of a republican government over its thirty-four States, now necessitates the destruction of slavery ; whether immediate or future be the result, the commencement of its destruction must be *now*. What measures are necessary, I am not qualified to say. It is a hard question. But pardon me this new reference to the great cause of the rebellion while I say a few things more.

I quote now from some conservatives.

Said I, to a girl of about sixteen, at the house of whose master I passed the night, " Do you know what we are here for ? "

" I specs you's here to free us."

" Do you want to be free ? "

" I does."

" Don't you like your master ? "

" No, sir."

" Why ? "

" He sold my mother."

" When ? "

" Twelve years ago."

" But your master looks like a kind man, and treats us kindly."

" I know he looks so, but he ties *me* up and whips me with a cowhide."

The tones of the girl were inexpressibly sad. I have never found anything but hopelessness and utter despair.

At the house of a Virginian near ——, the proprietor's apparent cordiality was induced by fear. While at table, we were waited on by a bright-looking yellow woman, about twenty-five years of age. I questioned her of the rebels ; she spoke intelligently but hurriedly, and in low tones, as if

desiring to communicate with us, and yet afraid her master
might hear.

" Do you like to live with your master?"

" No, sir."

" Then why do you?"

" Where shall I go?"

" North."

" What will I do with my family, and how shall I leave
my friends; we can't all go, and how can we be separated?
Besides, we thought we'd better wait for the law."

" What law?"

" Why, the law that is going to be passed to free us."

She added, also, " This is our *home*. We don't want to
leave it. We are willing to work."

There was a man near Snicker's Ferry who made many
abolitionists. Nobody suspected he was a slave. He was
no darker than a browned soldier. His hair was straight,
just turning gray. He was the son of his own master. His
wife was the daughter of her master. A more pious man it
would be hard to find. As he told of his early dissatisfac-
tion with his lot, there were tears in men's eyes. Now, he
was resigned. He thanked God that his children had not
been sold away from them. But, hopeless as he now was in
approaching age, he did wish his *children* might be free, and
live in a different sphere. Sad, yet religiously happy —
resigned, but ambitious for the children so fair, so white, so
intelligent.

Now I select these three cases out of *many*, as *fair* illustra-
tions, and for several principles.

1. In the mildest type of slavery, girls of sixteen are tied
up and flogged by their masters with cowhides.

2. Men hold their own children in slavery.

12

3. The slaves do not want to leave their homes, but profess a readiness to work for wages ; and if the resources of this section were decently developed, they could not do half the work.

4. The slaves exhibit the strongest family attachments ; repeatedly preferring to remain in a slavery they dislike, rather than leave husband, wife, or children.

5. They are peaceably disposed, but sad and depressed.

6. They are, as a class, more intelligent, more industrious, more civilized, than the " poor whites," though with less natural vigor of character.

7. They are looking, with intense longing, for legal redress.

NEAR NEWMARKET, VA., April 24, 1862.

WE move by fits and starts. A week ago this morning, after, I don't know how long a residence, we left Edinburgh. We had remained there, I suppose, as long as we did, because the corps lacked provisions and shoes. The intended, and partly accomplished, removal of General Williams' division to Centreville, had sent on the division supply train, and that had to come slowly back. In addition thereto, the miserable railway from Harper's Ferry to Winchester used to give out once a day or so. And still further, it was, of course, difficult to foresee that men would need shoes ; nor is it very wonderful that nobody supposed that shoes, given out new on the morning of a march over a plain, smooth road, would have holes clean through the soles at night, as various pairs did. But the various vexations overcome, we were to follow up Jackson ; and now a General Order congratulates the corps that the Virginia Valley is cleared of an armed enemy.

General Shields's division moved in the night. Ours in the morning following. Reveille beat at a quarter past two; we were in line of march at four. There was no excitement in following another division; the advance is far pleasanter. But we could enjoy the scenery and the day. The faint light in the east was struggling with, and soon to overcome, the clear moonlight. The denser column of fog, along the river, half hid the mountain-range rising beyond it, clear and sharp in outline. We crossed the creek at Edinburgh, after waiting till near sunrise, and moved onward in the most delightful scenery and air imaginable.

It is hard to imagine more beautiful views than one meets in this valley. Varying from ten to thirty miles in width, bounded by lofty and rude mountain-ranges, watered by rapid rivers or foaming creeks, the undulating lands, now wooded, now gently swelling fields, now green meadows, change the landscape almost constantly. The winter wheat was clothing many an acre with the liveliest green. Peach-trees were just making ready to bloom. Now and then one saw hyacinths and heart's-ease by the roadside. And robins and swallows were flying about in the greatest glee. Such it was, as sunrise bathed the whole scene in richest glory. But for the occasional roar of artillery miles onward, and the succession of burning bridges which we regularly met, it would have seemed the embodiment of peace. But the plough was idle in the field. The fences were broken down. The relics of straw and the brands showed the recent bivouacks. The men were away at war. The past thirty years of retrograde were rapidly accumulating the ruin of the valley. Beautiful, but decaying. Beautiful, but deceitful. Consumption and fever are the bane of this lovely spot; and tyranny and ignorance are ruining its population.

Every bridge for miles was burning. The hurrying enemy foolishly supposed this would delay our march; but there was a ford at every place, and where our artillery was stopped, Yankee eyes saw the railroad crossing a few rods above, and dashed over safely. So we went on to Mount Jackson.

There we waited for several hours. Why, I do not know, nor was it any of my business. Two or three miles onward was Rood's Hill, the place which Jackson held in force. Mount Jackson itself is not a hill, but a village. Here the enemy had built large hospitals, and evidently expected to remain. While waiting I went into them. The hospital flags were still flying, those little safeguards which are a sure protection in all civilized warfare. But the sick had all been removed ten days previous, to the number of nearly five hundred. The buildings were admirably contrived and constructed. In addition to two or three small ones, there were two completed and one nearly so, of perhaps a hundred and fifty feet in length, two stories in height, perfectly ventilated, and yet warm. The upper stories were entered from the outside by plenty of broad and easy stairways, and the whole showed better skill than usual.

Near by were two graveyards. In one, there were some fifty or sixty graves of soldiers, each with head-boards distinctly lettered. I noticed that there were buried there, in addition to Virginians, men from North and South Carolina, Georgia, Alabama, and Louisiana. Poor fellows; to die away from home, and in an unjust cause!

Near by was the railroad station, the terminus of the Manassas road. The rebels were determined we should have no use of it. The engine-house was in smoking ruins. The engine was as well broken up as they knew how to do it.

Remnants of passenger cars, and a long line of freight cars, were still burning. I cannot understand the love of the rebels for destruction of property. The bridges on the common roads they destroyed, the bridges their own South must rebuild, when it could not delay our forces ten minutes. And these cars they burned belonging to a private corporation, while their uselessness, if left unhurt, is clear from the fact that on the line of the road every wooden bridge, many a one of great cost and labor, is destroyed. And if the bridges were to be rebuilt, it is perfectly easy to obtain rolling stock from the other end of the road. But they seem to have a passion for destruction, even when at their own expense, and when perfectly useless.

Our waiting at Mount Jackson ended. General Shields's division was to advance on the main road; but to us was given as hard toil as we had ever had. Colonel Gordon's brigade, with two or three regiments of Colonel Donelly's, was ordered to make a flank movement to the right. Now we left our good turnpike travelling, and took a " dirt " road. Dirt road it was — muddy, stony, and rough. For two miles it led westward by the side of a rapid stream, whose power is wasted on a few little mills. Then we crossed it. It was fordable — that is, wade-able, and our soldiers emerged thoroughly wet. Bending southward, we were soon opposite Rood's Hill, and now and then a cannon shot came to our ears. They were speeding courtesies to the rebels, who, of course, saw the flanking process, and knowing that if it succeeded they were prisoners, left in disgust.

You suggest a doubt whether the report is true that many of Jackson's men being forced into the army, will not fight. There is every reason to suppose that it is true, so far as this, that he cannot rely on them. It is stated on good authority,

12 *

that Jackson asked the opinion of his officers whether to stand at Rood's Hill, which is a narrow ridge commanding open ground for a mile or two, itself guarded by a river on each side, and not overlooked by any accessible position. His officers favored a fight, but he overruled them, on the ground that he could not depend upon a portion of his force.

However, we plodded on, turning more to the east. We passed through a mean and dirty village called Forestville, probably because there is hardly a tree there; crossed another stream, where our pioneers had made a slight bridge; ascended and descended ledges; waited for artillery, stuck fast every now and then. It was bad enough by daylight; but when the sun had set, the march was execrable. It became *very* dark; the road led through woods; some of our men were even barefoot; and when, at half past eight, we turned into a wood, and built fires, and had our supper, and piled up leaves, and spread out blankets, everybody was ready for the slumber that awaited all but the guard. It was a beautiful night to sleep, and few, after eighteen miles of the hardest travel, moved till reveille.

The next morning we went on to rejoin the corps. The march had nothing noticeable save one ford. It was through the north fork of the Shenandoah. Water was high, the bottom rough, the river wide, the current exceedingly rapid. It took two hours to pass. Now and then a man was down; and now and then a horse. Six horses found it difficult to take a gun through; and one caisson obstinately refused to budge from the middle of the stream until horses were changed, and ten of them exerted their strength. It was a scene of order, but of exceeding bustle.

Two miles more brought us to Newmarket. For a description of this place, turn to any of my allusions to Southern villages. This one had, however, a rather pretty church, Lutheran in name. It had also a graveyard, from which, as we halted by it, I took from one of the best marble stones the following mixture of fact and piety : —

"He was taken sick the eleventh of June,
And only lived ten days ;
But he's gone to rest in heaven above,
And sing his Saviour's praise."

From which I gathered that it is considered extremely remarkable here that a man should go to heaven who was taken sick on the eleventh of June, and who had so short a sickness.

Yankee Doodle brought out the population of Newmarket extensively, but we could not wait. There is a strong Union sentiment here, as there is all through the valley, and of the most intelligent class, excepting the few wealthy proprietors. This sentiment only needs to be favored to make it extremely powerful ; that it has not been more attended to, I suppose is owing to the fact that the Union class is dark-colored.

Two miles out of Newmarket we went into camp. It had begun to rain a little before we reached the camping place, and we were glad to be located. Do not, however, have too exalted ideas of the shelter ; we had no tents, nor have had any until yesterday, although, saving yesterday, it has rained steadily. The shelters are improvised of rails, straw, and such like. Two rails, fastened together near the top, with legs spread out, form one support ; two more form another ; a rail is laid on top between the two, and from this horizontal cross rail, other rails slope to the ground ; straw is laid on, often plastered with mud ; some rubber blankets are hung up inside ; and if the wind happens to be right, the shelter will keep off about half the wet ; if the wind is wrong, it doesn't keep off any. Outside is mud, mud, mud. Yet our men are cheerful and manly. Notwithstanding they have done more work and borne more hardship, tenfold, than regiments sent by steam direct, and then allowed the opportunity to show themselves brave, notwithstanding the exposure to disease and bullets for months upon months, which the Second, the Twelfth, and the Thirteenth Massachusetts have had to endure, and for which they get no name upon their banner, while others, newer in service, get the glory of some fortunate opportunity, which our men are not allowed, yet they feel that the work they do is still for their country and necessary, and they bear it cheerfully. Though not always able to see why a rich government leaves them exposed to cold storms, without shelter, for days, while their tents are but a few miles off, and no enemy near, yet they endure hardness as good soldiers.

Contrabands are frequent. All tell the same story, all desire to be free, all seem ready to work. Here is one instance :

" Can you take care of yourself, Sam ? "

" I should think I might," is the reply. " I hire myself out, make my own bargains, and carry the money to my master."

Here is another :

" How is it with you? Can you take care of yourself?

" Gosh a-mighty, massa ; guess I can. Been taking car' of self and old massa dis twenty year. Guess can take car' of dis nig all alone."

Which was sound logic.

HARRISONBURG, VA., May 1, 1862.

HARRISONBURG, shire town of Rockingham county, is superior in appearance to any town in the valley which we have thus far seen, though quite inferior in size to Winchester. Its people certainly behave a great deal better. Winchester people, especially most of the women, act as though their hearts were " set on fire of hell." In addition to an evident lack of decent breeding, they show a want of all those humanized feelings which civilized nations show even to enemies. The barbarous institutions under which they live keep them down to barbarous levels. But in Harrisonburg, the inhabitants are decently courteous; and, indeed, there is, if true sentiments could be spoken without danger, a great deal of Union feeling. But who can wonder that they are afraid to speak openly, when they fear to be again deserted to the cruelties of rebels, as the Union people were last summer by Patterson, in the upper part of the valley? The evil result of Patterson's failure was not merely the loss of Bull Run ; his leaving Union people to the terrible vengeance of secessionists caused a sad distrust and fear. Better lose a battle than to abandon loyal citizens.

Harrisonburg is the centre of probably the best wheat county in Virginia. Nothing can be more beautiful, agriculturally, than the broad fields now covered with living green. The town itself has very good shops, a court-house, two or three hotels, and six churches, viz., two Presbyterian (New and Old School), two Methodist (North and South), a Lutheran, and an " Ironsides " Baptist, besides other civilizing institutions, which I will not venture to mention.

For this place we left our camp (I mean our regiment did) on Friday last. We were glad to get away from the mud, though with little prospect of improvement. Still any change would be for the better. Some of us had had our meals at a house near by, owned with, I believe, eighteen hundred acres of land, by a present brigade-quartermaster in the rebel service. The family, except the head, were there, and the conflict between hospitality and enmity was entertaining. A guard was allowed the premises, as is very common; and the good lady, on our leaving, felt bound to say that the men of our regiment had treated her and hers with courtesy; in fact, she said, Virginians could not have acted more like gentlemen. Our men always bear that character. The thirty or forty slaves of the place she notified to take care of themselves in future, as have others in the valley. She might as well, as the slaves evidently intend to do so, with or without permission.

It was a raw day when we made our march of fourteen miles, but it did not rain, for a wonder. We are now in camp, a little above Harrisonburg, in a pleasant, open wood. It rains now, of course. Of course it is muddy. Of course any number of brooks run across the roads. But we are well sheltered now, and the regiment is in very good health. It is a curious fact that wet feet hurt nobody if you keep them wet all the time.

Sunday was a beautiful day. I felt glad, because we could have public worship. But after arrangements were all made, suddenly there came an order to go out on reconnoissance towards the Shenandoah. On the other side of that river is Jackson, said to be reënforced. The bridge is piled with straw, and everything is ready to set it into a blaze as soon as we should attempt to cross. The road we took on reconnoissance is a "dirt" road, of a very mean kind, and very mean of its kind. Mud, brooks, and rocks are its constituents, with here and there a rod or two of decent road to hold the rest together. I have seen hard roads in New Hampshire, but never anything equal to a Virginia dirt road. Their only redeeming feature is rail fence, which makes a most beautiful fire when you stop for the night.

On this road we advanced until we were eleven miles from camp; we, the Twenty-seventh Indiana, and somebody's battery, and somebody's else cavalry, — Vermont cavalry, I think, — which, for goodness of horses and dash of men beats any other cavalry we have seen. Soon after leaving Harrisonburg we met Colonel Donelly's brigade, which was coming in from an advanced camp. I do not exactly understand what a reconnoissance was intended to discover, made to the same spot which regiments had just left; but I have no doubt there was some brilliant result obtained. A little brush between our cavalry and Ashby's took place, resulting in an exchange of one of our men for two of theirs. The day before their cavalry drove in our pickets; one man, I forget his regiment, did not reach cover, in consequence of taking the wrong direction; he hence was virtually a prisoner, but the rebels preferred to shoot him, and as he lay wounded, shot him again. This is rebel chivalry.

Farther on a few of us stopped for dinner. The men of the companies carry food in their haversacks, but some of us have to trust to the road. We stopped at a good-looking house, speedily obtained our dinner, and fed our horses. It was a very intelligent family; books were quite plenty, and flowers were far more common than usual. Many of the books were religious, and Presbyterian papers abounded, though few of late date. I should not mention, perhaps, this wayside dining, but that one thing carried my mind back suddenly to home. It was a " balm-of-gilead tree." Don't laugh at it, anybody. At the farm of my birthplace there used to be, by the gate, a noble tree of that kind. It had stood for many years, and there I used to love to sit or play.

When a boy I went once a year to see grandparents, uncles, and cousins. There was a house full of these. But one day there came a hail storm of unprecedented fury, and in it the old tree was killed. Out of the root, it is true, there came up little ones, but they never grew to be large and beautiful. When I saw this one in Virginia, my mind was full of the old homestead, grandfather then active, grandmother, a minister's daughter, meek and pious, and all the numerous household who made the home so happy. Gone the older; gone or scattered almost all the middle generation; gone, not a few of the youngest, into the world of silence; and the old place is different now. So do we often think here of home, at slight provocations. When rising from a prayer in hospital once, I heard " that seems just like my *home*," murmured almost dreamily by a very sick and weak man. Home! Happy those whose thoughts of home are so linked with prayer and praise.

We turned about. And a little after dark had reached camp again. Our men were sadly fatigued, but they had marched splendidly, over a road of twenty-two miles, equivalent to a good road of at least thirty, in little more, if any, than ten hours. Here we still are; and in this vicinity, I doubt not, we remain until Yorktown matters progress for the timing of our movement. But I *know* nothing about it. In the mean time we are eighteen miles from the post-office of the corps. Think of that, you who have mails two or three times a day.

STRASBURG, VA., May 16, 1862.

WE learn from the newspapers that our corps is now at Staunton, and aiming for Richmond. We learn, also, that

Jackson has evacuated the valley. Neither statement is true. We advanced; Jackson retired. We reached Harrisonburg; Jackson crossed the middle Shenandoah, and rested at the opposite end of the bridge which he had piled with combustibles, towards Swift River Gap. We threw out forces towards the bridge; Jackson watched them with cavalry scouts.

Then the corps retired. General Banks's headquarters had never advanced beyond Newmarket, eighteen miles north of Harrisonburg, and have now come back to this place, thirty-one miles north of Newmarket. Jackson has been reënforced, and appears to have re-occupied Harrisonburg, and even farther north. From General Banks's corps General Shields's division has been detached, and has gone over — somewhere. General Williams's division remains here, where fortifications were begun some time ago. This place is the key to the valley; the practical termination of the Manassas Gap railway, over which road trains now run to within two miles of this place, and will run in on Monday next; and a very strong natural position.

The slow advance of this corps is apologetically attributed, in newspaper editorials, to bad roads and deficient supplies. As to roads, your *Spectator* said, May 5, that General Banks found them in " shocking condition " in the same paper in which I spoke of " plain, smooth " roads. Now there is no part of New England whose main avenues are better than those of this valley. By-roads are bad; but the principal lines are direct, macadamized turnpikes, built in large part by the State. An army could advance with perfect ease and great rapidity. So far as the matter of supplies is concerned, there has been no difficulty which energy could not have easily remedied. The reason, therefore, of the exceeding

13

slowness of movements, and the present retrograde, is to be found in other directions, and is, in all probability, attributable to directions from Washington. Weeks ago, had it been desired, we could have been beyond Staunton, and have swept every foe out of our path ; but at the risk of having our communication cut off.

Our regiment remained in camp at Harrisonburg until on Sunday, May 4. About sundown that day tents were struck, and every one packed. We were ordered out to the road, and half a mile towards Harrisonburg, and there had the comfort of a sudden bivouac. At gray morning we marched — not southward as we expected, but northward, eighteen miles or thereabouts ; passed through Newmarket village, and had tents pitched by about eight in the evening.

But at one o'clock in the morning we were ordered out. A mile or more east of Newmarket is the Masanutten range, or part of a range which reaches from Strasburg just fifty miles southward, dividing the valley in two long parts. On the other side of the range was General Sullivan. In the evening we had noticed the lights of the signal corps on top of the gap, flitting backward and forward. They were telling some scarecrow story about the needs of General Sullivan against a threatening force of twelve thousand men ; and our brigade, tired as it was with an eighteen miles march over a dusty road, must climb up the hills and down the other side. There was no help for it.

Turning at right angles from Newmarket, the road gradually descended for a mile or more toward a rapid river. The air was damp and chilly ; the misty darkness allowed only vague and spectral views ; and to enjoy both, an artillery train, ordered to report at the covered bridge, stopped us for a detestable hour, until some piece of red tape somewhere could be accurately measured.

But we climbed the hill. There was no *hard* climbing,
however. The road over the gap was as smooth and firm as
any in Roxbury or Dorchester, and was made up of so many
acute angles as to give a grade of exceeding ease. Indeed it
is a beautiful specimen of engineering, and evidently costly ;
built on the principle of getting as much road into the given
distance as possible — and so contrived as to make you believe you are going down hill instead of up. Another brigade
was bivouacked for a mile or two by the road, and their
brilliant fires crackling all along on either side, now against
a wall of earth left by excavation, and now bringing into relief the wild woods over a precipice, while a brook near by
was rolling, scolding, or singing by turns, made a bewildering and fascinating scene. At the top we rested, and
turning to look, beheld a view of the utmost beauty ; a lovely
valley, of great breadth, confined by the distant Alleghanies,
whose tops the rising sun was just tinging.

Down on the other side ; a halt at the base, in beautiful
scenery ; a despatch ; the pleasant information that either the
signal officer had blundered, or else somebody had — made a
mistake ; two nights bivouac in delightful woods, and on one
of them a magnificent spectacle in the " woods on fire " near
the top of Masanutten.

Then we returned. Up the hill and down again, and back
to camp. On the way up, a few of us took short cuts from
angle to angle once or twice to gather wild flowers. There
was great abundance of several kinds. Wild cherry was in
blossom, and laurel, and what they call dogwood here, which
I think is found in Milton, in Massachusetts, and " red bud,"
without leaves, but gorgeous in its wealth of flowering ; and of
lowlier plants, the red columbine, mayflower, much like the
New Hampshire one, which is more beautiful than that in

the Plymouth woods (I have gathered both), the anemone, the iris, far more delicately lovely than any I ever saw wild before ; and above all, such profusion of wood violets as one rarely finds, of which many were colored so like pansies that they were easily mistaken for them at a little distance.   Sitting upon a rock to rest, the sight of belted men, with swords at their side and pistols ready, gathering flowers, awakened strange sensations.   But these " wood violets are the same we have at *home*," they said.

On Saturday, at sundown, tents were again struck ; but orders soon came to stop the wagons ; and so with tents less than half a mile off, we had two more nights and the whole intervening day of shelterless waiting.   What for, do you ask ? Shrug your shoulders and keep quiet.

But on Monday morning, at half past two, we were in the road ; fourteen miles that day, and woods at night, with plenty of luxurious leaves for beds, which, with good weather and a few blankets, make just the pleasantest summer residence imaginable.   Tuesday morning, at three o'clock, we rise again, and make fourteen miles more, — to this dirtiest, nastiest, meanest, poorest, most shiftless town I have yet seen in all the shiftless, poor, mean, nasty, dirty towns of this beautiful valley.

There is a considerable force — perhaps fifteen or twenty thousand — of rebels down the valley.   That they will be fools enough to come up, is not possible while Fremont is at Franklin.   So our chance to do something active seems small. Rumor has it that our division is to remain here this summer, to hold this place, which is a very important one in reference to operations in the valley, and to look after the Manassas railway.   We are all terribly chagrined at such a prospect. It would be too humiliating to a large, well-equipped, finely-organized, brave, admirably led force like ours. To sit down virtually to garrison purposes, while troops which came into the field far later are placed in posts of honor, would be hard to bear. To read the brilliant despatches from this place by the reporter to the " Associated Press," which have become here a laughing-stock for their stereotyped beginning, " Great rejoicing is exhibited in this corps on hearing of the brilliant victory at —— " one place after another — would be rather tough for summer employment. If this be the settled plan, I shall relieve you of one " army correspondent," as what is going on this summer in this quarter would not be worth reading ; and I would not insult your kindness by writing. But we hope better things.

In the mean time there is plenty of guerilla business. One of our men was captured not sixty rods from the roadside by the woods where we had halted ; but after four or five days' captivity shrewdly escaped from a rebel camp of thousands of men, and after two days' travel in the woods reached Union pickets. Another, in advance on a march, was shot at and very severely wounded. It is learned that citizens, and soldiers in citizens' clothes, are roaming the valley to pick off any one they can find outside the lines as well as pickets. This is in accordance with Governor Letcher's proclamation. There is but one way to treat these gentry — hang them when caught ; burn every house from which they shoot ; and in default of catching the scoundrels, seize secession residents as hostages, and hang a man for every man shot in this murderous way. This would stop it. But this will not be done ; we must *conciliate* the greatest scoundrels that ever went unhung.

13 *

CHAPTER V.

THE RETREAT AND THE RETURN.

WILLIAMSPORT, MD., May 30, 1862.

ON the night of the 11th of July, last year, our regiment encamped in this town, by the river side, having left Camp Andrew in West Roxbury on the 8th ; and now, after over ten months of campaigning, we have come to the same place again, very unwillingly.

I wrote you last that Jackson could hardly be fool enough to come up the valley again. He has been, however, and if government is wide awake, as I think it is, Jackson's folly will soon be made apparent. Good generalship cannot fail to annihilate him.

We have had to retreat, and to retreat in circumstances which insured disaster. But when the country learns fully the history of a retreat made by less than five thousand men, while an enemy of twenty-five thousand moved at the same time on converging roads, — a retreat of fifty-three miles, encumbered by five hundred wagons, — a retreat marked by fighting for miles upon miles, and by repeated stands to enable the trains to gain in distance, — a retreat which ended in a successful passage of a wide and rapid river, in which the horses had often to swim, — this retreat will take its place as a masterly movement ; and General Banks, with his gallant little corps, will take high rank in the esteem and affection of the people.

When the plans were fully consummated between the forces of General Banks and General Fremont to attack and destroy or capture Jackson near Harrisonburg, the very night previous to the intended movement there came positive orders to our corps to retire to Strasburg, and to detach General Shields from this command. Disaster was then foreboded. Remonstrances were useless, and we retired. We had then left but two infantry brigades of four regiments each, a regiment of cavalry, and sixteen pieces of artillery. The Manassas railroad was opened to Strasburg, and Colonel Kenley's regiment, the First Maryland, was spared to guard it at Front Royal, ten miles east of Strasburg. The remainder of the force was mainly at Strasburg, detachments being constantly on outpost duty.

On Friday, May 23, Colonel Kenley's force was overwhelmed. News came by an orderly, too late to help him, even if it had been possible. About midnight the wagon trains were put in motion, but the men, though under arms, were not moved until Saturday morning at about eleven o'clock. It did not appear certain until then that the attack on Front Royal was more than a mere raid. But it soon appeared that Jackson was in very heavy force, and instant retreat was needful.

General Hatch, with cavalry, and some few guns, were rear guard. Colonel Donelly's brigade led; Colonel Gordon's followed. The train was far on the road, but the forces, excepting the rear guard, reached some of it near Middletown, distant about six miles above Strasburg, and passed it.

We were (Colonel Gordon's brigade) about a mile and a

half above Newtown (sometimes called Stephensburg), and about twelve miles from Strasburg, when reports came that the wagon train had been cut by the enemy. General Hatch was thus intercepted, and it appeared afterward, had crossed over to a road westerly, and came by detour to the main force. Colonel Gordon was then ordered to go back with the Second Massachusetts, the Twenty-eighth New York, and a section of Best's battery, to relieve the train. On approaching Newtown, they found the Twenty-seventh Indiana (of Colonel Gordon's brigade) drawn up across the road in line, with four pieces of Corthren's New York battery. The Twenty-eighth New York was halted, and Lieutenant-Colonel Andrews, with the Second Massachusetts, was ordered by Colonel Gordon to take and hold Newtown. They passed the wagons along the road in every conceivable state of confusion, abandoned by the drivers. The enemy had posted artillery in the street, but the Second advanced without firing a shot, under a fire of shell; the enemy did not wait to be closed upon, but retired to an eminence near by. There the artillery was posted, and constant firing was kept up for an hour, during which the town was held. Colonel Gordon endeavored to procure mules to save the wagons, but none were sent, and he ordered the Twenty-seventh Indiana to burn them, which was accomplished. When this was done, Colonel Gordon ordered the forces on again. It was now twilight.

From that time the Second was rear guard during the retreat. No annoyance was then experienced for the two miles which the regiment had just retraced. There, when it had been ordered to return to Newtown, it had, in order to relieve the fatigued men, left knapsacks in a field by the road. The regiment here halted to take them. While this was being done, on came the enemy. It was now quite dark. Companies were immediately formed to resist cavalry. Down came the enemy's charge; but our men waited until they came to within seventy or eighty yards, when from the three directions an admirable volley was poured into them. They did not wait for a second, but wheeled in dismay. Again their officers tried to rally them. So near were they that their orders could be heard, and when they were disobeyed, the word "cowards!" was audible. But in vain. They would not risk themselves against such musketry. They brought up artillery, but it had no effect except to stampede some of our cavalry.

It was not long before the enemy's infantry appeared. They opened a severe fire, but it was well returned, and the enemy checked.

Everything being ready, the troops moved on. The enemy followed, but our fire was too hard for them, and they were wary. Kernstown was reached, and a halt took place, both to rest the men and care for the wounded, which had been unfortunately taken to that point only, instead of going on to Winchester. Ambulances were sent for, but they did not return. Half an hour passed. Again the enemy crept up in the darkness and opened fire. It was returned with spirit. But it was useless to wait. Artillery could be heard rumbling in the rear. The macadamized road brought our men out into relief, and it was necessary to move on.

About two A. M., the last of the tired soldiers reached Winchester, and lay down to rest. They needed it badly. But a company from each regiment was sent out, and skirmishing was continual. The enemy's advance, in about two hours, was evidently in force.

Colonel Gordon and Colonel Donelly had chosen positions

for their brigade.   It was just out of town, on the right and
left of the road going southward.   On the right (facing
southward) was Colonel Gordon.   A long ridge running
nearly parallel with the road is broken by a cross gully.
On the eminence nearest the town, a little sheltered by
broken ground, was placed the infantry, the Second Massachusetts on the right, then, in order, the Third Wisconsin,
the Twenty-seventh Indiana, and the Twenty-ninth Pennsylvania ; and several pieces of artillery were posted in the
rear.   The other brigade was on the left of the road, where
they fought bravely, particularly the Fifth Connecticut.

On the opposite height was the enemy.   As they showed
themselves, there were large masses, dropping soon out of
sight.   As Colonel Gordon's brigade ascended to its place, a
fire of grape was opened on them at a few hundred yards
distance.   The men were ordered to lie down, rising only to
fire, and the artillery was kept constantly at work.   Skirmishers were sent to pick off the enemy's horses and gun-
ners ; much exposed, they were soon ordered still nearer the
enemy, where they could be sheltered by a wall.   So accurate was their fire, with that of the troops in line, that one
gun was completely silenced, the enemy not daring to attempt
even its removal.

The troops fought bravely and coolly.   But by and by a
movement of the enemy threatened the skirmishers, and they
were called in.   Then heavy columns were seen moving to
turn the right of the brigade.   Colonel Gordon ordered the
Twenty-seventh Indiana and Twenty-ninth Pennsylvania to
take position on the right, in an oblique angle with the other
two regiments.   They rushed thither, and with shouts began
a rapid firing.   But seeing the force approaching they fell
back.   What could valor do against such odds?   Then the

guns were ordered away. It was useless to remain. Orders
came to retire.

So they entered Winchester, the enemy in pursuit. The
exultant foe pursued. They were the rear. Cavalry dashed
against them. Citizens fired from houses. Women shot
from windows, and threw hand grenades at them. Yet not
a break occurred. Volleys were poured into the houses fired
from. Riders were unhorsed. Past burning buildings, intensely hot, reckless of attack, the men stood steady.

So on to Martinsburg. Shells bursting over them; cavalry sweeping round; but unbroken still. And unbroken,
this regiment, the rear of the main column, before a foe of
twenty-five thousand men, it retreated. So on to Williamsport, fifty-three miles from the place it had left thirty-three
hours before.

In the action at Winchester this corps stood for three
hours and a half from the time the pickets were driven in —
four thousand men against twenty-five thousand; seven regiments against twenty-eight actually counted at once. Escaped
prisoners tell us that the enemy suffered severely. They
were astonished at the daring of this little force and at its
escape. They expected its entire capture.

In Winchester some stores fell into the enemy's hands, but
not a very great amount. Few wagons and few arms were
lost. The enemy took prisoners, however, of all whom
fatigue forced to remain.

The passage through Winchester illustrates again the infernal influence of Southern education. Women had accumulated pistols and hand grenades, and used them on *helpless*
men. What causes this? The education of *slavery*. *That*
brutalizes the people it curses. In this town of Winchester,
when we occupied it, not a house was robbed, not a woman

insulted. Such is the return. Woe be to that town when our troops see it again! As Sodom was, it is; as Sodom is, I trust it will be. But what else is to be expected? "Conciliate!" Conciliate rattlesnakes, if you will. The spirit of a slaveholder, as such, is the spirit of hell.

————

NEAR FRONT ROYAL, VA., June 19, 1862.

WE are gratified to find that our regiment is praised at home. I have always felt that all which was wanted for the regiment was opportunity to show the character of its material and the results of its drill and discipline. Few know the work necessary to make a really good regiment; the constant drill, the regular studies and recitations of the officers, the habit of unhesitating obedience of orders, to be obtained only by slow growth. These ours has had. Even last winter, daily recitations, in two classes, were conducted by the colonel and lieutenant-colonel, instead of allowing idleness. The result is, a regiment whose main idea is *duty*.

As to the character of the recent retreat, I see nothing to change in what I wrote you. We have since learned that the rebels were astonished and infuriated at the escape. They suffered greatly. Over seventy graves have been counted of men of one Southern regiment, the one, I think, which suffered terribly from the sudden fire of the brave Connecticut Fifth. The stand of our own regiment near Newtown, we have learned, puzzled the enemy. When they afterward learned from prisoners that only one regiment did it, they were surprised, and ashamed that it had checked their march.

Why this retreat was ever allowed, it is hard to understand. It can do no harm to state that the falling back from Harrison-

burg to Strasburg was sadly against the wishes of our commander, and only in consequence of peremptory orders. The
location at Strasburg was a poor one ; but it was ordered. A
fortification had been begun there by some engineers, which
was entirely commanded by several hills. The division of
the valley by the Masanutten range allowed the enemy to
choose which side to approach in safety. Our force was
small, especially after General Shields had been taken. It is
known that repeated attempts were made to convince higher
authorities of the danger of this position, but in vain ; indeed,
they at last excited jocular replies.

The *World's* account, by the way, which I see extensively
copied, has two items rather queer ; one day it says that our
regiment went through Winchester with colors flying and
drums beating ; another, that the Second, after firing one
volley, broke, ran through Winchester, and could not be ral-
lied for two miles. Both statements are untrue. There was
no drum beat. And on the other hand they never broke ; nor
was there a moment when the regiment was not perfectly in
the hand of the commander. They did not even take the
double-quick step, except twice when ordered, once in turning
a street corner, and once when passing five or six burning
buildings in a narrow street where the heat was insupportable.
The disjointed items of a youngster, who says he slept through
the conflict below Winchester, comfortably in bed at a hotel,
are, however, scarcely worth alluding to, but for the fact that
some Boston papers copy them.

This experience has had one evident effect on our regiment,
—to create the happiest feeling between officers and privates.
The coolness of our officers, their indifference to danger, and
their constant care of their men, have won respect and affection ; and officers feel the same toward the men, who did all

14

that men could do.   It had been enviously said that officers
like ours — young men, more than two thirds of whom were
graduates of some college (two of West Point), and reared
in comparative luxury — would neither endure hardships nor
manifest bravery.   The reverse precisely is true.   The great
difficulty with all was to keep them out of useless danger.
In the action at Winchester, those who had any breakfast, ate
it unconcernedly.   Some, not actively engaged, went to sleep.
One servant even passed along with food in the midst of a
fire of grape.   One officer there had a forcible appeal from
brother Trask, in the shape of a bullet from the storm, which
knocked his pipe out of his mouth, and so spoiled his smoke.

The brigade remained at Williamsport until June 10.   The
other brigade of our corps had left some days earlier.   On
that day it crossed the river, and bivouacked near Falling
Water.   The next day it went to, and camped at Bunker
Hill.   The following day it passed through Winchester, where
General Banks was, and General Sigel, whose forces had, a
week earlier, come up from Harper's Ferry, and camped six
miles south.   That place we left on Wednesday last, and we
are here a few miles north of Front Royal.

Much of this march was over ground traversed last July,
and so had its peculiar interest.   Some of its features, however, struck us as peculiar.   The conciliatory policy is extreme.   A guard from the brigade was stationed at every
house, and no person, officer or man, was allowed even to rob
the inhabitants of well-water ; fortunately we met brooks occasionally.   The general of the corps has just issued an assur-
ing proclamation to the farmers, to the effect that if they
gather their crops nobody shall touch them, unless government wants them, in which case their value shall be paid.
Considering that it is hard to find a Union man this side of

Martinsburg, this method of making war by furnishing an excellent market to the secessionists, is eminently forgiving. Winchester, with its villanous spawn of hell for inhabitants, is most carefully protected. Houses, from which, it is capable of clearest proof, citizens fired on our soldiers, are unharmed. The dwellers in that town are unharmed. I would not favor any indiscriminate pillage, but the policy which makes it for the interest of men to be rebels is queer. A rebel, he is protected by both Union and secesh soldiers. A Union man, he is protected by Union, but terribly maltreated by secesh; therefore — be secesh. Still, if that is the policy of government, doubtless there are sound reasons for it. In the mean time I have reason to know that rebel citizens laugh at us, and believe that we do not dare to be justly severe. Some cases of protection would make people stare.

As to the general situation, you know better where Jackson is than any here except the leaders.

The valley in which we are runs from Pennsylvania southwest. It is bounded by the Blue Ridge on the east, and the Alleghanies on the west. Two principal places of entrance from Maryland are Harper's Ferry and Williamsport. The valley is tolerably open until we reach Strasburg, where, in the centre begins a separate chain — the Masanutten range — which splits the valley for just fifty miles, where, near Harrisonburg, it abruptly ends. Now at the head of the western division stands Strasburg ; at the head of the eastern, Front Royal. When Jackson came northward, it was by the eastern side of the Masanutten, General Banks's force not being sufficient to guard either side. Middletown, a few miles north of both Strasburg and Front Royal, seems the strong point from which to support both places. This is now occupied. General Fremont holds Strasburg, and some dis-

tance below, and we are part of the force occupying Front
Royal.

These measures seem as if preventive rather than aggressive, but they can easily become the latter. The difficulty
here seems this : parts of, or the whole of *three* army corps,
have lately been occupying the valley, each responsible only
to Washington. It is a puzzle why all the troops in this limited area should not be in *one* command. General Fremont's
department, and that of General Banks, are separated by only
a *line in the road* for fifty miles. If this whole artificial cutting up of territory were done away, and if all the forces this
side the Blue Ridge were given to one general, would there
not be greater efficiency? In fact, ever since General McClellan was limited to his narrow area, and three other independent departments made in Virginia, matters have worked
badly. The army would rejoice to hear that the war in Virginia was under one general, and he McClellan.

For myself, I had enough to do in the hospital at Winchester. Several buildings are occupied for this purpose. Our
wounded are at the " Union House " hospital, under charge
of our own Doctor Leland, formerly of Milford. He has had
only one surgeon with him, and a hundred and seventy patients ;
but everything is neat, the care is admirable, and the men
quite cheerful. The surgeon has a great heart, and equal
skill, and has the warmest regard from all our men. There
is a post chaplain at Winchester, but he has several buildings
to visit, including those with the rebel sick. It is very
noticeable how the Winchester women send their delicacies
to the rebel quarters, few to the Union. Still our men do
not lack. It was a great privilege to go into the hospital,
though it was a six mile ride, and meet our own men. Take
good care of them, friends, when they go home, as they will,
to recruit. They deserve it.

I am not surprised that many persons are discountenancing stories of rebel insolence and barbarity, because it is hard to believe human nature sunk so low. One thing is true ; the wounded collected into hospitals were well treated. Whether the fact that they must and did leave a large number of their own to our care had any effect, I do not know. I am satisfied that no shots were *knowingly* fired into actual hospitals. But aside from these, there is no reason to qualify any statements which I have seen of rebel barbarity.* This race is not fully civilized yet. For ignorance and stupidity, I could tell you facts I never would have believed but for seeing them. And I tell you again, until slavery is broken, and until a new race is introduced, to a very great extent, there will be no true peace. Senator Sumner never uttered truer words than those in his speech — " The Barbarism of Slavery."

* Proof, in great quantity, of the firing from windows by women and others in Winchester, was afterwards collected to a certain extent. But the stories of our immense losses are perfectly absurd. So is the account of the panic equally untrue and ridiculous.

14 *

CHAPTER VI.

MOVEMENTS UNDER GENERAL POPE.

On the Road, Rappahannock Co., Va., July 9, 1862.

Last Saturday evening. as we looked at the red sunset sky, we said, " It will be hot to-morrow." Why we felt special interest in the expected weather was, because we were to march to-morrow. The tidings had come of reverses at Richmond.

It *was* a hot Sunday. Reveille was beat at the usual hour. All was made ready to move. Another brigade had gone in the night, whose rumbling wagons we could hear when we were foolish enough to lie awake. The morning hours wore on. At eleven o'clock, " Route step, forward ! " The sun was blazing hot when we started, and grew hotter and hotter. A few miles on was the Shenandoah, the junction of its north fork and main stream. There we waited under a hill, on an exposed plain, where the very leaves hung stupefied. Hours passed before the indolent wagon trains in front moved out of the way, and then we moved again. We crossed the temporary bridge built at the junction of the rivers ; passed over the site of Colonel Kenley's contest, where relics still lie in profusion, but which we left untouched, having long since got tired of carrying loads of old iron ; went through the rather pretty little town of Front Royal, which is well shaded, a mile or so from the railroad to which a branch runs, and camped a mile or so south of the town. No sooner had the ground been reached than men fell utterly exhausted, and passed under the surgeon's care. The march had not been long, but horrible for heat. On it we wondered why, as our destination was said to be Warrenton, government did not transport the troops by railroad, in one day, rather than break them down by a four days' march under a Virginia July sun. We also wondered why we might not have had our Sunday in quiet, and, starting at, say five o'clock in the afternoon, made the same distance by eight o'clock. Soldiers may " wonder," but they cannot help themselves. However, many of us had no scruples at taking a cooling bath that evening in a brawling brook near by, and having followed the Apostle's directions as to " pure water " and a " clean conscience," slept very well.

And on Monday, at three o'clock, reveille awakened us. At six o'clock we were in the road, toward the Blue Ridge. It was a lovely morning, and truthful, for it promised another hot day, and was right about it. It was an eventful anniversary too. For, one year ago that day we left Camp Andrew in West Roxbury, and left Boston, and left wives, children, and friends. Some wives, some children, are to be seen no more ; and some of that number of brave men have sealed their patriotic contract with their blood.

Four miles, or may be five, from Front Royal is Chester Gap, a break in the summit of the Blue Ridge. The ascent is gentle ; the scenery beautiful. The heat was severe, but when at last we reached the summit of the road, and began to descend, the breeze swept over us gently, and cooled the heated men. We were descending the Ridge, and I doubt if there was one there who did not rejoice that at last we were out of that hated Virginia valley, into which our evil fortune had sent us one year ago, and where our energies had been uselessly spent for that time. General Banks was now in Eastern Virginia.

Twelve miles that day before eleven o'clock. Then we rested in a beautiful wood, and toward night pitched our tents. By and by a refreshing shower came up, so that when next morning we marched on, the ground was delightfully firm. We were rear guard that next day, and so were troubled with the long wagon trains. Troubles easily borne, for this section is prolific in cherries; and as we halted for hours, the men luxuriated in cherries; they ate cherries among the branches; they picked cherries to take along; they cut limbs full of cherries and ate under the shade as they marched. Providence evidently made these cherries ripen for our march.

But, five miles on the road, we halted. We camped. Orders came, based on the facts that anxiety for General McClellan was over, and that sufficient forces were at Warrenton. What to do with our two brigades nobody seems to know, and we are waiting till somebody finds out. As usual, we are a kind of incumbrance, placed nobody knows why, and what to do with us, I think always puzzles the authorities. But we wait. Nothing is given us to do. Our brethren at Richmond we would gladly help. Our own comparative uselessness we lament. But if our government desires us to " spend the summer in the country," we can do so, though a little preferring, if our wishes were consulted, some sea-side spot. For instance, Nahant is cooler; or the line of the Lowell and Lawrence Railroad, ought not there to be a force sufficient to defend it? or say at Tewksbury, which, if my memory serves me, is quite warm.

Barring our wishes, however, clearly the country needs men. The call for three hundred thousand surprises nobody here. It will take half that number to fill up existing regiments. But I will tell you what to do. Send back our men who are wasted in other employments; employ "civil" nurses at Frederick; restore to a fighting position the many, officers and men, who are engaged in the trucking business (here called quartermaster's department), and the provision trade (here called commissary's department), and hire some good truckmen and pork dealers from Boston, infinitely better fitted than West Point graduates for such a service; cut down the hosts of men wasted on staff employ, as witness the late enormous list thrown out by General Fremont's being " relieved" of command, and then the terrible deficiencies of our six hundred thousand men would melt away one half.

But after that were done (which never will be), the country needs more soldiers. It has a right to demand them. After God, it has the first claim. When at home a few days last January, I could see no diminution in the street throngs; no want of men in business. *Here*, it is rare to find an able-bodied man; ask for one, and regularly you are answered, " He is in the army." In the army, to support the most infernal institution the world ever saw, and to overthrow the best government the world ever saw, while in Massachusetts there are multitudes who criticise and carp, as though they knew all about war, but never lift a hand. You, whose families *must* have your services at home, there are enough without you. But you, whose only trouble is your dislike at leaving them, — your fellow-men have left wives and children, with sore hearts, too ; *will* you? You, who are sick, stay at home ; but you, whose faces are white and forms slender, only because you need air and activity, come, and grow stalwart. You, whose highest work is to sell ribbons and laces, bonnets and slippers, — leave that to *women ;* be *men ;* a musket is more honorable than a yardstick for a man's hand ; a hard hand is better than flabby fingers ; an honest tan is a better color than tallow. A soldier is a *man.*

Influential men at home ought to set the example. *They* can fill up the army in a week. Let them throw their wealth, their ability, their persons, to this cause, and hosts of followers would fall in. If they have wealth, that excuses nobody from serving his country. If they *can* live at ease, that is no reason why they *should* live in ease.

And you, brother ministers, whose work is not, and ought not to be, to fight, — you, whose hearts are in this cause, and who would gladly be in it yourselves, — will *you* not use your powerful influence to fill up our armies? Tell the people what this war is for. Tell them it is a war holier than ever were crusades. Show them what the country needs. Explain what patriotism is. Convince your young men that the patriot *must* not refuse this call. Make them understand, what few do understand, the exigencies of the Age ; that this is the war of Civilization against Barbarism, Light against Darkness, Right against Wrong ; that now is the culmination of the Heathenism of two centuries ; that that Heathenism is indeed earnest. The ministry of Christ have a trust in their hands which this generation never equalled before, never will again. Thank God, I know they are TRUE.

———

NEAR WARRENTON, VA., July 16, 1862.

YOUR letter came a day or two ago. You say you have had none from me since one I wrote concerning the " re-

treat" of May 24 and 25. You inquire whether I have
ceased writing. " Ceased writing ! " when I have written as
often, at least, as once a fortnight ! Little did I know the
sad truth : how all my brilliant thoughts, my excellent dis-
quisitions, my beautiful descriptions, — had all gone, through
the post-office tunnel, into some paper-mill ! The world can
never know what it has lost. It is a hopeless loss : should
they come to light, alas, for their freshness ! A good brother
chaplain of my acquaintance had a bottle of champagne sent
him by a general. The excellent brother thanked the donor,
and stated to him that he never drank, but would keep this
bottle to use a little from time to time in case of sickness.
He learned his mistake. In case my letters turn up — they
are too long uncorked ; they are flat forever.

I do not know what I wrote. I never read my letters in
print, much less keep copies. But by way of recapitulation
as to our peregrinations, we left Williamsport, Md., June 10,
and crossed the river, to the inspiring music of " Carry me
back to Old Virginia, to old Virginia's shore ; " bivouacked
that night near Falling Waters ; passed through Martinsburg to Bunker Hill, and there camped ; next day marched
to and through Winchester in close order ; camped that
night at Bartonsville, a flourishing town of three houses,
about seven miles south of Winchester ; remained there until
June 18, when we moved to a spot about four miles north of
Front Royal, where we had the capital fortune to get back,
as brigadier, our own Massachusetts soldier, General Gordon. Sunday, July 6, we were ordered on ; one night a
mile south of Front Royal ; one night snug by a pretty locust-
shaded little village called Flint Hill ; two nights near
Gaines's Cross Roads ; here we pitched our tents late Friday
night, and here we wait for orders.

All along the roads are great wheat fields, into which no sickle will enter. Crops sufficient to feed all New England are to be lost for want of laborers. Owners have gone to war, and blacks have run away as the army moved. The strength of the rebel army is in slave labor. Able-bodied men can be spared to fight wherever the black laborers remain. The North has made a great mistake in supposing that slavery is an element of weakness at the South in time of war. Practically, the reverse is true. It need not be so. It ought not to be so. Had we given the slaves to understand that they are *free*, the crops now gathering would never have been food for rebel armies.

While waiting, we are amid a large army. Brigadier-generals are plenty. Regiments are on every hand. The Twelfth and Thirteenth Massachusetts are again our neighbors, and we revive old friendships with great comfort. Our baggage is cut down; one valise to an officer. Our tents are partly taken away; the officers crowd into a diminished number, and the privates have, or are to have, " shelter " tents. Ten days' rations are to be kept on hand, and each regiment to be ready to move any time, rations and all, at an hour's notice. General Pope's address to his army implies work. For myself, I am better fitted for a march than I was a week ago, when I had lost my horse! He turned up, at last, in the Fifth New York horse-thieves (known *officially as cavalry*). General Gordon lost a horse of his; it was found in, and with great difficulty (ending in the arrest of a captain) procured from, the Fifth New York horse-thieves. Our adjutant lost two horses; both were discovered — in the Fifth New York horse-thieves.

We are now, you see, under General Pope. That is, the lately separate commands, under Generals Banks, Fremont, and McDowell, are united under General Pope. We cease to be an isolated corps now, for the first time. How admirably General Banks behaves under this new order you know. He is a real patriot.

Everybody hopes we are to move toward Richmond. Whether it were wise we cannot judge. We have confidence in the Union generals. What little esteem we ever had for civilians who manage war was long since lost. Let them manage their politics, but let soldiers plan campaigns, — is the universal feeling. To meddlers are due the wails in thousands of households : to them, the prolonging of the war ; to them, the waste of untold millions of money ; to them, the imminent danger of foreign intervention : all accomplished, when men in civil life determined to dictate to educated soldiers what they, as soldiers, must do ; when they thwarted the best plans ; tried to balance the jealousies of parties by giving each general an inadequate independent command. I tell you the execrations of the army upon the authors of our disasters are deep. And while not dismayed, yet we are saddened upon hearing now that no change is to be made. Unless a *practical* change is made, I insist that the South *cannot* be conquered.

There are differences of opinion in the army as to the slavery question. Some want emancipation proclaimed. Some, practical and effectual emancipation without proclamations. Some, to leave slavery as it was before the war. The drifting is towards emancipation, mainly to the second position. In that I rather coincide, though I want the thing *done* at any rate, as necessary for the country. But all love their country first and best. If we can accomplish emancipation, it would be a glorious deed for our country. If not now, yet the old Flag must triumph. But, to emancipate, is

15

the way to succeed; and therefore the government needs policy, needs firmness, needs energy.

The more I see, the more I believe in the feasibility of emancipation. The difficulties in the way are not unconquerable; I mean, as to adjusting the elements of the new state of society caused thereby. The only obstacle is in the masters, who have so long made men work without wages, that, like all tyrants, they cannot bear to go to work for an *honest* living. The slaves could be freed, and remain on the soil. Compulsory colonization seems to me a perfect humbug, — unless you colonize the masters, the real encumbrances. To remove the industrious portion of the community is foolish. France tried that when it banished thousands of Protestant artisans. Let us not commit the same folly. Suppose Massachusetts were to expel from its borders its day-laborers, its working farmers, its shoemakers, its blacksmiths, — where would the wealth of Massachusetts be? The blacks are the workmen, — peasant laborers generally, but often mechanics. They do not wish to leave their native land. Why should they? What *right* have we to expel them? Is their race not a native of the soil? No more is ours. You who weep over " Evangeline," wherein have *we* a right to imitate the conduct of the arrant humbug nation of Europe?

Of course, in freeing the slaves, there would be trouble. They are unfit for liberty in some respects. But who made them so? What right have the masters — the criminals, to plead their own crime as an excuse for perpetuating that crime? Whatever troubles would ensue are the penalty of transgression, the price of reform. When our surgeon sets a broken leg, there is pain in the operation; there is subsequent inflammation in the very process of healing; there is, for a time, helplessness; but then there comes health and power; and in spite of, and at the cost of, pain and fever, it was better to have the leg set. Society here has both legs broken; better set them.

Better set them, because it is *right*. I thank God that we can stand at last, untrammelled, on the simple basis of *right*. I doubt all politicians who dodge the question of *right*. Your fourth of July oration is powerful, but I cannot see that it touches one point, viz., that the legality it argues for is iniquitous. Every man has a *right* to freedom save in crime. Every man who deprives another of that freedom is a robber. Every law which sanctions that robbery is wicked. In conversing with Virginians, there is one argument which they cannot answer: *every man has a right to his liberty*. On secession, or nullification, or republican party, or compromise, they will twist and dodge; but from that simple principle there is no escape. "I believe," I have told many of them, "in just what your own constitution of Virginia says, adopted in the last century, reënacted by convention in December, 1861, when in its preamble it declares that 'all men are created free and equal, and possessed of rights of which they cannot divest themselves or their posterity.'" That is the platform. It is astonishing how simple one's duty becomes when he gets at this fundamental principle, and means to adhere to it. I feel very comfortable now.

You will see that Congress, by recent legislation, has materially reduced the pay of chaplains, and possibly you will be curious to know its result. It is hard telling yet. There are two things involved; one is, the pay as to be established, is less than that of a captain of infantry, showing the estimation in which chaplaincies are held by the governing power. The other thing to be considered is, that while some chaplains will receive more than in any of their settlements, very many are already making comparative pecuniary sacrifice. The expenses of a campaign are very large. I judge from a year's experience that the pay newly established is inadequate, and must speedily send home all except the poorer class, who never had a parish of any size, or wealthy men, who can afford to stay.

But wherever our country wants us she should have us. And unless this rebellion is soon crushed we shall have war enough. Our country will then need all its sons. Never should I have any temptation to be more intimately connected with a soldier's life than now, unless foreign powers intervened. Then I should feel that any place was glory. To be one of an army to humble and cripple forever that hypocritical, arrogant, incarnation of selfishness, that Pecksniff of nations, England, the tyrant in Ireland, the barbarian in India, the hereditary ally of despots, haughty to the weak, fawning on the strong, " whose end is destruction, whose God is their belly, and whose glory is in their shame" — *that* would make ancestral fire burn in my veins; *that* I should recognize as a duty to the civilization of the century and to the voice of God. It would be a *holy war.*

Near Washington, Rappahannock Co., Va., July 24, 1862.

It is rather curious to reckon over the various titles and commanders of the corps in which, for one year, we have served. We have been in the army of the Valley, the army of the Shenandoah, the army of the Potomac, the army of Virginia; we " change the place, yet keep the pain." General Patterson has commanded our division, General Banks alone, General Banks under General McClellan, General Banks alone again, General Pope, and now, if rumor be true, General Halleck over General Pope. For brigadiers, we have had Generals Abercrombie, Williams, Hamilton, Greene, and Gordon,—varying backwards and forwards until one tenure of each would not average a month. As we have been kept in a limited locality, and formed part of but one army, the simplicity and straightforwardness of this management is pleasingly illustrated.

Now matters seem to have come to a stop. The army and the country pause to consider. Richmond will not fall this week. The rebellion will not end the week after. What is the look of things?

After more than a year's fighting, after untold expenditure of treasure and blood, we seem no nearer the end than when we commenced. The forebodings long entertained by experienced men have been realized. A year ago, and repeatedly since, high, very high authority predicted to me just this state of things. The predictions were based upon the course of public matters, and upon the misunderstood energies and resources of the South.

Yet there are some hopeful matters with us.

One is, the union of the forces in Upper Virginia under one general. It has long been waited for. The evils of the opposite course have been most painfully felt on the ground. While the people have been amused with pompous headings in the dailies about some little skirmish, they did not know that our strength has been frittered away, our resources wasted. Who should tell it? Who could venture to speak in view of the stringent rules against communicating "information"? Now the troops are under one head. Of General Pope himself the country knows. His deeds declare what

15 *

he is. The recent inaugural (so to call it) did not favorably impress the soldiery; but the subsequent orders are received with delight. They indicate a vigor and policy which have long been waited for. Baggage, well called *impedimenta* by the Romans, has been reduced. Wagons are in order. A hundred and fifty rounds of ammunition per man are kept with the regiment. And all are quietly and courageously waiting to second him in what he may do with the army of Virginia.

There is sense, also, in the appointment of General Halleck (if it be true) as general-in-chief. Not merely that it is General Halleck, but that it is a general-in-chief; and also that it is one whom we may hope will not be interfered with. A soldier is to plan our campaigns; let civilians attend to their civil duties. What could be more proper? The contrary has cost the country enough woe. Thank God for this symptom of reason. Why a republic has been considered incapable of carrying on wars with success, is evidently because political leaders cannot willingly keep their fingers out of military affairs. Rome, in time of peril, committed its powers to a dictator, charging him to see that the republic met with no harm. The universal demand of our people for unity and efficiency have virtually done the same thing. The head of the armies should not be interfered with. Wielding the vast resources of the North, and eminently qualified, he cannot fail. The civil authorities can settle political questions; the military must rule the armies. If this be not done, I see no successful issue to this war; nor do men infinitely better qualified to judge. Now, we may hope that General Pope, in Upper Virginia, will have more men. We may hope that General McClellan will have what he needs.

The new indications as to the vigor with which all proper warlike measures are to be pushed are hopeful signs. Government has been very slow to be severe enough. It has long been a matter of astonishment that the importance of the occasion has not been recognized. The South is in earnest. It takes what property it wants. It impresses its citizens. It scourges Union men. We play with the rebellion. We treat Union and rebel alike. We have kept negroes at work to support their masters in the rebel army. We have guarded rebels' straw stacks while our men slept on the ground. We have used the labor of negroes with hesitation and apology. That is, we formerly did. Now we shall take rebel property. We should receive, organize, arm if advantageous, our black allies. We could make the South tremble by the statement, "your slaves shall be free, and they shall help conquer you." I have seen the effect a suggestion of such a policy makes on rebels. It angers them, but it terrifies them. Of all the Union generals, they tell me that they consider McClellan the most of á military man ; but the man they are most afraid of is *Fremont*. They *dread* him. In the rebel army at Winchester, there were plenty of black soldiers, *actual soldiers*, as many will testify. Why should not *we* use such ?

But there are reasons which account for indecision. One is, the stupefying air of politics. It benumbs one. It is hard for anybody to realize the condition of the country, immersed in petty details and surrounded by corruption. But another is, the people have not spoken in a clear and decisive tone. ·A ranting demagogue makes as much noise as a true patriot. " Conservative " patriots are afraid to venture on anything out of the old track. Even old Massachusetts presents a divided front in the councils of the nation, and its delegates have been congratulated after speeches by the remnant of traitors there. How, then, can the President see what the people want? If we could but rise above even such considerations, and ask " what does GOD want," then the pillar of fire by night, and the cloud by day, would go before us in our war of escape from our slavery to Southern despots. But is the old Bay State to be misrepresented forever? Is it to resend to Congress shaky politicians or open mis-representatives? If you want more of your sons slaughtered, choose again such men at the next election ; but if you want to conquer, give us a loyal delegation.

Congress, at its last session, has, on the whole, done well. It has voted men and supplies. It has pledged the country. It has made and urged stringent and energetic measures. Of course, whatever Congress should do, *we* are bound to respect it ; for that pleasant literature, the Articles of War, say, " Any officer or soldier who shall use contemptuous or disrespectful language against the . . . Congress of the United States . . . shall be cashiered, or otherwise punished, as a court-martial shall direct." But apart from the respect thus secured, I really think that Congress has done well in its late session. Yet there is a feeling of relief that it has adjourned. Nobody knew what it would do. Now it has done its work well and gone home we are glad. They leave power enough in the President's hands. They authorize the calling out of men, the equipment of armies. So soon, therefore, as our armies are filled, the rebellion must suffer.

So soon as our armies are filled. When will that be? The dark spot in our horizon is at home. The fact is evident that men come in slowly. The worse fact is evident, the more disgraceful one, that large bounties have to be offered to secure enlistment ! We read your papers with amazement.

Glowing meetings are held in this and that town. Great speakers are called out to address the people. The honorables and reverends speak; the rich offer money. Is this needed?

Is it possible that Massachusetts has fallen to this? Must its sons be coaxed and hired to fight for their country in a war in which all are agreed? Have our fellow-citizens so sunk that they must be *bought* for a hundred dollars? Talk not, after this, of the Hessians, who sold themselves in the war of the Revolution. Is patriotism so precarious as to need the weight of a hundred dollars?

Is it true that the authorities have themselves lost self-respect to such an extent as to *offer* these bribes? Has not the country a *right* to the service of every able-bodied man? And as it has that right, why should not the manly course be taken? call for the men on just the pay that thirty thousand men of Massachusetts have already gone for. There is the power to do this; is there not the courage?

The argument seems to be that it would be a confession of weakness to draft. Is it any less so, besides the disgrace, to *bribe?* The subterfuge is too apparent. Your great gatherings, and your hundred-dollar bribe, are confessions that simple volunteering is ended. That there are not fifteen thousand men ready to go, if needed, cannot be true. Many a man who hesitates would be willing to submit to the draft. The conscription is the true method. I believe in it, because it is *democratic.* The conscription, which will take rich and poor alike, high and low, and so guarded that the rich man's money will not secure his immunity. The idea is preposterous that only certain social classes ought to fight. Men fight, not your dollars. I know no man too good to fight for his country. It *was* a noble sight when six hundred thousand men rushed to arms. It *is* a disgraceful sight when recruiting officers buy men at a hundred dollars apiece.

The emotions of the army, to a great extent, I know. The soldiers are disgusted with the able-bodied speech-makers. Why do not they, at the close of their speeches, say, " *I* go for one." Their country *they* love it dearly — at a safe distance.

The soldiers feel a sense of injustice in this matter of bounties. " We," they say, " came in time of doubt. We have borne the hardships and dangers of the war for a year. We have had hard fare, hard work, and bullets. These new men have had all the comforts of home for that year, and now they are to be rewarded with a hundred dollars apiece ! and we, so far as we have property, are to be taxed to pay for this ! "

The soldiers feel that this whole business is fostered by many men who wish to secure themselves. They will not volunteer; they might be drafted; if drafted, it would be disgraceful to secure a substitute. They talk loud ; they vote bounties ; but *they* will stay at home, buying and selling and getting gain.

The soldiers see the prodigality and reckless waste of this system. Towns vie with towns in proffers. States rival States. Is Massachusetts so affluent, that it wants to throw away fifteen hundred thousand dollars before it puts a gun in a man's hand, or a pair of shoes on his feet, or a piece of bread in his mouth? Are taxes so light, are expenses so small, that this bagatelle of a million and a half is of no consequence? If so, offer the soldiers already in the field the three millions they deserve. Give the old soldiers the bounty too, or when they get home some men will go out of office in a hurry.

It is humiliating. It must be that Massachusetts is not aware of the imminent dangers of the occasion. It may not know that General McClellan cannot stir without new aid; that the army of Virginia is confronted by heavy forces, which may be hurled upon it any week; that — I dare not say how many — thousands are the sole and anxious defence of the Potomac? And instead of ordering a conscription, a hundred-dollar bounty and huge speeches are gathering driblets. An active, wise, unscrupulous foe is threatening, with great forces, even the North itself; the North refuses to take the only manly course to fill up its exhausted armies.

Your paraphernalia of recruiting is an abomination; your bribes are disgraceful. There is a cheap, simple, fair way. Call together your able-bodied men. Select by lot the requisite number. Take care of their families while they are gone; or, better, draw first only from unmarried men. If the people will not submit to this, a republic is a failure. If the administration is afraid to risk its popularity, the administration is a failure.*

Near Little Washington, Rappahannock Co., Va.,
July 30, 1862.

How we came here was by road from Warrenton, across Carter's Creek just above its junction with Hedgeman's River, and then across the river itself, over a temporary bridge, (very temporary — a freshet started it toward the sea two

* I leave this letter as written, because it expressed real principles. The men were procured, and so far the predictions were incorrect. As to the administration, it has shown pluck enough in the matter, and can afford to laugh at the closing hypothesis. As to bounties, they are a nuisance. The fair thing is, to make a soldier's pay equal to home pay, and go no further. Our men do not risk life for bounties.

days afterward), on whose bank we camped that night, July
20, in a beautiful thunder storm; then, next day, through
Amissville, a forlorn, deserted village, to Gaines's Cross
Roads (so called, because no roads cross there), and turning
westward, travelled in another thunder storm to a steep hill-
side, where we made a stay quite long for this pilgrim life.
It rained when we camped, and rained next day. Sunday
morning it did not rain, and we had public worship, but it
rained in the afternoon.

A beautiful view was visible from that camp. Broad
fields, broken now and then by woods, were bounded only
by sharply outlined hills, wooded almost to their tops. The
little village of Washington lay nestling under the shadows of
the Blue Ridge, with white houses gleaming out of the dark
green foliage, and a church or two visible, a third of a mile
away. Even in rainy days it was pleasant to watch the
riotous clouds on the mountain-sides. I was sorry I went
into Little Washington one day. Centred in green meadows, watered by a tree-fringed brook, overshadowed by mountains, that is the first impression; but within, dirt contends
with whitewash, nasty streets lead nowhere, and three mean
taverns intimate the ancient character of the place. In fact,
it images Southern chivalry; fair to view at a distance, a
sham when inspected.

I hate shams. And so I was glad when we left the hill-
side, as we did to move a mile or two, for military purposes,
last Thursday. It was irritating to sit in our lofty camp,
say at sunset, and look down to the village, so quiet, so fair
to view, and yet feel "you are a dirty sham." I appreciated
the sensations of the little girl, when she learned that her
pretty doll was filled with sawdust. Not for this, however,
did we move. War does not care for scenery.

Why we came here, was to occupy a more appropriate position for the purposes of the campaign than we did at Warrenton. Indeed, I have heard it stated that some mistake sent us down there at all. General Banks's whole corps is here or hereabouts, barring one brigade which is at or near Culpepper. Somebody else is at Sperryville, six miles southwest of this. Somebody at Luray, not far westward of that. Somebody at Warrenton. And so forth, and so on. All are under command of General Pope, whom we should be glad to see. I am told that he has lately moved his headquarters from Washington, D. C., to Warrenton, probably because they are " in the saddle." Our forces are within supporting distances of each other, from the Potomac to the Blue Ridge ; while in the valley, just over the ridge, troops hold Winchester, rather shakingly, and the railroad to Harper's Ferry.

Yet I see no prospect of immediate activity. True the troops are kept in readiness, but so they ought always to be. Should the rebels dash up this way, there would be work. Should they conclude to try the valley again, perhaps there would be work. The crops there are well worth their efforts. And I do not see why they may not be gathering them in the vicinity of Harrisonburg. But that any movement is to be made toward Richmond does not appear. General Pope, however, keeps the rebels well irritated below. We want troops to accomplish much.

The new orders of the general are well received. Every one feels that we have played at war. War is to destroy, not protect an enemy. Some Union people in the valley told us, and always told us, that our course was weakening. If " we are coming, father Abraham, three hundred thousand more," it is a comfort that it is intended now to fight. The

16

orders requiring the inhabitants behind our lines to take the oath of allegiance or else travel southward, is exceedingly disliked by rebels. But this is just what has been long needed. We want to do things the rebels dislike. I am satisfied that, were the people sure the rebel armies would not return, they would almost all take the required oath without objection. This county was unanimous for secession ; but terror made it so. And genuine seceshers will submit, without feeling any loss of honor, so soon as their cause becomes hopeless by the defeat of their main armies. Curiously enough, the people were told that secession was the only way to prevent " war," and were fools enough to believe it. They *are* an ignorant set. Passing through quite a village in the valley, we found the people troubled as to the instruments of our military band ; they had never seen any ; they imagined them some terribly destructive kind of fire-arms. " Yes, ma'am," replied one to a questioner, " *this* is the *bell-teezer*, to fire grape at short distances, and is awfully powerful ! " The wondering people gazed in dismay.

We have public worship quite regularly. Rarely, this spring and summer, have bad weather or movements prevented. Our colonel is very exact about it, and where that is the case, few interruptions are necessary. Last Sabbath *you* would have enjoyed our meeting-house better than yours. Ours was an open, yet shady and beautiful wood, just above a rapid brook ; yours was a hot, confined, four-walled building. Your cushioned seats are not equal to our grassy sod. Nor your miserable penitentiary of a wooden box to be compared with our level sward for a pulpit. Some in your house went to sleep ; ours do not. It is humanizing, in war, to have the Sabbath, however inadequately observed, and public worship — the text, the old tunes — so like home. Yet there was a lack — no wives, no bright-eyed children, nothing but armed men. Such as the worship is, it is growing less in the army. Many regiments are without chaplains now. These officers are leaving quite rapidly. Several have tendered resignations within three weeks, and I think many others intend to do so soon. Then batteries have no chaplains. I had a funeral service in one last Saturday ; a youth of twenty years, whose name I knew not, whose home I had not heard of, whom I had never seen ; but the tears stood in the eyes of the officer who came to ask me to officiate, as he said, " He was a good boy, and the only child of a widow." The whole force of the battery went to the grave, and a sight at them would cure, I hope so, at least, the officials who want to leave our Sabbaths unnoticed, our sick without religious comforters, our dead buried like beasts.

One of our own number, too, was buried on Sunday. Two miles from camp his company, officers and men, carried him to the village graveyard, overgrown with weeds and neglected. Other dead were there, newly buried. Ours was reverently placed in their line, and a plain board tells where the stranger lies. These scenes have never lost their first sadness.

Last week I wrote somewhat plainly, I believe, as to the bounties offered for enlistments. I hope that letter went safely. Most of the dailies now arriving try to conceal the real results of the plan in vogue, but it is easy to see through the deception. Recruiting is a failure. In spite of " eloquent remarks " and " soul-stirring resolutions," in spite of bounties ranging up to $150 per man, recruiting is a failure. The army feels ashamed of such methods ; indignant at their injustice ; astonished at their recklessness. If the fifteen thousand had come forth spontaneously, well. But everybody knew that could not be. The adventurous had gone already.

Thousands upon thousands remain, equally courageous, and who are willing to go if actually called upon, but who do not care to volunteer. A draft would have brought out the best material in the State, and have organized a splendid soldiery. You have tried bribes, and in that very thing confessed your weakness. The slowness of enlistment, even with the bounty, shows what anybody might have seen, and what many did see, that the draft is necessary. Foreign powers will say that the war is growing unpopular. Had an instant draft been ordered, there would have been no room for the allegation. To read, at this distance, the accounts of war-meetings, with their imported enthusiasm, and their impotent results, humiliates every son of Massachusetts. Its regiments have covered their State with glory; its politicians are doing their best to disgrace it. Stop the foolish, wasteful, useless humbug; give us the conscription!

CHAPTER VII.

CEDAR MOUNTAIN.

Culpepper, Va., August 13, 1862.

I HAVE never felt so sadly in writing you as I do to-day. Last night we went into camp for the first time since the recent battle. How touchingly our emptied tents reminded us of our loss! Our beloved major wounded and a prisoner. Our excellent surgeon wounded. Of seven captains who went into action, four gallant men dead, two prisoners, of whom one is wounded. Of eleven lieutenants, one killed, four wounded, and one wounded and a prisoner. And lying in a soldier's grave, or shattered by bullets, one in every four of our men, as noble a group of soldiers as ever graced a country's name.

Last Wednesday we left Little Washington. Friday night, at twelve o'clock, we bivouacked at Culpepper. Next morning, after varying orders, we were moved six miles, hastily, to support General Crawford, known to be threatened by the enemy, who, having hastily crossed the Rapidan with his advance, was hurrying up his main body. That army, if I may rely on the statement of a rebel colonel whom I met on Monday, consisted of three divisions, Jackson's, Ewell's, and Hill's, — numbering forty-five thousand men. General Pope's army consists, as you know, of the commands of General

16 *

McDowell, General Banks, and General Sigel (who took the place of General Fremont in charge of the troops formerly in Western Virginia). Why these were not concentrated is known only to those in power. As it was, General Banks was thrown forward; General Sigel was still at Sperryville, or perhaps on the road, and General McDowell was too far to help, — no, we passed one brigade at least, less than three miles from the battle ground, which had lain there since four A. M., waiting for orders, and which lay there till we were done fighting, — while an inadequate force was opposed to the enemy, as usual.

Losing one man that day by sun-stroke, at twelve M. we reached the position assigned us, the extreme right, which was slightly bent from the enemy, and were stationed on a height important to be held. A mile and a half due south, or very nearly so, is Cedar Mountain, in front of which, and round its sides, lay the rebel forces; troops being stationed westward, however, holding as their left a wooded eminence, but the bulk of their army running southwest, back of their right. Part way up the mountain they had posted artillery also. On the side of the mountain was Jackson himself, and from that eminence could see all our movements, as I have found by a personal visit to that place. Not a regiment of ours could go into action without his knowledge. Almost parallel with their line was ours, five brigades, in this order from right to left, viz., Gordon's, Crawford's, Geary's, Greene's, and Prince's. General Gordon's original position was never attacked. Our right was on a wooded swell; our centre and left on rolling land, almost a plain. We had withdrawn before from an advanced position. But it was early in the afternoon when the enemy advanced their skirmishers. They were met in the same way. Then the enemy opened a fire of artillery, to which our guns responded. Going some-what in front of our brigade position, I had a full view of this artillery fight, which was almost entirely confined to the centre and left. The firing was rapid and with effect on both sides. The shell from the enemy's guns would raise clouds of dust as they ploughed the ground, when they did not strike fatally ; while on the other side, the number of slain horses I have since seen there, attest the accuracy of our fire. So an hour passed. A cavalry movement now and then ; the withdrawal of our guns a short distance ; movements of in-fantry to support them, — all were visible.

But about five P. M., Gen. Crawford's brigade was hard pressed by a concentrated force of the enemy's infantry. Im-agine a wood of perhaps an eighth of a mile in thickness, on elevated land, running east and west ; the front edge of that is General Crawford's position. Then, an open oblong field, somewhat rough, two hundred yards wide. Then another wood parallel to the first, and of rather less thickness, and the northerly front line of that is the rebel position. And at the western end of the intermediate field was another wood, making the field bordered by wood north, west, and south. General Crawford was holding the north side, with his own brigade increased by a portion of the Wisconsin Third, — as gallant a regiment as there is in service, the statements of some liar in New York papers to the contrary notwithstanding. That wood was the key to the enemy's position, and behind it, also, was artillery firing on our centre. General Crawford's brigade fought well. He was not the only general there, nor were his troops all that were worth mentioning, although a correspondent of the New York *Times* of Tuesday seems able to see little else : the date of a letter in juxtaposition, from the same writer, accounts for the character of the letter. General Crawford's men finally made a charge across the open field. The moment they entered that field the storm of death began. Yet most nobly did his men press on. Through the field, and into the rebel wood about thirty yards (I found their dead there afterward), when they melted away like snow placed in a July sun.

General Gordon was ordered to change position and support General Crawford. With the Second Massachusetts, the Third Wisconsin (restored to its brigade), and the Twenty-seventh Indiana, he instantly hurried to the line. General Geary was then endeavoring to operate on the centre, but the artillery had ceased, and nothing but musketry was heard. It was furious. General Gordon went to *support* General Crawford, but he *replaced* him; for that brigade had vanished, and its scattered remnants I saw coming singly back. One fourth of it was found the next day.

As the new brigade took its place the fire was terrific. Backward and forward the bullets flew like hail. Then the dead began to fall. There hosts of wounded men were carried off. Among the first wounded was our surgeon; both assistant surgeons were away, one sick and one sent to Alexandria with sick men; and it fell to me to keep steady the movement of ambulances to and fro. Our division hospital was established in a house and grounds from which I had witnessed the fight in the centre, where Dr. Chappel, our admirable division medical director, was in charge.

What could men do outnumbered as ours were? Where were reënforcements? What could one brigade accomplish against a foe steadily replaced by fresh troops? Why was not a force stationed to prevent the flanking on the west? Yet for more than half an hour those gallant men fought steadily and coolly, outnumbered, and worse, outflanked; for

the enemy filled now the western wood as well as the opposite. Then his line advanced. In front and obliquely on our
right, came *three* fresh brigades against our shattered *one*.
The cross fire was savage. The right of our line, the Twenty-
seventh Indiana, withered before it. So company after company shrivelled up in the fire till the Second Massachusetts, the
left, stood alone. It *stood* — alone. Its fire thinned the advancing line every moment, but under the enfilading aim, the
ranks grew less every moment. Enough was done for honor,
but none fell back till the order was given. One terrible
volley it poured in when the enemy was within sixty yards.*
Then the order came, and it retreated, with *one third* of
its strength gone.

The enemy occupied the wood, but did not pursue. The
brigade reformed in its earlier position. " This must be held
to the last," was the general's order. But the centre and left
had fallen back, and orders came for this brigade to leave its
position and take a new one in the front of the centre of the
new line of defence. And now it was night.

But I was not with the regiment then. Our colonel could
not bear to leave his own wounded men without some care
from his own regiment, and it was my privilege to remain.
We expected — we were told — that in half an hour the enemy would occupy this important height. We were agreeably
disappointed. Though he pushed up his force on the central
plain past our house and lay there, not three hundred yards
off, though toward the battle field we were outside our lines,
yet no man molested us. And all night, with our flickering
lights almost eclipsed by the full moon, yet under the solemn

---

* The line advancing in front now got nearer than that sixty yards.
Our fire stopped it, bewildered; so our own officers, prisoners, afterward
told us.

trees we kept on our sober work with our three hundred injured men.

It was a strange scene. Within the house lay wounded, dying men; without, they covered the ground. Then the surgeons, with every one who could bind up a wounded limb, were busy. Dr. Chappel was the soul of order, and the good surgeons worked hard. A few hundred yards off, to the east, we could see the glittering musket-barrels of the enemy as his sentries now and then emerged in the moonlight. About eleven o'clock a flash, a report, and a whizzing shell flew screaming by into the woods just north of us, and another, and another, then over us, and a storm of them. Then our own artillery came into play very near them, and soon the thunder was continuous, and the lightning never ceased flashing from their muzzles.* After half an hour it ceased. We could not tell which had driven, but still the enemy's muskets gleamed in front of us.

The removal of our wounded men was determined upon. Through a rear path in the woods (the main road covered by the enemy, but I knew, fortunately, another), we sent them away. How slowly the number seemed to diminish! How few seemed the ambulances! But patience succeeded, and after the rebel shell ceased to fall on the road we had to use, up to morning there was no cessation.† A little past five the last of ours in hospital was sent on, and my duty was accomplished in that regard. The director had assigned to me the task of filling and despatching the ambulances, for the surgeons had especial work to do; and I was rejoiced when one trip only of the vehicle was necessary to take all. Dr. Ben-

---

* I afterwards counted eleven dead horses of the enemy in a space not four rods square.

† Among the number was the brave Colonel Donelly, mortally wounded, with whom I had considerable conversation, as with others.

nett, a true man, volunteered to stay for them. It was a relief when that trip ended; for at three o'clock General McDowell, who had come near, had sent us word that that spot would be untenable in the morning.

And when, as the gray of morning came on, we looked to the right, near a mile away were the rebels drawn up in a long line of battle. As we looked to the left, our brigades were defiling into position. So when the work was done, the house was left to itself, or to a family of women and children, whom I had urged to leave, but who, irresolute, knew not what to do. Of that family there was a beautiful child, a boy of eighteen months, who, on the day before, while the air was filled with the heavy artillery thunder, slept on as sweetly as though only the pure summer air fanned him and only his mother's lullaby was charming him to rest. When, next day, a way was found to remove this little child of a rebel family, and the women also, by General Gordon's pass, and under escort, I was glad. As I saw this child, into whose home a stray shot might at any time send death, perhaps there had been thoughts of another little one, as beautiful in face, as princely in form, for whose memory's sake I would pity such, though *he* is with the angels of God forever.

After securing the commencement of the removal of our own wounded from the second hospital, I returned to the regiment, and was directed to remain. All day the armies were sullenly watching each other, but there was quiet. At night, late, a wounded man who had crept off the battle-field said that the rebels had left most of our wounded there. It was a statement hard to be believed, — it was barbarous, — but it was true. A party was immediately and cordially detailed by our colonel, at the suggestion of our general, to go thither, it being rumored that the rebel pickets had been drawn off. Lieutenant Abbott commanded it. We went three miles, but, half a mile from the field, General Sigel refused to allow the risk of losing the party. It was midnight, and we slept by our outer pickets. Early in the morning we went. Telegrams say that the rebels " asked leave to bury their dead!" Asked leave? They had held the ground for thirty-six hours, and I saw not one rebel corpse. It chanced to me to be in advance. I went to the edge of the wood. Rebel sentries were in the open field. I waved a handkerchief, and pointed to our wounded. The rebel nearest waved his cap and nodded. So I had the indescribable happiness of being the first to tell to the wounded men still there that help was at hand. As we came to each they cried for joy. They put their arms around our necks. Our strong men, who had fought well, and now came back for their comrades, cried too. Though the rebels had been guilty of the barbarity of not taking to hospital our severely wounded men, and of not informing us of the fact, though the field was in their possession, — while we always treat both sides alike, — yet rebel privates had been kind. They had built shelters of boughs; had brought water, and sometimes biscuit and apples. But all the dead, and many of the wounded, had been stripped of everything valuable, even to outer clothing.*

We removed our wounded. We buried our dead. Our dead! The pride of Massachusetts! There lay one with whom, just as the regiment moved into action, I had been in conversation. He was ordered to advance with his company

---

* I shall never forget an interview with one officer (not of ours) lying mortally wounded. He knew me. I was giving him some water, when he feebly said, "I know I must die. I am a Catholic. I die a true Catholic, though a poor one. Understand that. But I wish you would pray with me." He soon died — a Christian. What did I care that he was a Catholic?

as skirmishers, and I noticed then the clear, ringing, brave voice with which he said " Fall in, men ! " And another, the frank, straightforward, courageous man. And another who had left an ambulance to go to the field, and who, as I had asked him, " Are you strong enough to go? " had answered with a smile, " I *cannot* stay when my men go ! " and buckled on his sword. And another, lying there as though asleep, falling with a miniature on his breast — a true, brave man, who had, a little before, said to me, " If anything should happen to me, it would kill——" And all around, the men, the noble men, so uselessly slaughtered. My heart was full. How long, O Lord, how long before these men, slaughtered by infernal ambition, be avenged? Come, Lord, and tarry not !

Southern men were about us. I went to the rebel lines, for we heard there that it was now truce. I met colonels and a general. They were courteous and kind, and far from exultant. On learning that I was a chaplain, the general showed the greatest regard for an office which some Union generals treat with contempt ; * so did one of our generals, who late in the day found me the only one on the field except enlisted men, and put me in charge of the burials.

But it took till far into midday to bury our dead. Those

---

* I could not write then one fact. The rebel general had come to the line, as I saluted him for the second time. I inquired for some of our missing, and he kindly sent an officer to ascertain, but uselessly. Seeing my disappointment, he said, " Come over yourself ; of course (with a smile) on honor." " Of course," I replied, as I thanked him. Passing the sentries, and going beyond the wood, until I saw the valley stretching off on the west side of the mountain, I saw that the rebel army had gone. Only a shell was left. He noticed my astonishment, and smilingly said, " You are on honor, you know." It was not till some time afterward that a reconnoisance discovered the fact, which, of course, I could not mention. I went where I pleased, but I could learn little of our men.

17

of ours (and we identified most) are in two graves near together ; and I had trees around them marked deeply, each with three cuts, that if any one should ever wish to know where these men lay, the spot should be identified for the holy pilgrimage.

As soldier hands were laying our brave men in their graves, and we were covering them first with green leaves, my eye was attracted by a leaf, which with others had evidently been in the hands of some dying man.   And my glance fell first on these words : —

" Seeing then that all these things shall be dissolved, what manner of persons ought ye to be in all holy conversation and godliness.

" Looking for, and hasting unto the coming of the day of God, wherein the heavens being on fire shall be dissolved, and the elements shall melt with fervent heat.

" Nevertheless, we, according to his promise, look for new heavens and a new earth, wherein dwelleth righteousness."

We left our dead.   But the leaf I reverently folded and carefully keep ; and I will leave it to my child, and tell her to honor the dead of the brave, gallant, Second Massachusetts, whom her father loved.

CHAPTER VIII.

POPE'S RETREAT.

ON THE ROAD TO SOMEWHERE, September 3, 1862.

To somewhere : but where to?

My last letter forwarded told about the Cedar Mountain battle. My next was stopped by orders which prohibited all mails from leaving, expelled reporters, and denied the use of the telegraph. Instead, therefore, of reliable information, the people have had unfounded rumors, lying statements and gross deceptions. They have learned, however, the general fact that the army which was recently on the Rapidan was soon on the Rappahannock, next at Bull Run, and now, doubtless, near or in the fortifications in front of Washington ; that, day after day, the thunder of artillery has been the music of our armies, while hard marches and hunger have taxed our strength, and pitched battles have drawn the blood of the gallant soldiers of the Union. But they learned this only by the gradual sifting of the statements it was impossible to confine.

Of many of the recent movements, and of the recent battles, I know little from personal participation. Our corps was not called upon in the battles of last week. Why, we do not know ; who does? But a part I saw ; and of the general bearing of events it is easy to learn. And, in the army we are constantly saying, " What is the use of lying ? " Things transpiring under our very eyes are so grossly misstated that we become sceptical to *all* accounts. I am reminded of a map of the battle-ground of the 9th of August, which appeared in the New York ——. I tried the top as north ; I made it east ; I made it south ; I made it west ; but not the least resemblance could I trace. Such are many accounts of affairs until the public press — which may God preserve free as the refuge of our liberties — examines and sifts.

We are congratulated on the victory at Cedar Mountain ! Cedar Mountain a victory ! One brigade almost annihilated ; another losing one third of its strength ; all badly suffering ; our forces driven from the field ; the ground occupied by the enemy for two days, and then left at their pleasure ; our dead buried, and our wounded brought off at the sufferance of the enemy thirty-six hours after the fight ; what a glorious victory ! *

Then these successive stages of affairs appear. First, the movements between the Rapidan and the Rappahannock, ending in our retreating over the latter river. Secondly, the various operations on that line, ending in Jackson's appearance at Manassas in our rear. Thirdly, the various manœuvres and fightings by which we and the enemy reverse positions, he establishing his line of communication with the south, and we with the north, following which are the battles of Friday and Saturday last. Fourthly, the attempt, or appearance of attempt, to turn our right while we still held

---

* It has been alleged that General Banks brought on this action in a place not contemplated, and contrary to orders. There is no truth in it. I knew what the orders were. An officer came with them the morning of the 9th. " General Pope directs that you will do " so and so. " Please put that in writing," said General Banks. It was done ; and that writing is doubtless in existence.

Centreville, and the necessary falling back to the line of the fortifications. In all this, that we were tolerably clearly out-manœuvred, and partially defeated, is evident, though the relative size of the armies may have rendered any other result impossible.

First, General Pope appeared bent on a vigorous pursuit of Jackson. He advanced to the Rapidan. He threatened battle. Jackson had retired thither after the battle of the 9th, and is reënforced. On the day that Jackson awaits the attack, General Pope — the 19th of August — suddenly with-draws. He had been sending all his supplies and trains to the rear. They were all safe, and rapidly and in perfect order the various columns move northward to the Rappa-hannock, cross it before Jackson can harass the army, and accomplish most successfully a skilful movement. Our forces were not sufficient to hazard a battle at the Rapidan, but were enough to engage attention while General McClellan accomplished his withdrawal from the Peninsula. That object attained, General Pope retires, to unite with General McClellan.

On the Sunday after the battle of the 9th of August, we moved to a wood about two miles and a half from the battle ground, where we bivouacked two nights. On Tuesday we returned to our camping ground, just outside of Culpepper on the north, where our wagons had been left, and where our tents were then pitched. It was a sad evening, because so many tents were empty. But there we staid until Monday, when, in the afternoon, tents were struck, and wagons des-patched to the Rappahannock. We remained until midnight, finding rest as we could under rather unfavorable circum-stances; then moved a mile or so, and built fires, and slept somewhat till day; then, after various vexatious delays,

17 *

moved several rods; then waited for orders and got them, and moved several rods more; and by fits and starts moved along, vexed by somebody's trains, several miles; then left the trains entirely, and marched to the north side of the Rappahannock River, at the crossing of the railway to Culpepper; there we bivouacked — our wagons still ten miles onward. Then, the enemy having soon followed, the Rappahannock River is the scene of operations. The day after our arrival, about noon, we hear rapid firing, and soon see on the plain across, the movements of cavalry and skirmishers. So for day after day the cannon gives the morning reveille, and up and down the river we move. At first our right is General Sigel; our centre, General McDowell; our left, General Banks. But each corps is movable, and General Reno is added. The enemy felt our lines at all points. Every ford for miles was tested in turn. August 21, our corps moved down the river a mile. The next day up the river five or six, where brisk cannonading was going on, and a Union battery driven off. The next morning, Corthren's gallant battery of ten pounders, which our brigade supported, silenced and shattered *two* batteries of twelve pounders, and we could see dead and wounded carried off, while Corthren's loss was one man wounded, one caisson demolished, one horse struck. That day up the river again, and a damp bivouac; the next day the whole move up, passing a terrific fire from the opposite enemy near Sulphur Springs, his shot crashing through the woods for several hours, but at last nearly silenced, with little loss. Next day down the river, and next day, and so on, until our corps was near Bealeton.

Accounts tell how the enemy was repulsed at all points on the river. I could not see that he ever made an attack in great force at all. He kept the line alive, but for three days he was visibly sending his columns up the river, infantry in long lines, and artillery. Where was he going? Amusing our army below, he was steadily crossing somewhere above, and suddenly we awoke to find that, on Friday night, the 22d, his cavalry had dashed through Warrenton, pushed on to Catlett's, burnt General Pope's baggage ; that a little later his columns had occupied Manassas Junction, where they burnt supplies and property worth hundreds upon hundreds of thousands ; that he held Thoroughfare Gap, through which his forces had poured, tidings which two blacks had brought ; that he was in our rear, our communication with Washington cut off, our junction with the Peninsula army incomplete.

Then our front was changed. Jackson was " in a trap." On Wednesday, August 27, Warrenton was evacuated by the Union troops. General Banks remaining near Bealeton. The army moved to Gainesville, — General Sigel toward Manassas, — and a portion of General McDowell's corps toward Thoroughfare Gap, to prevent a junction between reënforcements and Jackson. An action took place there, from which our troops " withdrew." On Thursday night General McDowell was on the Centreville road, looking northward — where I saw it, being sent thitherward with sick. Friday morning commenced the great battle. Of that I know nothing personally, leaving Gainesville early with General Rickett's division, which was moving towards Manassas. That day's fighting undoubtedly resulted favorably to us. But on Saturday heavy reënforcements reached Jackson. He had skilfully changed position till a junction could not be prevented. On Saturday we were defeated. Not pursued, but still defeated, and with great loss. Then our lines fell back to Centreville, and held a strong position.

In the mean time General Banks was near Bristow Station, four miles below Manassas Junction. Valuable stores were there. General Hooker had driven the enemy away from the Junction. The stores were being rapidly removed. But during Friday, during Saturday, the corps was not summoned to the field. All day Friday we impatiently heard the steady fire. Saturday night found us still between Bristow and Manassas Junction. Sunday morning we were suddenly ordered to burn stores, burn heavy baggage, and make a forced march by a long detour. Our direct communication with the army was sundered, So past the flames of long lines of burning cars, past exploding ammunition, we hastened to Brentsville, forded the rapidly rising Occoquan Creek, and by noon had safely come into junction with the main army.' It was well done. General Banks did it.

Centreville was a strong position, but it could be turned too easily. So backward to Fairfax ; backward still. Fighting here, fighting there. Immense lines of ambulances loaded with wounded. Laid upon the ground for transportation to come, they covered acres. How they cursed one man !

Sunday night there was a rumor that General McClellan was to command. How it thrilled the army ! How it electrified the soldiers ! I should not have believed the enthusiasm had I not seen it in passing through two corps. I saw some of his own soldiers. Said one to me, " If General McClellan should say to his old soldiers, ' Boys, who will go back with me to the Peninsula and try it again?' every one would say, ' I will, general ! ' "

That disasters have come is undeniable. That anxieties must prevail for some time is clear. But we have a great army. We have courageous soldiers. Reënforcements are rapidly coming. The great North is not defeated. Every day of delay will strengthen us. While McClellan remained on the Peninsula, the enemy dared not send away too heavy a force. The order for his return freed the hostile army, and therefore we have to meet it. But be not discouraged. The army is not hopeless of remedy, though several features of affairs do depress it. So far it has not been broken. But as to its confidence in present leaders, the less said the better.

But Jackson skilfully passed the river above us. He threw himself boldly in our rear. Supposed to be trapped, he yet held his own, and so manœuvred as to secure his line of reënforcements. He destroyed immense stores. He has changed our positions until he has an untroubled rear, and a clear road from Richmond. He has transferred the war to the vicinity of Washington. He has made us the defenders — put himself in the aggressive.

MARYLAND, September 10, 1862.

I WROTE a somewhat general account of the recent events. Before you received it, I am asked for " personal observations." This request presumed that our regiment was in some of the battles, which was not correct. Nevertheless, I will follow my own line of travel as to what I saw. I *had* seen a rebel general, whose prayers, as pitted against outrageous profanity, I was more afraid of than of twenty thousand men. When a high commander selected Sunday as the day to review our corps for the first time, I felt badly, so did others. It was partial relief, that General Banks, who regulates the choice of day, but could not help himself, directed religious services to be held with the whole corps immediately after the review; but the high general galloped off in a hurry, doubtless from " military exigencies."

While we were moving up and down the Rappahannock, where the enemy were amusing our general by little attacks along the line, I saw rebel columns on the opposite side of the river moving northward. Where they were going, nobody knew. Where they were to strike, who took the trouble to find out? But they struck in our rear, destroyed millions worth of property, cut off our lines of communication, reënforced their moderate army, and defeated the army of Virginia.

I saw there, on the Rappahannock, soldiers faint with hunger; considering whether to eat a biscuit, or save it until morning; glad to receive the remnants of meat which some others had to spare; roasting green corn, not as a luxury, but to satisfy hunger. This was in an army whose general had, in his first order, ridiculed having " bases of supplies."

I saw, on eventful and disastrous days, a whole corps lying idle within sound of the battle.

I saw millions of dollars worth of property destroyed, all of which could have been saved, had the general not laughed at " lines of retreat."

I saw the order which prohibited all mails from leaving, all use of telegraph except by the general, and excluded all newspaper reporters.

More particularly and personally, when news came that Jackson was between us and Washington, we were near Sulphur Springs. It was immediately thought that the enemy had rashly exposed themselves to capture, and movements appear to have been made with the view of accomplishing that result.

Our corps was sent toward Bealeton, on the railroad, and took no part in subsequent activities beyond marchings.

It was on the 23d of August that we heard this, but I do not learn that any marked movements were made until the next Wednesday, the 27th. On the 26th, while we were on the road toward Bealeton, I was sent to Warrenton, in charge of a sick man, a member of General Gordon's staff, with the hope of sending him through to Washington. Reaching there about noon, I found hospitals full of sick men. They were in churches mainly, but in the afternoon were placed in cars and started for Washington. They were brought back that night, the road not having been repaired. My own charge I concluded to put into a house in Warrenton.

But the next day it was determined to evacuate Warrenton.* The sick were again put into cars, to be sent as far as the road could allow. General Sigel and General McDowell were in town. General Sigel started early in the day, General McDowell towards night. Unable to return to my regiment on account of unsafe roads, indeed, ignorant of its position, and without transportation for the sick man, I concluded to join friends and keep with a column. So, finding the brigade (in General McDowell's corps), which held the Twelfth and Thirteenth Massachusetts, being cordially received and furnished with ambulance for my friend, I left Warrenton with the corps about five P. M. It moved through New Baltimore towards Gainesville, on the Centreville road. It was a weary march. The road was rocky, the numberless streams (of course bridgeless) seemed to run lengthwise of the road, and it was dark. The column grad-

---

* I have been surprised to read that Warrenton was evacuated "immediately" on hearing that Jackson had cut the road. That information came on the 23d. I was at Warrenton when the evacuation commenced, on the 27th.

ually wasted away, until about one A. M., when a halt and
bivouac was ordered.

Of that wearisome march I have a marked recollection,
because it was the last time I saw Colonel Fletcher Webster,
as kind-hearted a man as ever lived, and a brave officer. We
rode side and side much of the way. The remnant of the
night I lay near him, and we slept soundly, though he had
only (as I did) a rubber blanket and overcoat, and it rained
a part of the night. He shared with me his breakfast,
which he ate without grumbling, though it was only coffee
(without sugar) and hard biscuit. He seemed to me on that
march rather thoughtful, though by no means sad, and play-
fully indorsed me, as I had been received into their care with
my sick, as their " acting chaplain." He was a noble-hearted
man ; God hallow his memory.*

In the morning, providentially, I met two wagons of our
own (one an ambulance), loaded with supplies, but unable
to reach the regiment. One wagon-master, one ward-master,
a driver, and three soldiers as wagon guard, were of the
party, and gladly did I greet it. We kept with the brigade

---

* I venture to insert, with some hesitation, the fact that the last previous
occasion on which I had seen him, was when he had just heard of the death
of a daughter. I was in his camp one day, when I was told of it. He had
been refused leave to go to the funeral, and had shut himself in his tent.
They told me that he appeared strangely, no one daring to speak to him
even ; and some of the staff urged me to go to him. I did so. I remembered well the little girl who was the life of the camp at Frederick.

I went into his tent. He did not look up. I ventured to take his hand.
He looked then very sternly. But I said nothing. Waiting a moment, he
saw I was not going to try to comfort him, for how hard that is to bear I
sadly know. Then as if feeling I was a friend, his countenance changed.
He pressed my hand and said, "Ah, it was my *last born*, my treasure !"
and then the tears gushed forth. The stern fit had passed as the tears came,
and he was himself again.

until it turned off, about two miles back of Gainesville, to
go to Thoroughfare Gap, with the hope of checking the
advance of the rebels through that entrance. They had
there a fight that afternoon with partial success, and retired
near to Gainesville that night, which I did not learn till the
next day.

After that brigade turned off, I continued with General
McDowell's corps to Gainesville — a railway station, with
two or three houses. The corps went on the road to Manassas a few miles, — the same road by which General Sigel,
I was told, had gone in the forenoon. Here our small party
halted, built a fire, and cooked its dinner, in the midst of
immense wagon trains, cavalry pickets, straggling soldiers,
enough to make several regiments, and opposite a house
whose hospital flag showed its use. An hour or two afterwards we tried the Manassas road, in the presumption that
General Banks would be moving thither, to strengthen our
then right; but a few miles on, before we had emerged from
General McDowell's regiments, we learned that the road was
unsafe for so small a force as four guns and two pistols. We
could hear, also, vigorous firing in that direction. So, remaining a while quiet, we watched events. General McDowell
himself was on a hill near, to the right of the road to Centreville, studying a map, and sweeping the country with his glass.
Soon and suddenly his regiments began to move, and steadily
poured towards and on the Centreville road. Curiosity led
to an investigation, and discovered that he took position on a
beautiful ridge across the road a mile or so, looking northward, and about three miles from Gainesville. Here a very
pretty little fight took place. The enemy attacked, but our
men repulsed them with great ease. This was Thursday,
about sunset. A little earlier, we had been told at head-

18

quarters that Banks was at Thoroughfare Gap, just the
other end of the line from his real position. I knew better
of course.

Moving back a mile or two, our little party camped.
That is, it turned into an open grove by the roadside, unhar-
nessed and unsaddled, and fed horses, cooked supper, and
went to bed; that is, wrapped " the drapery of our couch "
about us, viz., blankets, and laid down under the trees.
Just opposite was a party of cavalry in charge of rebel prisoners. I visited the party, and talked with the prisoners, a
very good-natured set of men. One was a South Carolinian,
of good education. Pardon me, patriot, if I, for the love of
my child's kindred of that State, helped him to something
better than the confederate paper, which was all he had for
his captivity.

That night we could hear the rumbling of artillery wheels,
apparently moving westward, though there was no firing.
Where they went, or how our army changed its front, I cannot yet understand. But in the morning I found Gen. Rickett's division already on the road from Gainesville to Bristow,
south of Manassas Junction. We followed, and seven or
eight miles on, found General Banks's corps.

That day, Friday, we heard — all day long — the sound of
the battle. Impatiently we waited — in vain. It is said that
ten thousand men more would have given the country the
victory. Why, then was General Banks's corps kept idle?

At night, just after tattoo, came orders for our brigade to
go out on picket. So we did, moving about two miles, to
near Broad Run, where we lay down by the side of a graveyard. No alarm took place whatever. The next day, the
corps began to move northward, by Manassas, saving one
brigade, which remained to see to the removal of long trains

of supplies, as well as of sick and wounded. About noon we crossed Broad Run ourselves, moved on a mile, and then returned and took up our position on the north side of that stream; and here, before dark, came back General Banks's corps, with tidings that General Pope had gained a great victory. But while we were cooking our suppers the battle was raging, that Saturday evening, which proved so disastrous to our arms; and our corps was left uncalled for.

Next morning we had sudden orders. " Burn all baggage but two ambulances. Move instantly." At seven we started, but saved our little train. We saved it, on condition that at the first delay from it, it should be burned. The corps was said to be cut off, and we must hasten to Occoquan Creek before the pouring rain should render it unfordable. A half mile on the road we crossed the railway; on it were scores upon scores of loaded cars, wrapped in flames. The melancholy and useless loss of property, to be paid for by the hard toil of our citizens, accompanied by occasional explosions of ammunition, the drenching rain, and the exigency of the march, made it a spectacle I never desire to see repeated.

Passing through Brentsville, fording Occoquan Creek, never stopping for five hours, at last we saw the railway again, near Bull Run, with the road open to Centreville — a virtual junction. Of the real exigency I know nothing. But under the orders which he received, the promptness with which General Banks moved, the steadiness of his march (with our SECOND leading), and the perfect order of his movements, are characteristics of a man whom Massachusetts delights to honor.

At the railroad I was again sent forward with sick, in the hope, finally to be accomplished, of finding an open road to Washington. We went on by the rebel corduroy roads of

last winter to Centreville. This new observation of the rebel
position only strengthened my old conviction that an attack on
the rebel stronghold last winter would have been madness.

At Centreville, on the heights, were immense forces. It
was difficult to conceive how they could have been worsted
the day before ; but all whom I questioned as to events, had
no lack of confidence in the soldiery.

I had no time to delay. Already I saw signs of backward
movement, and to be entangled in trains would have been
unpleasant. Besides, I heard orders which evidently contemplated movement. I had but just started, when Providence favored me with a sudden meeting which delighted me.
It was with my friend Mr. John A. Fowle, the excellent
chairman of the executive committee of the association in
Washington for the relief of Massachusetts soldiers. He
had procured a government ambulance, loaded it with supplies, and, with his brother and — I will not say whom else —
worked for twenty-four hours among the wounded, binding up
hurts, comforting and relieving the helpless. I have seen him
in hospitals in Washington, too, and know his faithfulness.
The widow and the fatherless bless him ! Of him I procured
supplies ; joined a long, long train of ambulances ; reached
Fairfax Court-House, and was then ordered to Fairfax Station.

The sight there cannot be described. The floors of cars
and the roofs were covered. Acres of ground were strewn
with the wounded men. Train after train had gone. Yet still
the ambulances came on, on. Camping there, the shriek of
the steam-whistle broke the hours of that Sabbath night, and
morning showed loaded trains still. I did not see any chaplains there, but I think there were some ; indeed, I know
there were next day, for I met my excellent friend, Chaplain

Gaylord. The wounded were as well cared for as possible, lying upon hay, and attended by surgeons. The most disconsolate men were divers government clerks, who had come out to assist, and who were distressed beyond measure because they could not return to Washington in cars, every inch of which was needed for the wounded. " I came out by invitation of the secretary of war ! " pompously remarked one. " Well," said the sentry, " we don't know that individual here." " But where *shall* I stay to-night ? " " Just where you please," said the sentry. I advised him to sleep on some hay, if he wished to sleep. He was horrified. He wanted to know, with a triumphant air, if *I* had ever slept out of doors. I rather thought I *had*. Had I ever slept when it *rained ?* (It was sprinkling just enough to make it pleasant.) I intimated to him that he was a great baby to fuss that way, with acres of wounded men lying around him, and gave him up. Perhaps I ought not to despise him ; I suppose I was just such a fool once.

Monday morning I went back to Fairfax Court-House, and direct to Alexandria. Still the long trains of ambulances were on the road. The eye wearied, the heart grew faint, in seeing them. I was appealed to for water, as I had some. Now every ambulance of the kind there used has two kegs for water. I examined, and found that in those long trains moving a score of miles, there was not one drop of water in the kegs ! I am happy to say that in our division such a fact would court-martial somebody !

The army was now in retreat. I saw no disorder. There was no panic whatever. And, within the fortification line. I rejoined ours,

18 *

CHAPTER IX.

THE ANTIETAM AUTUMN.

BELOW BOONSBORO', MD., September 16, 1862.

SUNRISE! After the long dark hours, light dawns. Mc-Clellan is restored to command.

The dispirited soldiery, lately depressed by knowing that they were steadily out-generalled, and without confidence in leaders, have become enthusiastic. The man whom they have always respected and loved inspires them.

Yesterday, while we were on the road in several parallel columns, McClellan rode through. Without orders, out of the enthusiasm of their hearts, sprang deafening cheers. The sound rolled up from regiment after regiment, brigade after brigade, until the voices of scores of thousands swelled the shouts.

We are, for once, following the enemy. He took his own time, chose his own positions, occupied hills of wonderful capacity for defence, but Northern valor forced his fastnesses, and drove him.

On the fourth of September our own corps left Virginia for the third time. We crossed at Georgetown, soberly. That day we camped a mile or two above Tenallytown. The next day we moved to a brook a mile and a half above Rockville, where, attached to General Sumner's corps (General

Banks remaining in Washington for other service, and, indeed, in poor health still), we formed in line of battle. General Sumner's force was on the right, ours the centre, and General Couch on the left, which rested, I believe, on the Potomac. The enemy appeared to threaten on our road with thirty thousand men, while the remainder of his force was moving towards Frederick, which he soon occupied. It was doubtful where the foe would strike. General Burnside came up on our right still further off, and on the 9th, it appearing that the enemy had moved his whole force toward Frederick, we began our march thitherward, General Burnside in advance. Our corps bivouacked at Middlebrook that night; near Damascus next night; still nearer Damascus the next; half a mile from Ijamsville, on the Baltimore and Ohio Railway, the next; and Saturday night, we were less than a mile out of Frederick. The whole movement, considering that it was necessary to watch the development of the enemy's plans, was remarkably rapid.

General Burnside had entered Frederick the evening before, with no action save a slight cavalry skirmish in the main street, the enemy having evacuated the place the day previous. I revisited old friends in Frederick on Saturday afternoon, and had good opportunities to learn a few facts derived from high rebel sources. They had over ninety thousand men in that army, with one hundred and sixty pieces of artillery, — the latter by actual count. They admitted that McClellan had worsted them in every one of the " seven days' fight " on the Peninsula, but left Richmond with perfect confidence in their ability to beat General Pope. Had he still been in command, they said they would have conducted their campaign differently in Maryland. But General McClellan's appointment made them more cautious, and they fell back to an immensely strong position west of Frederick. In Frederick they conducted themselves peaceably. What they could make useful they purchased, but they paid in confederate money, by which some secessionists there suffered nicely. It was a favorite amusement to tie the American flag to their horses' tails, whereby they made plenty of Unionists out of the lukewarm or even secessionists. In their main design they were terribly disappointed. Not only baffled in their purpose of invasion, but they found Maryland a Union State. Their pompous proclamation fell dead. A few hundreds were all the recruits they obtained in Maryland, where letters had assured them they would find a general uprising of the people. They left Frederick, cursing it as a Union city. When I remembered the almost supremacy of secessionism there last winter, I was delighted to witness the change. Our forces were welcomed with tumultuous cheers. The city swarmed with American flags. Frederick is a loyal town, and confirmed in its loyalty by its disgust with the secession soldiery — the leaders educated and iron-willed, the privates usually the poorest of "poor white trash."

We had expected to rest on Sunday. But at eight A. M. we were put in the road — a road we were on for *sixteen hours.* Long halts, but in tiresome places, and not for rest; road obstructed by trains and artillery ; immense bodies of troops, two or three columns abreast; on by-roads, across fields, wading brooks — up to and over the Catoctin range of hills, four miles west of Frederick. Here the rebels had made a stand, on a ridge capable of great defence. But, on Saturday, General Burnside had attacked them, carried their position, and drove them beyond the river in the Middletown Valley, where they burned a bridge.

The view from this ridge is delightful. The Middletown Valley is wonderfully fertile, and its whole breadth of nine miles is covered with beautiful fields or green forests. Had it only a broad river like the Connecticut at Mt. Holyoke, or a lake, the scenery would be unsurpassed for quiet loveliness.

But we heard the sound of artillery all day, and we pressed on. We were in hearing and sight of the battle of South Mountain. The march was a singular one, bearing north, south, east, west — by road and fields indifferently. At sunset the flashes of guns on the opposite range, the Blue Ridge, and the black puffs hovering in the air, marked the site of the artillery. Our object seemed to be to reach the slope by night. The general in command found a good place for supper, and we went on directly across the country a while; through cornfields, the tops of whose products one could not reach by standing in the stirrups; through brooks, and at last wading a river; resting in damp air and on damp ground; found at last, at ten P. M., by an orderly of the general's, hunting for us; going on until midnight, and at last camping, in lack of higher orders, by direction of our brigadier; exasperated, tired, some of us supperless as well as dinnerless; having marched over twenty miles to reach eleven in distance; wondering whether it is wise to break soldiers down without need.

We were to go into position at three A. M., as support to General Sturgis, in the repeated renewal of the fight. In the morning we found ourselves half up the hill, but the enemy were gone. Some of us visited the field.

The position they had held should have been impregnable. Imagine a range of lofty mountains, with here and there a winding road through " gaps " themselves very elevated, the ground often rocky, with plenty of wood, and commanding every approach for miles. At their own pleasure they planted their batteries, and placed their infantry, having all the forces needed, and occupying a succession of crests as you ascend the hills. This was the line which General Sumner, General Burnside, and General Hooker attacked.

From crest after crest the enemy were driven, up to the last. When night came on the enemy held the highest land on our right, our troops having driven them back from two positions, and lying within a few rods of them. In the centre the height itself was taken. They were well sheltered behind the crest of a slope, and walls and fences, yet General Burnside's troops had pressed up, driven their batteries, slaughtered their infantry, and held the ground. On our left, General Hooker had succeeded equally well.

In the centre the rebel dead, in their strongest position, I saw actually heaped one on another ; almost all shot through the head as they had risen from behind a stone wall to take aim. Near by was a secluded road where they had evidently taken care of their wounded. I rode half a mile and found relics of their hospital work the whole distance. Our loss was slight in comparison.

The enemy began to retreat as soon as night covered their movements ; all night they moved, pressing to the Potomac, and at daylight our forces were in rapid pursuit. The enemy not only left their dead, but frequently we found along the road their wounded, abandoned to our mercy. In Frederick, indeed, they left six hundred sick men, paroling a hundred and fifty of ours, sick there in hospital.

I believe that the campaign is now to be active. A battle is probable. The men are confident of success. They feel now that the army is one, instead of detached pieces as heretofore. They are satisfied.

For ourselves, we have a new general. General Mansfield takes General Banks's place. I may be pardoned for referring to our late commander again, although I have before repeatedly told you how brave and fearless, as well as discreet, he was as a soldier, and how much he was respected by his command. The poorest soldier had a friend in General Banks. Modest, keeping all grievances to himself, obedient to his orders, he has won great respect in the army. Had his opinion been listened to, the now famous " Banks's " retreat would not have been needed.

I had known our commander earlier. Holding a State educational position during the whole of his service as governor of Massachusetts as well as before and after, I had occasion officially to know the judgment, integrity, and firmness with which he acted in the board of which he was chairman in regard to most important interests, pecuniary and others ; and often to see in his general administration, how firmly he adhered to the good of the State, regardless of mere partisanship. And now, while no longer under his command, I can say that the same qualifications he applied to his military position. Yet he is more. I speak with reason, in saying that he is a sagacious statesman. His predictions have been fulfilled, his opinions gradually adopted.

Speaking as a chaplain, I know that General Banks has always been on the side of right. Every chaplain has had all opportunities for usefulness which the general could give. For that I owe him, and the people owe him a debt of gratitude.

NEAR KEEDYSVILLE, MD., September 18, 1862.

I CANNOT describe the battle of Antietam Creek.

I heard the thunder of cannon all day long; the horrible whirr of shells; the musketry which · sometimes became a mere roar; the cheers of success; the groans of the wounded; the whisper of the dying.

I saw the smoke of a battle-line of five miles; the fierce, flashing fire; the wounded and dead; the advance, the waver, the recovery.

But what it then meant, or what our commander was trying to do, who, confined to near one spot, could tell? So far as I could imagine the next day, as I examined the county map, it seemed as if it was wanted to drive back each wing, so that the rebels would be shut within a kind of peninsula of the Potomac River.*

On the Sunday preceding the battle of Antietam (Anteetam the neighbors call it, without any exception, to my knowledge), the Blue Ridge had been carried by our forces, excepting one point, which, of course, became untenable. During that night the rebels evacuated the ridge, and hurried to and through Boonsboro', towards the river. Our forces rapidly followed. It was generally reported by the inhabitants that the enemy were crossing, and undoubtedly a portion had. But they returned; and as it appeared, the whole force which had been investing Harper's Ferry, also joined Lee's main army in season for the battle. Monday evening our corps found itself south of Boonsboro' a few miles, where it biv-

---

* Of the history of the battle, no other account I have ever seen at all equals that by "Carleton" in the *Boston Journal,* from whose inferences I sometimes differ, but whose comprehensive statement of facts has no peer among correspondents.

ouacked. On Tuesday morning no orders came until about
nine o'clock, when we made ready to move. General Mansfield
rode up, saying, "You are going immediately into battle," — a
declaration received with as much coolness as if he had said,
"You are going to dinner." He was mistaken; we were
moved about a mile and a half only, where we came suddenly
in view of our large forces. On the crest of the hills were
posted batteries for a mile or more. Down the slopes were
drawn up long lines of battle, first and second. Just below
were still other forces. And off to the right was a dense
mass in reserve — perhaps the most impressive sight I ever
witnessed — black, motionless, silent, but like a thunder cloud
in its threatening. We took our place as reserve, and were
near, I think, what was the centre of the battle line the next
day. No battle ensued that day. For two or three hours a
smart cannonade only enlivened the scene. I saw movements
were, however, steadily going on. A corps was going to the
left, to the vicinity of the bridge. From the front nothing
could be seen but a gun or two, and a few sharpshooters; the
rebels lay behind the slopes as ours did; at least they were
hidden when I rode up to the front with our colonel.

At night we lay down there. But about half past ten there
came low, quiet orders to be ready to move. In ten minutes,
"fall in," and General Mansfield led us by road through
woods, across the river at Keedysville, up to the vicinity of
Smoketown, where, at about half past ten we went to sleep,
under a gentle rain in a field new to us, but destined to be
better known, for within musket range the rebel forces were
occupying one of the hillocks of ANTIETAM.

It was about five o'clock, when the rattling fire of skirmishers awoke us. That broke the last slumber of thousands.
It was followed by the heavy sound of artillery. Looking

19

around us we saw our thousands destined to be the right wing,
for in the night our corps had traversed half our line, and in
the darkness bivouacked in the midst of an army.   It was
half an hour, perhaps, before our column was formed.   Silently
we moved forward to no drum, no bugle, nothing but the
word of command and the savage war of artillery.   We
moved by brigades, in column by divisions, dark and heavy
spots on the field.   But our corps did not yet go into action.
A little distance, and the order is to halt.   Then the men, like
old soldiers, kindle fires and begin to make their coffee, while
General Hooker is steadily pressing backward the rebel left.

But before the coffee is ready, the corps moves up to
support General Hooker.

He held the right.   Our corps joined his left, though a
little to his rear, and next to us was General Sumner.   All
the morning Hooker had led his heroic men, a heroic leader.
The rebel advance had fallen back, but it was to their stronghold.   He had pushed up to the right so far as to threaten
their flank.   Then they began to mass their power against
him.   Our left was silent as yet, and they saw where the
great struggle was.   Hooker's force is inadequate.   Our corps
is ordered to support him.   Nobly does it respond.   It pours a
steady and terrible fire into the enemy's line.   Its effect is
tremendous.   Backward falls the foe before General Mansfield's tremendous attack, and General Hooker is relieved.
But the latter is wounded, and must leave the field.   Mansfield receives a mortal shot, and General Williams takes command.   But the time rolls on, and the conflict is terrible.
Then the enemy bring up new lines.   The reserves are all in.
The line is forced back, but it stands splendidly.   The anxiety
is intense.   Can it be that we shall fail?   Is defeat our fate,
and with it the march of a victorious foe upon our capital?

No. We have left an untenable position in front of that rocky height; that is all. Then General Sumner's corps comes on. How reviving the sight! Up they come in mass, then deploy into line amidst the cheers of our shattered troops, and rush into the conflict. They dart upon the stony position; they cannot carry it; but the ground gained at first is held, and the effort to turn our right is a failure.

It was about noon, I think, — but it seemed night, — when the thunder sounded on the left. Burnside was at work. Far down the valley was visible the smoke of his guns, but with what success we could not tell. Doubtless it relieved our right.

There is in our wing a lull in the iron storm. Soon after one P. M. there is almost entire cessation. By and by the cannonading is more intense than ever, and so, with hardly varying fortunes, it is sunset before the guns sullenly and gradually ceased firing. Then the sky is red with conflagrations. We do not know the entire result; but we know that the power of a confident foe, greater in numbers, is broken.

Our army has fought as never before. "I was in all the seven days' peninsular battles," said a wounded rebel officer, whom I assisted, "but your men never fought as they do to-day." And ours — our *own* men — have increased their heroic record.*

But all this time I had a sad work. The wounded must

* General Gordon led his brigade like himself, and General Mansfield's early wound, with that of General Crawford, put him in command of the division. General Gordon's aid, Hon. Charles R. Train, was in the hottest of the fight. This gentleman had left the comforts of home — though a member of Congress — to take the moderate position of an aide-de-camp, where he found his services needed. He plunged at once into the hardships of veterans of a year's experience, and bore them well. And in this battle, his first experience under fire, like a true and brave man, he deserved well of his country.

And our own brave colonel, so cool, so ready, fit to command the gallant men whom he led!

be cared for. From the excitement of battle to the help of the suffering is a severe change, but a needful one. How nobly the men bore their hurts!

How faithfully many a surgeon labored! Our own assistant surgeon was a hero; regardless of bullets in the hottest fire, he kept coolly on his work, — while near, Dr. Kendall of the Twelfth Massachusetts was killed. The nearest hospital, that of our own corps, was necessarily in range of the enemy's shell, which every now and then fell around and beyond. Near by were five other hospitals, all for one wing. Here were generals and privates brought together. General Mansfield I saw dying, and a few feet off, an unknown private; General Hartsuff badly wounded, and by his side a throng of others now on the same level. There is no distinction as to what body or soul needs then.

Our own regiment helped fill these hospitals. Our gallant dead, they are remembered with all the other gallant Massachusetts dead. But one we lost, — hard to replace, — our brilliant, brave, generous, kind-hearted lieutenant-colonel, Wilder Dwight, shot mortally, but living two days; of wonderful promise at home; cheerful, resigned, ready to die, — his only wish ungratified being to see his father and mother; strong in faith and trust; hard is it to part with *him*, my friend, my more than friend. While lying in the garden, moved only on a stretcher, he sent our own surgeon to relieve the wounded lying all around, unattended to by the surgeons busy cutting off limbs of men even death-struck; and again and again sent water provided for him, to the poor fellows calling for it. Yet he was not free from brutal insolence. While waiting there into the night for an ambulance into which to place Colonel Dwight for shelter only (as he could not bear its motion), some men of ours, detached for that purpose, were waiting to help, while all was quiet save the groans of sufferers covering the ground, suddenly a harsh voice insisted on turning out all our men. I found a pompous little surgeon angry and furious. I informed him why the men were there, assured him of their perfectly good behavior, and requested permission for them to remain, as we were momentarily expecting the ambulance. It was all in vain. Colonel Dwight himself was treated most harshly, although of higher rank than the brute himself, and although I told the surgeon that it was a man mortally wounded. He ordered the guard to turn them out at the point of the bayonet, and to prevent their return even to move Colonel Dwight, — refusing to tell his rank and even his name, until I obtained it of another party. The men *were driven away while actually giving water* to wounded sufferers who had been calling in vain for help. I assured the brute that I would take care his conduct was made known, knowing, from several opportunities to see that day, that he is, from brutality, pomposity, and harshness utterly unfit to be in charge of wounded men, and from gross disrespect to an officer higher in rank, unfit to be in the army.*

———

NEAR SHARPSBURG, MD., November 13, 1862.

WEEKS have passed by since I wrote. I do not remember how many. I know that my last letter was written just after the awful day of Antietam, by the dying bed of a heroic soldier, dying in Christian peace, the memory of whose friend-

* This fellow's name was said to be " King," — a medical director in General Reynolds's corps, Pennsylvania Reserves, — too good troops to have such a fellow among them.

ship is forever sacred to me. Then followed a sick bed, —
with the nervous prostration and malarious fever which the
Rappahannock campaign had originated. Then, as strength
was gained, there were the meetings with wounded of our
regiment at home; with convalescents, whose highest comfort was to drop into our recruiting office; with some not
seen since Cedar Mountain, whose grasp of hand was accompanied only by starting tears as we remembered the gallant
dead of that mournful day. Alas, for the weeping hearts
which write the history of this war!

If I ever appeared to write cheerlessly, I must say that I
always have written as encouragingly as I *could*. There is,
first, the wearing upon personal sympathies. There is, or
was, next, the knowledge to be uttered only delicately, of
useless and needless disasters, of a lack of vigor where vigor
was essential, and of opportunities wasted, of time, means,
and men thrown away. I *will* tell you now, that many a
man in this army, in high stations and low, for months
believed this war to be utterly hopeless except as to the mere
question of boundaries, and that men high, very high in civil
life, have privately admitted the same opinion; and this, not
from the strength of the South, nor from any inability in the
nation to restore its authority over every spot in its domain.
Not that there is the least hesitation as to fighting on, but
that there is a desire to fight usefully. I am speaking now
from a tolerably wide knowledge, not from speculation, nor
from my own purpose.

But I do not feel, I have never felt, that the war is hopeless. I believe, on the contrary, that it never promised as
well as now. We have a magnificent army. It is well led.
It is brave. There is much loss yet to be had, but we can
succeed. A winter campaign will destroy, by death or dis-

ability, one half of our numbers, but if the country wishes the attempt at that cost, the attempt can be made. I say this, notwithstanding two facts which look, to one or another, unpromising.

These two are, first, the result of the recent elections. They look as if the war was unpopular. But I do feel confident that while there are some double-dyed traitors in the successful party the great mass is truly loyal. They have voted against the administration, because they meant to rebuke it. But I am more mistaken than ever before if that party as a whole does not demand a vigorous prosecution of the war.

The second is, the removal of General McClellan. Of course, the intimations that the army would not fight under anybody else, are perfectly foolish. Our men fight for their *country*, not for a *man*. Yet, while I cannot answer for any other corps than ours in ours there is a feeling of deep sadness at the loss of our beloved, our trusted leader. I have hardly yet seen the man who does not mourn over it, although ready to give his successor all their help. Indeed, the new commander is personally liked. I remember the cheers with which he was greeted the morning after the battle of South Mountain, and how the cheers redoubled when General Burnside, after entirely passing the line, stopped to shake hands with a wounded soldier hobbling along on crutches. But we remember how General McClellan reinspired the shattered, despondent troops who were gathered in front of Washington, and by the magic of his name and presence made an invincible army; who, instead of remaining in the fortifications, boldly assumed the offensive; who marched onward, waiting only to be sure of the enemy's plans. and marched to victory; who, against superior numbers (I say what is

true), saved the North at Antietam ; who restored the wavering fight of the right wing ; who infused life wherever he
went ; who ordered an advance, which he stopped only at the
urgent request of commanders ; who would not throw his
brave men into a hasty advance and a winter campaign without suitable clothing.* The soldiers remember these things.
But they will follow the directions of their leader ; they will
give all their powers to his successor ; they will imitate the
patience, the patriotism of their late general, who loves his
country too well to make his personal position any cause for
weakening that country's power.†

But now the army advances. It moves down along the
side of the mountain ranges, watching the enemy. I regret,
on some accounts, that I cannot chronicle its movements ;
but we have no anxious longing to retravel either the east or
west side of the Blue Ridge. Our own corps is guarding the

* There has been much discussion as to whether McClellan ought to
have attacked the next day after Antietam. I have never believed it was
prudent, shattered as we were, to risk it. We were terribly cut up. It is
true the rebels had to retreat across a ford ; but that ford was a mile in
extent, and the water hardly knee deep. We had baffled an exultant foe,
and saved the North.

Whether the army should have moved earlier after the rebel retreat, is a
question. If one knew how poorly provided it was, I think that the question would be answered. I remember that five weeks afterwards our wagons went to the railway stations day after day for supplies, and unsuccess-
fully.

† I should not respect myself if I suppressed this old record of our sadness at the loss of our general. We loved him. But that love was not in-
compatible with the most ardent performance of duty, as the heroic record
of the Potomac army, and especially our own corps, will testify. The government has seen that that army was true and obedient. We respected the
general, but we loved our country more.

I ask, besides, that it be remembered that love for a leader, as a military
man, had nothing to do with political views.

Potomac line, which is necessary, as the enemy hold the Virginia valley, and Maryland is therefore exposed to sudden raids. Harper's Ferry is thus to be defended, and the river lined, up I do not know how far.

General Gordon has charge of a long stretch of river. That is, all the fords are guarded carefully. Our own position is at the main ford hereabouts near Sharpsburg, and but a few miles from the old battle-ground, which extends for a mile up and down the river. It takes nearly a third of our regiment at once to do picket duty. General Gordon's care is most active. He knows every part of the line himself for some thirty miles. We are in General Morell's division.

The excitement of a battle is sublime. But I am not earnest to see many more for our regiment. I wrote very dolefully last summer because we were likely to see no active service. Then immediately came Banks's retreat and a battle at Winchester. Then. Cedar Mountain. Then, Antietam. Ours has made its name honored. It is now ready for onward movement, having gone up from less than two hundred to six hundred men fit for duty. But battles — ah, a sunset finds too many gaps in the line. Such men as Abbott, Cary, Goodwin, Williams, Perkins, Dwight, — dead. And now we are sad at the loss of another, Major Savage, who died in Virginia, of wounds received at Cedar Mountain. An honorable, brave soldier ; refined, gentle, warm-hearted, and one of the purest-minded men I ever knew ; an only son, whose parents may God bless ! Nobody knew James Savage but to respect and love him.

And such men in the ranks. I miss too long a list to be written out, though they deserve it, and some day shall have it in permanent form. Men, like one of my Christian brethren, dying after just time enough to say, "Lord, receive my spirit!" Or, like one dying day before yesterday, a warm-hearted Christian, but lately returned from a captivity of weary months, long ago freed from the captivity of sin, now released from the captivity of the body, into the glorious enjoyments of the children of God — of perfectly consistent Christian example always, meeting death in peace.

Brave men. Patriots. Long is the list. And long in many another regiment besides ours.

———

Near Sharpsburg, Md., November 21, 1862.

WE have little share in the great movements on which hang the destinies of the campaign; but we watch with intense eagerness. With all the affection borne to our late general, everybody feels, as that chief himself teaches us to feel, the warmest interest in the progress of his successor. With success before January, we insure the masses to determined measures; we dispirit the rebels. With defeat, we create a party ready to recognize the South; we encourage the rebels; we give opportunity for foreign meddling. With undecided results, we insure a disgraceful compromise, worse than separation. Without success in this war the North crumbles to pieces. National life is suspended on present issues. Often have I thought, in such anxieties, of the remark an honored soldier uttered to me — "This nation has forgotten God!" But no. There are too many praying men and women to allow us to believe so fatal a statement. But does the nation have an adequate conception of the things at stake? When a weak measure was adopted early in this war, that soldier referred to said, "I never felt so sadly but

once ; that was when my child died." National destruction
is a worse personal loss than loss of children ; worse than
death itself.

Our work is picket duty. We are in front of a ford, of
which the water is but knee deep for a mile. It is the ford
by which the enemy retreated after the battle of Antietam.
The enemy still hold the valley. If Jackson went southward,
it was only in a parallel line with our army on the east of
the Blue Ridge, and he returned. Whether he still remains
is doubtful, as General Lee will need him. But the enemy
are still opposite us, though rarely showing themselves. A
few days ago a man who went over for his family was stopped
by a rebel party just as they were embarking. One man
took to the water, was wounded, and finally killed. Two
days ago the deepening twilight brought into view at least a
mile of camp fires, which were speedily extinguished. Yesterday we heard cannonading half the day, apparently from
some supposed reconnoissance from Harper's Ferry. The
ease with which a rebel.party could make a raid into Maryland, keeps here a large force ; besides the possibility, now
growing less, that Jackson might seek to divert troops, by a
sudden threatening this way, as he succeeded in doing when
he forced General Banks to retreat from Strasburg. The
river is not yet raised to any noticeable degree by the light
rains of this week, but we have not yet heard from the
mountain regions. It is *their* waters which swell the Potomac.

Our own regiment maintains its morale, notwithstanding
the loss of its colonel, Andrews,* to the gain of General
Banks — a modest, unpretending, but wonderfully skilled and

* Now commander of the Corps d'Afrique, and commandant at Port
Hudson.

energetic soldier is our late colonel. He is a graduate of
West Point, whose pupils prove altogether the best soldiers.
I have been somewhat surprised to see jealousies fostered at
home against educated soldiers.   I have seen a good many
of the graduates of our military schools, and from observation I have acquired the highest confidence in them.   That
they often feel superior to mere militia officers, is doubtless
true ; they are superior.   That many volunteers feel distressed
because they recognize their own comparative inferiority, is
true ; they ought to feel distressed.   Educated soldiers are
as much superior to one beginning without any training, as
an educated physician is to one who begins practice utterly
ignorant of medicine.   The latter may learn by years of
experiment ; so may the raw soldier.   But each sacrifices life
to do it.   I could instance slaughters which no educated
soldier would ever have allowed to occur ; they were the cost
of teaching raw men.   I could point to a brigade uselessly
sacrificed ; and to our own, saved in similar circumstances,
by having a soldier for a commander.   West Point cannot
make a soldier out of a blockhead ; but other things being
equal, its training is invaluable.

The public press, just now, is speaking of the great
number of deserters from the army ; and government has, I
believe, issued stringent orders.   The evil is by no means
magnified.   In battles, too, there are many who go to the
rear.   I saw at least *thousands* at Antietam.   Even when
men carried off the wounded — which was not their business
— surgeons kept them from returning ; I saw it.   But is
there not a reason why men do not fear to desert?   I know
of a case where a man deserted, and was afterwards appre-
hended, in citizen's clothing, a salesman in a store in New
Hampshire.   He escaped after being taken, but was recap-

tured. He was tried and convicted. The sentence was entirely remitted, because the powers that were could not see sufficient evidence of the crime of desertion ! He was returned to his regiment, but, before being put to duty, deserted again, and was not heard of more.

Another matter of public interest is the new system of the ambulance corps. All ambulances are taken away from the regiments, and put under charge of one brigade officer. When the sick are to be moved, the surgeon sends a written requisition for ambulances. The new plan has some merits ; in one place, viz., the field of battle. But for regiments, as such, it is exceedingly unpleasant. For instance, on leaving a recent camp, ambulances were wanted to transport the sick. The ambulances were four miles off. On sending for them, they were not to be found. Again, suppose at this point the enemy came suddenly, and in such force that it were madness to remain: There would be no time to send a requisition for ambulances. The sick, in such a case, must be left to the enemy. Or, suppose a regiment is ordered suddenly to move ten miles on a dangerous service. It has no time to get ambulances. Such occasions I have seen repeatedly, when, having ambulances, there was no difficulty. It is hard for soldiers to feel, going on such a service, that if wounded, there is no way to remove them. The old system of having all ambulances with regiments had evils ; but it is just as bad to give them none. The true system would be to give a limited number to each regiment, and have a general ambulance corps besides for emergencies.

Let me allude to the matter of gratuitous supplies. Many presents sent to soldiers are worse than useless. What a soldier needs, as to clothing, is what government gives him, only a supply of better flannels and stockings. Now, indis-

20

criminate giving is useless.   First, know what a soldier lacks before sending anything.   Our own regiment is partially, and sometimes entirely, supplied with under-clothing, by a systematic method of donation.   This works well.   It saves the soldier's money, and gives better articles.   Such a systematic method is good.   The Sanitary Commission's attempt to make itself the medium of *all* donations, is absurd, although that would be better than indiscriminate presents.   Whenever persons can supply and keep supplied a regiment, let them do it.

So as to donations of reading matter.   If anybody has money to give for such purposes, for a particular regiment, well, I want to say more on this matter.

———

CAMP NEAR SHARPSBURG, MD., November 28, 1862.

MATTERS continue tolerably " quiet on the upper Potomac." There is reason to suppose that the ubiquitous Jackson has left the valley himself, to assist in the defence of Richmond or Fredericksburg.   But reconnoissances discover quite a large rebel force somewhere near Berryville, which is about ten miles from Charlestown.   That force is said to be under command of one of the Hills.   It is rather difficult to account for the fear of Jackson.   He has one quality — suddenness and rapidity — of high excellence.   But in actual fight he has never shown great generalship.   He was foiled last winter by General Lander.   With forces quite even, he was beaten by acting Brigadier General Kimball in the first Winchester battle.   With an overwhelming force, he fell upon General Banks in May, and utterly failed of his purpose — an army only one seventh as large holding him at bay for three hours. In the return movement, he fled before General Fremont.

The last battles at Manassas were under General Lee, not Jackson.

I wrote you last week of a murder — mere murder — committed on a man trying to get a family out of Virginia. The men were actually enticed over by the apparent distress of some women, purporting to be refugees ; went over on an errand of mercy ; fell into the power of the guerrilla Captain Burke, for whose apprehension a reward was once offered.

The appendix to the affair is a very pretty operation of our own commander, Captain Cogswell, with sixty men. Ordered to cross in the night, he moved off about nine P. M., and by making a cautious, and rather circuitous march, entered Shepardstown after midnight. The houses wanted were easily found and surrounded. In one of them was Captain Burke and five of his gang. The captain was dressed and armed, and the horses of the party stood saddled. As it proved, Burke was to have started on one of his plundering expeditions in about an hour. As ours were preparing to enter, a man suddenly sprang from a door, and attempted to escape. Captain Cogswell ordered him twice or more times to surrender, and then told two men to fire. A ball entered the heart of the rebel, who, on examination was found to be Captain Burke himself. The other five were captured, and their horses, arms, and important papers brought away. The expedition was a perfect success, and Union men in Virginia will breathe free now this miscreant is gone.

Captain Cogswell, with the same men and some cavalry, was sent again the day following, in broad daylight. They crossed and occupied the town before the people had any suspicion of the approach. They arrested the man they wished for, paroled three officers and twenty privates in hospital, took some arms, and returned in perfect safety. The rebels in that

neighborhood express no very kind feeling toward the Second Massachusetts. They vow vengeance; but our means
of defence at the river are such that our men would hail a
brush for amusement.

On that night, while our men were descending the valley,
another man, in our hospital, was entering the valley — the
valley of the shadow of death. From his bedside I heard
the tread of our men. As they were crossing the river, he
was crossing the river — the final river. As they landed, he
died. They were victorious. Trust in God that he was.

Yesterday was Thanksgiving day. The weather was
lovely. The air was mild. In sight of the river, almost
hearing its ripple (we do hear it at night as we lay awake,
and our men hear it as they pace its shore all through the
darkness), we had our public services; our old New England
singing; our prayers. How many of us kept home in mind
all day! How many at home were praying for us! The
preacher told them that what was a crime at home, was a
crime here; what they would be ashamed of in their homes,
they should be ashamed of here; what they would not do at
home with their good mother's knowledge, they should not
do here; what they had been taught of truth at home, was
truth here.

Then the men had their quoits and ball. Some tried the
speed of their horses. All — I hope — had their good dinner; the turkeys, the geese, the chickens, the plum puddings,
were many. Our hospital inmates all had such peculiar
luxuries as would not injure them. The officers dined together; and as at home, members of families return to their old
hearthstones on Thanksgiving day, so yesterday there came
back to us all the officers in our vicinity who had gone from
us into other commands — back to the good old regiment,

whose men have been tried in the furnace of fire, and stood by one another like true comrades. Among officers and men were many who had felt the bullet, and a multitude more who had had them in their garments. Many were not there. It was like the vacant chairs in a household — to think of the departed heroes.

In the morning we had visitors. They were ladies, part of whom had come from Chambersburg, Pa., thirty-five miles off, to bring some gifts for our hospital; some home bread, fruits, butter, jelly, pillows, and other needed articles. "Verily, verily, I say unto you, they have their reward."

In the midst of the merriment in the evening a sick man was dying. Some relatives were by his bed; so was a good man, whom I found bending over him, and commending him to God. Soon he passed away. "I wanted to go home before I died," said he, "but I hope I am going to a better home." These were his last audible words. "Home." How every sick man's heart grows sicker because he wants to be at home. It is the hardest feature in a soldier's life. But when the surgeons are anxious to send a man home, in cases where home would save his life, it takes so long to prevail upon higher officials somewhere to sign the papers, that the favorable time often passes. But the home above is always ready.

I have said nothing yet on the Proclamation. I preferred to wait. At home I did not hesitate to praise it, in the solitary half day I had strength enough to occupy my own pulpit; nor to denounce the infamous utterance of an infernal press, whose great comfort was that slavery would be preserved whether the Union was restored or broken.

I have taken some pains to see the effect of the Proclamation upon the army. A few, very few, are distressed about

20 *

it. They love slavery. They admit, upon questioning, that
they deem servitude the proper condition of the " inferior "
race. But the number is incomparably less than a year ago.
One year has brought about an immense change of opinion
as to the character of slavery and the civilization of slaveholders.

Many like the Proclamation on the grounds of decided
opposition to all slavery. They receive it as a matter of
justice.

The great bulk of the army, however, look at it only in the
light of a military measure, and feel no excited interest in it
whatever. They regard it as perfectly within the power of
the President as commander-in-chief of the armies, while
most would dissent from his right to issue such a decree as a
civil magistrate. As a military measure, they believe it
proper and needful. But it is no new thing in practice. We
have been freeing the slaves in a rebellious State these nine
months. We never think of returning a fugitive. A slave-
hunter would be kicked out of our lines. Contrabands are
everywhere, in public service and in private, and are treated
as other men are. The Proclamation only enlarges what we
have been doing this long while ; and therefore creates far
less talk than it does at home.

The army, moreover, is in a different state of discipline
from what it was at the beginning of the war. When it was
what Governor Andrew felicitously called a " collection of
town meetings," such a measure might have made great
trouble. Now the army is under control. It understands
obedience to be its duty. Its work is to fight, and not discuss ;
hence it gives such a measure much less consideration than it
would once.

Again, we have become accustomed to seizure of blacks on

the other side. When Jackson came to Winchester last May, he seized all blacks, free and slave, except some belonging to rebels there. When he went southward he swept the country clear, carrying many freemen into slavery. When the rebel army captured Harper's Ferry it seized all blacks, and they are still in the hands of the men-stealers southward. Nor do we forget that the blacks who drove the ambulances when the wounded were gathered in under a flag of truce after the late Manassas battles, were seized and carried away. Southerners steal negroes whenever they have an opportunity; steal them to make them slaves. Are we to regard their slave property as sacred?

Nor can we distinguish between seizing slave property as property and seizing wheat. Whatever the rebels have that we want, government takes. We are not worshippers of slavery, and we can see no more harm in taking slave property than the products of slave labor. It is all one. If the constitution gives no right to touch slave property, no more does it to touch the wheat the slaves raise. If the right is a military one to take wheat, we cannot see why it is not the same to take slaves. Those who can find nothing of such a power in the constitution, remind us of the man who said, "As to liquor, give me whiskey-punch; other liquors are forbidden, but there is not a single word in the Bible against whiskey-punch!"

Nor do we relish the statements which come to us from Richmond, how the rebels everywhere impress slaves to build fortifications. Have we got to encounter those fortifications? Has Northern blood got to flow because of those fortifications? Have Northern fathers and mothers to believe that the work which slaughters their sons, is a labor not to be meddled with? *We* do not see it so.

I met a rebel officer once who spoke of slavery. "You thought," said he, "that slavery made us weak. You are mistaken. It doubles the number of guns we can put into the field." I thought over it, and I believed him. I saw, one day, as noble a regiment as ever was raised, go into action full of genuine men. The best blood of Massachusetts was there. Two days after, I buried its dead. Shorn of one third of its numbers was the regiment. Lying on the field were the pride of their homes. Men of education, character, ability, industry. Apart entirely from the fact that but for slavery there would have been no war, slavery doubled the guns against them. Fathers and mothers, of every two guns levelled at your sons slavery fired one. I lifted your sons ; some to bury, some to send home. It was slavery that killed them all.

I saw, on another day, that same regiment undaunted in the fiercest battle of this continent. One fourth of its number came not out. Its good men, how they fell. One of the noblest, who cared not for his life if victory was ours, had come to hate slavery as I do. Of every two guns at Antietam, slavery fired one. I saw countless bleeding men there. Slavery wounded them. I saw countless maimed men. Slavery maimed them. I saw countless dead there. Slavery killed them.

The product of slave labor doubles every gun the South could without it put into the field. To sustain slavery the South keeps both guns there — without slavery they could keep none there. And shall any man tell me that the system which killed these gallant comrades is one whose continuance, it is his comfort, is sure, whether we succeed before January first, or whether we fail finally, and I not loathe him as I would a snake? Is Massachusetts sunk so low as to breed such reptiles?

Therefore, as the South has made slavery the great test, the great object of this war, — as the only grievance of which the South complained was interference with slavery ; as they call us all abolitionists ; we say let that be the test.

I hope and believe that the President will stand by his Proclamation. We never had a doubt of his honesty, his patriotism, his conscientious firmness. He will be sustained. The country will sustain. God will help him.

That it will have no effect is absurd. That the slaves will not hear of it is absurd. That the blacks will rush North is absurd. That the South has feared it as the hardest blow, Southerners have repeatedly told me.

It is a *right* step. There is but one more, — universal emancipation. I have now but one article of faith on this point : *no man can own another ;* no, not for a moment. All laws saying he can, are, of right, void. It is only a question of the best way now to treat them as void. But void they are, and cursed with a curse. This is the simple platform on which every man can stand : No man can own another.

As to this matter of slavery and the Bible, I am reminded of a conversation I once had with a Virginia schoolma'am. She was not of the kind they put in jail ; she taught only white children. She was sound, very sound, and a real hearty, solid Presbyterian, and of a " certain age." But I offended her terribly.

She attacked me several times quite ferociously. It was a great comfort to her that I had voted against father Abraham, but she concluded I had " fallen from grace."

" Now," said she, one day, " you abolitionists reject the Bible."

" Not by any means ! " said I, with great horror.

" What if the Bible authorized us to hold slaves, wouldn't you reject the Bible ? "

"No, ma'am! God can authorize it if he chooses," said I.

"Well, then," said she, exultingly, "I can convince you it is right for us to hold slaves."

"Go on," I replied, "and I'll give it up if you bring Scripture fairly to prove it."

She got her Bible, and turned instantly, just as if she had read that place a good deal, to Leviticus xxv. 46., and with forefinger extended, read triumphantly, "They shall be your bondmen forever." "They shall be your bondmen forever!"

"There," said she, "does not that settle the question?"

"What question?" I asked innocently.

"Why, that we have a right to hold slaves."

"Well, not quite," said I. "First of all, who are 'they'?"

"The heathen," said she, after reading a little, say the 44th verse.

"Correct; but 'thy brother' 'waxen poor,' it says, shall be 'as a hired servant,' and shall be free when the jubilee year comes. That's Scripture, isn't it?"

"Ye-e-s," was the rather reluctant reply.

"But you have been telling me that the slaves are better off because many of them are converted. You don't think it right, according to Scripture, to keep *them* as slaves?"

She was nonplussed. But still, —

"Well, those not Christians we have a right to hold," said she.

"Why so?"

"They shall be your bondmen forever!"

"You remind me," said I, "of the old schoolboy way of proving the duty of hanging one's self, by quoting 'Judas went and hanged himself,' with 'Go thou and do likewise.'"

Whereat the schoolma'am waxed wroth.

"*This* applies to the subject directly," said she.

" What subject? "

" It proves that it is right to hold slaves."

" Right for *whom* to hold slaves? "

" Why, for anybody."

" Not at all, madam. If it proves anything, it proves it was the privilege of the *Jews*. Are *you* a Jew? "

She was vexed.

" If it was right for the Jews, it is right for us," she said.

"I don't see that," said I. " I admit that God could authorize certain parties to hold slaves; but it does not follow that others not so authorized have a right to do it. The privilege is limited by the special permission, because contrary to natural right. Show me a provision anywhere from God authorizing the South to do it, and I will submit; but I want the documents! "

She began to think I was an infidel. But I pacified her by insisting that I believed in the five points of Calvinism clear through.

Then she laid down again the general principle that what was right for the Jews is right for us.

" Very well," said I, " Abraham was ordered to sacrifice his only son. Do you believe it is everybody's duty or privilege now? "

She did not; but that was a peculiar and single case.

" Very well," said I ; " take a general case. Jewish men had several wives apiece. Am I to understand that you advocate that arrangement now? Or, is it your idea that slavery is called a ' patriarchal system' because it comes as near to this arrangement as possible, if I may judge from the color of the slaves hereabouts? "

The indignant schoolma'am was filled with wrath, and I have not dared to argue with a woman ever since.

CHAPTER X.

THE FREDERICKSBURG WINTER.

NEAR SHARPSBURG, MD., December 5, 1862.

"ALL quiet on the Upper Potomac." Two rebel brigades
at Winchester. Constant reconnoissances from Harper's Ferry, and more noise about them than is profitable. Waiting
for news from Fredericksburg, where the remarkable rapidity
of advance shows some hidden strategy.

So we read the President's message, and ponder over it.
And the secretaries' reports, and ponder over them.

Of the President's message, I am puzzled to say what impression it makes. Its honesty, its earnestness, strike us at
once. Renewed and strong determination that the South
must and shall be conquered, would have suited well, I think.
Of the matter of " compensated emancipation," I believe
nobody cares. Our way would be to carry out the proclamation by force of arms ; hang all men at home who dared to
proceed to " give aid or comfort to the enemy ; " and reply to
any rebellious cities of Northern rowdies by infantry, cavalry,
and artillery.

But it is a delicate matter to discuss a President's message, — especially as our assistant surgeon was " dismissed,"
according to the papers, for " absence without leave," whereas
he was not absent a day without leave, although for weeks

prostrated by malarious fever, and placed in charge of a surgical ward at Washington while hardly able to walk, — and another officer was " dismissed " after he was dead.

I began, in former pages, to say something about gifts for the religious and moral improvement of the army, and for general reading. I feel impressed with the need of some public utterance, in view of the sums which the large-hearted friends of soldiers are making. It is due to them that they should be informed of the best methods. They are not alone in this benevolence. I have in my possession a little religious tract, one of a series printed at the South for distribution in the rebel army. I remember also seeing, the morning after the battle of South Mountain, a large number of Testaments which had been taken from the bodies of killed or wounded at the rebel roadside hospital, with letters and other papers. So far as I can learn, the Southern army is quite well supplied with chaplains ; nor has their congress cut down their pay to so low a rate (as ours has) that no man from an expensive place of residence can support his family upon it.

Of all the organizations which minister to the comfort of the soldier, the Sanitary Commission is, beyond all comparison, the most useful. I think I could point out some evils connected with it : I think it has some defects in itself. But it has done, it is doing, a vast amount of good. The expense is great, the waste considerable ; but the work is great, and would not otherwise be done at all. Its facilities for forwarding supplies instantly in the emergency, as after the battle of Antietam, form its great excellence in my opinion. Government could furnish the same necessaries, but while requisitions were going the round of the circumlocution office, a thousand men might die. Government is not much to blame for such slowness ; for, a certain amount of formalities is essential to a proper regulation of expenditures. The Sanitary Commission is bound by no such official routine, inasmuch as its business is in one board, able to act instantly. Of the donations of the Commission I have seen but little indeed. But the character of the men constituting it is a perfect guarantee of integrity.

The recent recommendations of the Commission, as to the sending of articles direct to soldiers, are in the main good. They make the exception of such articles as can be sent by mail, which is also good. Socks, and even boots, come through our mail. When our first colonel was applied to by a benevolent association in Boston and vicinity for information as to the best articles to send to soldiers, he replied, " The same things that government furnishes, only of better quality." All such save the cost to the soldiers. Our regiment is very generally supplied in this way, with excellent effect. Care is taken to have the boxes sent only when and where we are likely to be stationary. A bright official at Hagerstown, indeed, stopped a box of clothing the other day, on the ground of its suspicious appearance, not opening it, but keeping it back for days. It is seldom, however, there are such fools as officials, and such matters come safely. To recommendations to make the Sanitary Commission the sole medium of donations, I advise our friends to pay no attention. The society for the Relief of Massachusetts Soldiers, located at Washington, is a specialty worthy of support.

As to other departments of general benevolence, it is a little unfortunate, in some respects, that there is a multiplicity of organizations doing substantially the same work. The Christian Commission and the Tract societies occur to me, besides some minor agencies. The different mediums must of course distract attention in some places. But as they probably operate on different fields, and so differ in some particulars of working, perhaps they will not interfere with each other ; and some ground may be occupied which would otherwise be neglected.

It is to be remembered that chaplains are the author-ized officers charged by government with care for the religious and moral condition of regiments. For post-hos-pitals, other chaplains are appointed specially. There remain, therefore, only the temporary assemblages of sick and wounded after a battle. Even these are cared for by reg-imental chaplains, except when the forces move on, in which case voluntary effort like that of the Christian Commission in its plans (if I understand their plans) is invaluable. Even then, one or two workers, remaining while the temporary hospital remains, are better far than twenty men volunteering for a week or two, to be replaced then by twenty more. There is everything in having a system in such a place ; in knowing the entire ground, and arranging accordingly. If gov-ernment had extra chaplains — as they have surgeons — to be detailed for such special duty, it would be a far better plan than any voluntary organization can supply. Until they do, the efforts of outside friends are at such times indispensable.

Beyond such extraordinary emergencies, there are some regiments without chaplains, the number of which is, in our vicinity, diminishing.

But wherever there are chaplains, it should be always remembered that the work is in their care, however great it may be. They will always welcome all suitable help ; but for others to attempt to do their work, is an irregularity which would prove disastrous. In a well-regulated regiment, it would not be allowed ; no more than to allow voluntary sur-geons to prescribe to the sick. If a chaplain tries to do his

duty, he will be glad of all help in a legitimate way. If
he does not try to do his duty, there is ample field for
usefulness in interesting him in his duty. If I remember correctly, Dr. Nettleton once directed a person who
came from a particular parish for spiritual advice, to go
to his own minister, notwithstanding the fact that that minister was uninterested in such cases. The doctor judged that
such a call would interest the pastor. The minister was
aroused, and with him his whole church; and vastly more
good was accomplished than if Dr. Nettleton had tried to do .
the pastor's work. If a man wants to work a mill, he will
do rather better to put water in the boiler, and fire in the
furnace, than try to work the crank himself. A systematic,
kindly visitation of chaplains by a Christian Commission
would be a capital plan. The idea is novel; but don't start
another society to do it. Come, agents of some old one, and
we will be delighted. Come, see just what we need, —
as the agents of the Sanitary Commission do in the sister
work, — whose ministrations have saved many a life. Come,
and we will tell you what we do and how we do it, and how
we are crippled for want of help. Employ some minister of
experience, and ripe, genial piety, and send him to visit, in a
brotherly way, every chaplain in some one corps; to see his
privations, perhaps, and cheer him with Christian fellowship.

Gifts — we come to that — are sometimes useless. I have
before me a lot of tracts addressed to sellers of ardent spirits;
that business is not carried on by our men. I have had a
quantity addressed to distillers; but we have no distillers. And
tracts to Sunday school children on their behavior in Sunday
school; which is of another meridian. And tracts to Sunday
school teachers on the preparation of their lessons, or how to
greet their classes, and on visiting their pupils; which is a

work adapted to places where there are children. And tracts on dancing ; a fault to which there is little liability, — as I remember but one instance, and was glad when that took place, — on the ground, closing at tattoo. I could multiply the list, but you have specimens. What do we want of the unsalable lumber taken from cobwebbed shelves of some institution glad to be rid of it — but reckoning it at the usual price in their demands for more contributions? Or of bundles of worn out Sunday school books? Or of piles of volumes of some Christian truth adapted to certain states of mind, of which ten copies are enough for a year? Or of tracts attacking Catholicism, to distribute which, even by chance, would effectually destroy all influence with many men, even if a chaplain was fool enough to suppose it his business to try to make Protestants — which tracts I have carefully put into the fire.

Again, many bundles of good reading are mere heaps of duplicates of what has already been widely circulated. Societies cannot tell what has been distributed, and they glut the market with some particular work. Or volumes come, to be thrown away the first march.

Or works which excite only ridicule. For instance, here is a little book entitled " Valuable Hints to Soldiers." It tells what a soldier needs : A " Bible " — no, he doesn't ; he needs a Testament. A " cheap portfolio of —— ; " won't any other maker's portfolio do as well? " A filter ; " of which he disengages the tube to smoke through. " Three flannel undershirts, ditto shirts, ditto drawers, four or five pairs of woollen socks ! " I wish the man who wrote this had to march the miles our men have, with such a load on his back. Then it tells us that the soldier " should never sleep at night in the flannel shirt, drawers, or socks worn during the day." How, when off on picket duty, one night in two or three?

How, when at the close of a march he is too tired to do *anything?* "No one should on any account be in wet clothing." Suppose he bivouacs in the rain, as we have over and over again? Suppose he changes, and gets out again immediately? "Blankets must be aired in the morning." Of course, when up before daylight to march on, with just time enough to pack one's knapsack. "Soup may be omitted at one dinner, and beef at another." How many courses do soldiers have? They are glad enough to get *one* article, even if they get down to green corn, as we all did on the Rappahannock. "Never be afraid of good beef." No, nor of turtle-soup or blanc mange. "An entire meal should never be made of beans." What *will* he eat then, when beans are the only dish. In certain cases "increasing" the quantity "of vegetables." He *can't* increase it, especially as two thirds of the time in marching he does not have any. Soldiers laugh at such directions. It may be a very good book, but it doesn't suit the latitude of a regiment that has been out a year and a half.

Men have an affection for particular publications sometimes. I gave an almanac once to one of our officers. He kept it a while, but afterwards told me that it did not seem "quite natural." So I gave him the other one, "the Family Christian Almanac." "Ah," said he, after looking at it, "this is the one. This is the kind my mother used to read me the stories from every Sunday, when I was a boy." And he kept that for many a long mile.

Now, when people have money they wish to pay for reading matter to be sent to a regiment, the best thing to do is this: Write to the chaplain first. Tell him how much money you will spend. If you wish it to go to any particular publishing house, tell him so, and send the catalogue of their publications. Ask him to say if he has any choice ; what he can use to the best advantage. You will thereby avoid sending useless matter or heaps of works already distributed. If you have a particular fancy for sending some one book, mention it. The chaplain will be glad enough to reply. Then send the publications — paying express charges, in which, from an expensive experience, I have a feeling interest. And remember that some of the best minds of the whole land are in the army ; that there are educated men in the ranks as privates ; that soldiers are men of common sense. In reading some of the books got up for soldiers, I am reminded of a good brother, who, happening to preach at the Mariner's Church in Boston, got along very well, until, in describing a storm in the middle of the Atlantic, asked, when attention was intent, " What would you do ? " and himself replied, " You'd instantly let go the anchor ! " Just as many occasional preachers think they must " talk sailor " to sailors, so many writers " talk soldier " to soldiers, with as much accuracy as letting go the anchor where the water is any number of miles deep. I am aware that I didn't know an adjutant from a company cook eighteen months ago, but the books are just as ridiculous where men do know ; just as that most excellent book, the " Life of Adjutant Stearns," which I have read with the deepest liking, has one rank for him in the volume, and another on the shoulder-straps in the likeness, — a very slight matter in a volume of such touching interest, and so admirably written. Such a book soldiers will read.*

If any one wants to feel sure that what he gives for reading will be used, let him subscribe for such number as he

* Of later publications, there is one, the most touching, most beautiful little book possible. It is " The Sergeant's Memorial."

pleases of some good religious newspaper, which he can usually get at half the usual rates, and have the copies mailed direct to the chaplain for distribution. These will be read eagerly. For myself, I never have a quarter enough. . With the *Christian Banner*, I never get over one third through the regiment. I have had copies of various papers, religious and secular; some donors have become weary in well doing, for which I am sorry. It is the readiest and steadiest way of supplying good reading matter.

FAIRFAX STATION, VA., December 15, 1862.

SUDDENLY we were turned out of our anticipated quarters. We were tumbled into the " winter campaign." We did not know of the movements on the Rappahannock, but we were modestly satisfied that if anything was to be accomplished they would want us.

We had built huts. Some had log-houses. The surgeon and myself were building an elegant log-cottage. We were satisfied that the capacities of logs for ornamental building had not been developed, and we intended a model. Our logs were straight. They lay close. The corners went up vertically. We had the foundation of an elegant stone fireplace, — already having a brick one.

But on Tuesday afternoon orders came. So on Wednesday morning we started. Our house was left. For no fault; the owner, being about to leave town, had no further use for it. Camp was hardly left, when the place swarmed with people to search for goods. A deserted camp is wealth to many a Marylander.

We were ordered to be at Antietam Iron Works at nine

A. M., a mile and a half from camp. We were there ten minutes early. At fifteen minutes past, an orderly came with a document certifying that we need not be at the iron works until *noon*, — which was very comforting, considering that we were there, and had only three hours to wait on a cold morning. The change was made — too late — because other regiments had miles to move, and the Third Wisconsin had not had orders at all at nine o'clock. Was the fact known the night before — that the other regiments could not possibly be there until twelve M.? Of course, but what matters it that the soldiers must have reveille at four A. M., leave a comfortable camp in winter, and lay three hours uselessly in the road?

Twelve o'clock came, and one, and half-past one ; and then we moved on. We had studied the history of the dilapidated iron works, — disused four or five years since, — whose pig iron, accumulating at Harper's Ferry, had repaired the ford there. We had inspected a capital stone bridge, and an arched channel for the canal. And the men snow-balled.

About five P. M. we went into a light wood about five miles from Harper's Ferry for a bivouac ; built our fires ; made excellent beds by piling on the snow some cornstalks, and topping off with pine branches ; and, wrapped in blankets, slept well.

Reveille at half past three, to start at five. Orders came at half past six. What mattered it that we were deprived of an hour and a half's sleep, uselessly?

The horses slipped badly on the icy roads, and we **had to** "wait for the wagon." Early we were at Harper's Ferry, and crossed into Virginia for the *fourth* time. Three times driven out — the fourth should be a better advance. The pontoons passed over the Potomac, and over the Shenandoah, into Loudon county, round the base of Loudon Heights, up the hill skirting the eastern side of the heights, and resting in a field whose fences fell suddenly. Out came the owner; he tried to stop it, but in vain. Then he came to the commander: " Your men are taking my fences." " Yes." " Isn't it hard," said he, excitedly, " for me to lose my fences?" " Yes," said our sensible commander, " but it would be a good deal harder for my men to be cold. Government will pay you."

So we waited five or six hours. Then we were ordered to move, — which resulted in several rods. Then a halt of half an hour, in the road, waiting for orders, which started several regiments but did not reach the regiment next before us. That regiment finally started without orders, and as our business was to follow them, we followed. Soon it was dark, but we kept on — on — through half frozen brooks, half frozen mud, over rocks and ruts, for several hours of darkness, and then bivouacked. We had very gloomy views of public affairs, until after supper, when, with good fires, we became altogether more hopeful. Orion watched us going to sleep. What mattered it that we had waited hours in the middle of the day, and stumbled on in the darkness?

Reveille at three A. M.; to be ready to move at half past four. We were ready, and of course waited until half past one. Then, orders to fall in; in less than five minutes, orders *not* to fall in; in five minutes more, orders again to fall in, — whereupon our commander sent a lieutenant to ascertain which órder was *the* one; " the last," and we went on. We had waited because " the brigade train was not up;" but ours was up close, and the man responsible for the other ought to be broke, — only, what matters it that soldiers are up at three A. M., and wait ten hours needlessly?

Through the pretty little stone-built hamlet of Hillsborough, which is beautifully located in a cleft of the " Short Hills," and a mile on. Then, some guerillas, only half an hour before we reached that point, had daringly captured a wagon. A party of cavalry trotted off and recaptured it, and we went on, having waited only two hours, which would take three of horrible stumbling with sore-footed men over a wet, rocky road at night. Three miles from Leesburg we bivouacked, on the western slope of the Kittoctan. What mattered it that two hours of daylight had been wasted?

The first day we had made six miles; the second, fourteen and a half; the third, ten and a half.

The fourth day reveille at four; to start at half past five. At half past, a message *not* to fall in immediately, as the brigade would not start as early as expected. The orderly could not help smiling, respectfully, as he delivered the order. We did start, to our astonishment, at half past six; climbed the Kittoctans, wound round the height still crowned with a former rebel earthwork, passed through the shabby Leesburg, — which has one pretty house, which I thought I recognized as copied from a plan and view in Godey's Ladies' Book; saw lots of fellows who we knew would mount as guerrillas as soon as we were gone; and reached Gum Spring, a "shoddy" village of nine houses, a spring (whether "gum" or not I don't know), and a church, probably Dunker, Tunker, Dunkard, or Tunkard, whether these names denote one, two, three, or four denominations, I don't know; reached the turnpike to Fairfax — turned into a wood; found a good wood; discovered STRAW, and had glorious beds in front of splendid LOG FIRES; having accomplished seventeen miles and a half. Wagons attacked in the rear; guerillas beaten off.

Reveille at four o'clock, to start at five. Fancy our intense astonishment when we found that the foremost regiment actually took the road at that hour! It seemed like the old times when our own Brigadier-General Gordon (now sick) was with us. Trains were up also, — which reminded us of the same commander, who would have dressed down somebody handsomely for such delays and hitches as had disgusted us for the several days gone, — only such delays don't often occur where he is. Nor will we be bored by the yellings of some of our neighbors when he gets back.

Next day was pleasant. Indeed all were good marching days, if decently used. Saturday threatened to be wet, but the storm was " postponed on account of the weather." Sunday morning we overtook the bulk of the corps, which had a day's start of us, and we entered Fairfax (Court-House) in the afternoon. There we learned, indefinitely, of the fight at Fredericksburg. But no newspapers, no really satisfying news.

Fairfax is in a terribly injured condition. Roads cut up. Ditches everywhere. We left it, over a most horrible corduroy road, for Fairfax Station, five miles away. That road I traversed, with sick, last summer, when it was a smooth, well-fenced, well-shaded, pretty road. Now it is a corduroy, fences gone, wood cut down. Only one fence remains — that around a graveyard, which stands entire, though large armies have camped all around and passed on. Near Fairfax Station we bivouacked in a pine wood, where trees are lying in every direction, utterly defying order. And we sleep very sound. Rations are, however, given out at night, which were needed. Before leaving Sharpsburg, there had actually been delivered *flour*, for a march! It reminded us of the night before the battle of Antietam, when for the first time for a long while the coffee was sent to us in the *berry*, to men without the possibility of burning and grinding it, and who were to go into battle next morning. On this march, too, we had to pick up forage for horses as best we could, although entitled to a supply. It is not strange, of course, on a march, and nobody could complain. It was worse when, in camp, receipts had to be given for two hundred and five pounds, while the actual weight was one hundred and sixty. Don't think I blame the government for such hitches — as to flour, coffee, or forage ; there never was a government which lavished so much on its armies, or which was more ready to punish fraud or incompetency ; but some of its intermediate officials are — well, not angels.

We had a new illustration, in this movement, of the friction of the new ambulance arrangement. It was necessary to send all the sick to the Smoketown hospital before starting. The senior medical officer of the brigade made a requisition for ambulances. It was not answered until *next day*. Men got sick on the road ; we had one ; no ambulances within *nine miles*. Our surgeon had to put him in a house and leave him, but he was, fortunately, brought on afterwards. The officer in charge of the brigade ambulance train is under nobody's orders except the medical director. Our medical director at Sharpsburg was eleven miles off. Have a brigade train, but let the regiments have each three or four ambulances, subject to the colonel's orders, in care of the surgeon. On the march of Saturday they had to come down a little, and gave each regiment one.*

There is fault in some hospitals, I know, for I have visited them much, and have acted as chaplain temporarily by request of a major-general. I know that coffee (without milk) and bread for breakfast ; bread, boiled potatoes, and boiled meat

---

* Time remedied the friction of the new system. It soon came to work well, with some modifications.

meat for dinner ; and coffee and bread for supper, are not precisely the suitable diet for men just able to sit up ; particularly when government allows most liberally for support — means
to purchase milk, eggs, chickens, &c., being at hand, besides
such portions of the army ration as may be asked for — rice,
molasses, vegetables, &c.   I was told, a day or two since, by
a chaplain of high character, of a hospital he had often visited lately, for which chickens and the like are *paid for* by
government, but he could never find a patient who had seen
them.

The root of the evil is the " military command " of those
in charge.   Sick men should be treated as such in hospitals,
not as mere soldiers.*

I am afraid I am grumbling, but I do not mean to.   Indeed,
I presume that the majority of the hospitals are well managed.   I have seen most excellent ones.   At Frederick, the
one organized by our present surgeon was admirably conducted.   But at Sharpsburg, the surgeon in charge (whether
subordinate or not I don't know) of one building showed himself a pig, and a brutal pig at that.   A fierce " I order ! "
was his natural grunt.   He absolutely refused a sick man, left
there one night by his comrades through mistake, bed, supper,
breakfast, nurse, or medicines, though entreated by a surgeon
who had a heart — the man being low with typhoid fever.
But such swine are rare ; I never saw but one who was his
equal — the pompous pig at Antietam.

—— Still on our march.

---

* The Austrian system of putting the military charge of hospitals into the
hands of a military officer, and giving the surgeon only his proper work, has,
I think, been tried. I know that many surgeons desired it. It relieves the
evil of making the medical attendant a military commander.

FAIRFAX STATION, VA., December 18, 1862.

THOUGH dating from the same place as at last writing, we have not been here in the intermediate time.

On Monday we left the Station.   Reveille was at five A. M., but as we were the rear regiment, to guard the brigade supply train, we had to wait until the train came in with supplies to be loaded into wagons.   It was therefore near two P. M. before we started.   The last previous regiment had over five hours' start, but at Occoquan Creek it was but an hour ahead.

But such a road !   Mud, ruts, corduroy, holes, — such a mixture was never known to me before.   A mile and a half an hour was handsome progress.   About sunset we reached the Occoquan, which we had forded a few miles above, last August ; forded it anew six miles and a half from Fairfax Station ; climbed the opposite hills, still crowned with last winter's rebel earthworks ; moved on a mile, and bivouacked in a tangled wood.

The stars cheated us.   The clear sky promised fair weather. But toward morning it rained ; it blew ; it poured.   We pulled our rubber blankets over us, and went to sleep again. Reveille at five, in a cold, drenching rain.   The men stood it good-naturedly, however.   At seven we moved on, one regiment in advance.

The roads the day before were the worst possible.   That day they beat possibility.   Mud, mud, mud.   The road was ascertained to be fordable in several places, however ; but men who could not swim staid on the banks.   By noon the column had made three miles, but it took till night for the wagons to get so far.   At noon orders came from below to halt, — nobody knew why.   The halt was turned into camp, which means, on the march, building fires, and sitting down on the ground. The wind blew the clouds off, and it came warmer too. We had luxurious quarters — we did. A young pine thicket, with the interior cut out and the walls thickened up with pine branches ; a bed of pine boughs fit for a king, and a huge fire in front. There we slept, five of us in one enclosure, soundly.

Up at five again. Two days' cooked rations in haversacks. Soon on the road — for Dumfries? No, northward! Then we knew that fifteen hundred rebel cavalry, and nobody knew how many infantry, were at Brentsville, threatening Fairfax Station, and our division was to march back to defend that depot of rations. So we did, yesterday, nine miles and a half. Nothing special occurred save a snow squall, — and a little trouble by reason of a brigade running up to us, and trying to get ahead of us, as we were ordered to bring up the rear of ours next behind the wagons. I did not know who the officer was that made the trouble, but he showed importance enough to be lieutenant-general, at least, if not President of the United States.

It seems to us very queer that a whole division should be sent back merely to guard Fairfax Station, a place of no consequence except from its deposit of rations — two thirds of which are kept in cars for fear of accidents. Needed so much elsewhere, it looks strange to see our armies scattered in petty service. So we suppose it presages a general backward movement.

The defeat at Fredericksburg we now learn of with sadness. The papers do not say " defeat," but what else is it, where the army, having crossed the Rappahannock, is three times repulsed in its attempt to carry the enemy's works, — repulsed with terrible loss, — retires across the river in a dark and rainy night, and pulls back all its pontoons to destroy communication? It is simple defeat — that is all. Call it so. Look at it as it is. Give the rebels credit for using, in fortifying, the time in which our army lay quiet in front of Fredericksburg. Their army is no braver than ours. They are miserably deficient in supplies of which we have abundance. They are no *better* armed, have no *more* nor *better* artillery ; but our only late success is Antietam.

Eight days we have been on the road. The weather has generally been wonderfully favorable for this season. But we have had cold and wet, toil and sleepless hours. We try the winter campaign under pleasant circumstances, and we do it cheerfully. But we often wish that the wise people at home, demanding a winter campaign as they sit by their comfortable firesides, with their well cooked food to eat, their warm beds to sleep in when they are tired of urging on the army — could try a week of march and bivouac even before the snows come. We are willing to do what is needful ; but, wise men, let those control the campaign who know enough to do it.

Yet I do not wonder that civilians are astonished at the results of this war. Who is not? With such an army, so large, so brave, always equal, in an open fight, to Southerners, man for man, it is humiliating to see such failures.

FAIRFAX STATION, VA., December 24, 1862.

A WEEK ago it was said to our commander, as we were halted in the road, " Put your regiment into the wood, stack arms, and wait for orders." So it was done, and we have been waiting ever since. Waited so long, indeed, that we are

22 *

about to begin the building of huts, to be made of the small, straight pines which are plenty hereabouts. The weather has been remarkably pleasant for the week past, and little real suffering has been endured.

In the mean time we tender our heartiest sympathies to the Massachusetts men at East New York, on account of their exposure. We read that " the men have passed the last two nights in barracks and tents, sleeping on straw, without any stoves to take the keen edge from the air." Poor fellows! No stoves! The "keen edge from the air!" How could they survive! For the eight days, of which the two were a part, we were marching into the darkness, in bivouac at night, with neither barrack nor tent, rarely ever seeing a wisp of straw, and on part rations; in cold, in wet; eating our dinner in the air when the water in one's cup actually " skimmed over " with thin ice between two drinkings at the same meal. Poor men at East New York! " Barracks and tents! " " Straw! " Why didn't they board at the Astor? or, say the Fifth Avenue, which is thought to be a tolerable hotel? A sad thought strikes me; *have* they been furnished yet with umbrellas, or rubber shoes, or parasols for warm days? have arrangements been made for hair mattresses, or feather beds? *are* they provided with hair oil, and pier glasses? with cologne and hair-dye? These things should be looked into immediately, *immediately !*

These remarks are exclusive of all reference to their rations, which were doubtless villanous. But what say you to short rations, to a regiment within two hundred rods of a commissary's post, on a railroad, eighteen miles from Alexandria? Short rations in spite of the utmost efforts of the regimental officers? So it has been. The ration prescribed by law is not given. The old rule, that rations not drawn should be credited to "company funds," so that needful articles might be purchased, was revoked last February for men in the field.* And, still worse, no back rations can be drawn at all. That is, if a commissary is unable, on some day, or too lazy, to furnish the ration which the men are entitled to, they lose it *forever*. If a sudden movement is ordered, and an article like flour is on hand, which is useless on a march, they must go hungry, although there may be thousands of dollars worth not drawn. The fact is, the ration guaranteed by law is large ; but whether the men get it depends on some commissary's whim entirely. Of course, in such circumstances as those of the Rappahannock campaign of last summer, unavoidable hitches may occur. But, with communications all open, in the very vicinity of Washington, with government furnishing most liberally, — the men who will let soldiers go hungry are scoundrels, if not swindlers.

For the present our corps forms part of the reserve, General Sigel's grand division. We believe in General Sigel, too. I do not believe that any important movement will take place immediately. It always takes time, I have noticed, after every failure, to get ready for another enterprise. But the delay cannot be long. The country demands action. The cabinet crisis of course disturbed all plans ; its passing away restores possibilities. The army, I believe, would have been glad of a reconstruction, but not in the direction things were tending.

I have had two letters attacking my politics. They want to know what party I belong to. They say I believe in a general who is Democratic, and in emancipation, which is Republican. Bosh! I do not "belong to" any party. They never bought me, and of course I don't "belong to" either.

* So it was said then ; but I now think that the ration money is still credited.

I always vote. It is a duty. I never had the good fortune
to vote for a successful candidate for Congress but once ; and
I wish I hadn't done it, for he said in Congress the other
day, that the " old Federalist party was as honest and patriotic a party as ever existed." I sorrow over a vote for an
old Federalist ! But it was done " ignorantly and in un-
belief."

I believe in Union, first, last, and forever. I judge of a
general by no party predilections. I judge of measures by
their need for the restoration of the Union. Slavery is now
to me the greatest obstacle to the perpetuity of our government. The President cannot abolish slavery, but the President has, I believe, just as much right to seize slave property as he has to seize horse property. He claims no right
to abolish slavery, but merely to seize slave property, —
which is a marked distinction. I could not support the administration in anything I believed unconstitutional. I can
support it in what the commander-in-chief does as a soldier.
He wishes to deprive the rebels of their strength ; freeing
their slaves will do it. The regeneration of Southern society
is another matter, something beyond present duty, something
whose devising may appall the wisest man.

Party is the bane of this contest. Party ! I remember a
good church-member in New Hampshire, sound and ortho-
dox, who said he " would vote for the devil, if he was on
the Whig ticket." That's party. I would vote for a pair
of Andrew Jackson's old boots. That's not party, that's
patriotism !

Why need there have been these present dissensions? How
glad we were, after Sumter, to see all party lines obliterated
in love to the Flag ! I remember how, that Monday morning, very early, I took up the familiar *Boston Post* with a lit-

tle trembling. I was rebuked. There was the FLAG. My
hat flew up to the ceiling, to the intense astonishment of several grave people. There was the true ring in that *Post*.
There has been, ever since, true patriotism, though I differ
from it as to some measures. I have read it much, and find
no factious opposition to the administration. So I read
Republican papers. I find true patriotism. Why need they
quarrel? Why were partisans allowed to renew party lines?
Why were calls issued for mere party conventions? Why
was it deemed " necessary to preserve the party organizations," when, if either old party had held aloof, the war
could not have gone on a month? Why exclude one party
from the pettiest town offices? When I was at home —
after Antietam — it seemed to me as if madness had seized
many people. Men calling others " traitors ; " men fighting
their neighbors, when they had better been handling a musket
in Virginia. I was grieved and sick at heart.

The Democratic party is not, with few exceptions, going
to favor rebels. It will prosecute the war in earnest. It
will not hamper the President, much less his generals. The
Republican party, with few exceptions, are in favor of carrying on the war. Let it not hamper the generals. " The
Republican party, *with few exceptions?* " Yes, there are
exceptions. It is well known in some circles that there are
some prominent Republicans who regard the war as a mere
question of boundaries, nothing else.

FAIRFAX STATION, VA., January 2, 1863.

Two things : How we met the enemy at the Occoquan ;
and how I went to the President's reception on New Year's.

News came on Saturday last that the rebels had taken Dumfries. We could hear heavy artillery in that direction. We afterward learned — on the road — that the enemy had captured three regiments at Dumfries, and also two pieces of artillery. Of the artillery loss, there could be no doubt, for we were told by men of the same battery. The stories were true, except that the enemy had not taken Dumfries, nor any regiments, nor the artillery.

But, on Saturday night, an orderly (one always reminds me of the printer's devil), brought commands to be ready to move at any moment, in light marching order. "Light marching order" meant — no knapsacks, but three days' rations in haversacks, and thirty rounds of ammunition per man. The whole corps was under the same orders. So we packed up, in case of accidents while we might be gone; but, knowing the indefiniteness of "a moment's notice," went to bed — or our substitute for bed — as usual. It was wise. In more juvenile campaigning, we should have kept awake. As it was, we slept all night, had a breakfast, and were on the road in less than ten minutes after the order came to "fall in," and so lost our Sunday service.

Six miles and a half to the Occoquan, over the road travelled and retraced a week or two before. The road had greatly improved, however, and artillery and the extra wagons with forage, moved steadily along. Wolf Run Shoals reached — a halt. Then came an orderly to the division commander, with tidings: "Cavalry of the rebels had attacked Dumfries, but had been driven off." "They were passing up toward Fairfax Station." "They had occupied Fairfax Station, and captured our camp, and paroled the guards." It seemed so good a joke that the rebels had gone round and taken a camp and baggage just left, that roars of laughter were heard on

all sides, which would break out anew every few minutes.
When, however, reflection recalled the various items in our
baggage, we didn't see the joke. And gladly did we learn
about nine P. M. that the rebels had not captured the station,
but were only approaching it, while our men left there were
fighting bravely, though steadily being driven back by the
superior force of the enemy. By and by we learned that
the enemy had not attacked our force there, but if they did,
as was evidently their purpose, our men *would* be driven
back. Still later, it was ascertained that the enemy did not
appear to intend an attack there, but were several miles
another way. And still later next morning — the rebels had
gone by way of Burke's Station, four miles above Fairfax
Station — and passed out of our regions.

And that was how we met the enemy at Occoquan River.

But it was a very pleasant sight — that of a whole division
on the two sides of the river. One brigade had been sent
back on the first tidings, but all the rest remained. Some
lovely pieces of artillery, Napoleon guns, marked " Revere
Copper Company," were put in position. And we bivouacked
in the beautiful starlight. There are no such pyrotechnics
as a few thousand bivouac fires. I went once to see the fire-
works on Boston Common, of a fourth of July ; but, pshaw !
they do not compare for a moment with bivouac fires —
particularly in a night of thin mist. One night there, however, was clear and cool. When we woke in the morning,
the water in our canteens was solid ice.

In the forenoon we were ordered back. It took one hour
and fifty minutes to reach camp — six miles and a half. It
seemed like getting home to reach camp again. They had
been somewhat alarmed ; wagons were packed, for precaution's sake, and things generally made ready to move. At

Burke's Station the railroad had been torn up — only to be replaced in a few hours ; the telegraph wire cut — after Stuart, the humorous rebel, had telegraphed to Washington that the last lot of mules was not satisfactory, and he wanted better next time ; and then he had escaped. Mules ! He ought to be satisfied with some of the mules in our army.

I went to Washington. Not to attend the President's reception, for I had forgotten they had such things, but to do divers errands, regimental and personal. One was, to see if the paymaster had frozen up — that worthy having last paid us up to June 30, while some of our men's families were actually suffering at home. I wonder if the paymasters have been paid *themselves* in that time ; or the clerks in the Treasury or War Office, &c., &c., &c.

The railroad to Alexandria is in good order, run as a government road. So, having leave of absence, I got transportation to Alexandria ; showed my pass at the Ferry, which convinced the officials that I did not intend to capture Washington ; hurried about divers errands ; found where the trouble was with our mails ; had a shrewd suspicion that the army would be paid so soon as their clamors brought about some new legislation ; and I went to bed. To bed ! None of your piles of straw ! In a hotel ! None of your bivouacs ! But somehow, I did not sleep much. It seemed unnatural. There was no tattoo — so barbarous are they in our Capital ; no reveille, even.

At Washington City they have evils, such as paved sidewalks, which soon tire one. All sorts of lies were posted on all sorts of stores, about the " best goods in town," the " cheapest store in the city," and all that. Young boot-blacks, with a trap made of a raisin box, wanted to " Black yer boots ! Make 'em shine ! " Newsboys and apple women abounded.

Everybody wanted to sell something ; and being " just from the country," I was *afraid* of city snares.

But the President's reception was to come off January 1st, — for the public at twelve M ; for officers of the army and navy at half past eleven A. M. Of course I preferred the more quiet half past eleven, and the column to be led by the general-in-chief. Thereby one gets rid of the rush. You see they grade things here. The ambassadors went earlier still. It is as somebody said — David Crockett, I think — about dining ; common people dine at twelve ; common clerks in departments at one P. M. ; head clerks at two ; representatives at three ; heads of departments at four ; senators at five ; ambassadors at six ; and the President — he doesn't dine till the next day.

Of course the rush was great — of officers. Even the fossiliferous strata were upturned. Plenty of gay staff officers are in Washington, crowds of doctors — I beg pardon, army surgeons — and several visitors. I had a little repugnance to helping swell the throng ; so did the officers with me. Still, as to the great many officers in Washington, there is a deal of humbug. At the time of the Fredericksburg battle, some New York paper says, a hundred officers were about Willard's. Well, what of it? Willard's is the news rendezvous. Consider how easily a hundred, interested to read the bulletin there, could assemble. First, the general-in-chief is in Washington, and he has a staff, necessarily. Secondly, the quartermaster-general, the adjutant-general, the military governor, the paymaster-general, and the surgeon-general, have each a staff. Third, what military force there is in the city has officers. Fourthly, there is a multitude of surgeons, easily mistaken for army officers, as they wear uniforms. Add to these the convalescent officers just able to move about, and you have *hundreds* necessarily in Washington. Of course the display of epaulets was great.

In the forenoon I went to the " Soldier's Free Library " in Fifth Street, under the care of John A. Fowle, Esq. He has accumulated, mainly from Massachusetts help, about or over two thousand five hundred volumes, excellently selected. I am glad to say that many came from Jamaica Plain, and many from Dorchester. The soldiers in hospital have the free use of the library, which is open daily. An inspection of the entry book will show astonishing results as to the number and character of the books taken. For the first time, novels are rejected by the borrowers.

On New Year's the room was open all day. Coffee, cake, fruit, &c., was furnished freely to all soldiers, with a little present of some books and papers, and Testament (where needed), to each. The crowd was dense and continuous, and the poor fellows seemed *happy.* " This is the most like home of anything yet," I heard one man say. " Yes," responded the others. One of the assistants was a most excellent lady from Dorchester, who took a journey to be present. God blessed her in the gratitude of the soldiers.

Among other gifts was a shirt made by a little girl. The soldiers cheered her again and again. Some of them looked at it and at her picture as if *they* had little girls at home, and it did them good. I copied the writing attached :

> " THE LITTLE FINGERS OF ALICE HEATH,
> Of Bunker Hill,
> Charlestown, Mass.,
> Aged 4½ years, sewed every stitch in this shirt.
> *She loves the Soldiers.*"

Over two thousand men came there, and the soldiers felt better, New Year's, for looking at her work — as well as the pictures and other things provided to make the room cheerful. That soldier's free library is a good thing. I have examined and know.

As to how the President looked at the reception, and what he said — I almost forgot to say — that I did not attend the reception.

But that evening I read the honest, manly, earnest proclamation of freedom; and, apart from the object — the manner in which that object was framed into expression has increased my respect for its author a hundred fold. Who can read it without feeling that the writer is a noble man? So unlike Davis's tissue of lies and bombast — so simple, so direct, so devout. Every man who believes in freedom must do everything in his power to uphold the hands of the President.

FAIRFAX STATION, VA., January 8, 1863.

THERE is no change in our position, barring some re-arrangements of picket duty. Our own regiment has moved into log houses, except that the field and staff are not yet furnished.

Last Sunday I had hoped that we could have public worship. The Sabbath before we had been away on a march to the Occoquan. The weather on the last Sabbath was beautiful, but, alas! there came an order for a corps review. General Slocum reviewed his command. It occupied most of the day, but I cannot describe it, for I did not attend. It was a matter for regret, that, when work on the new log village had been suspended till Monday by our commander, a review should usurp the sacred time which a soldier needs for both bodily and spiritual help. I had purposed a prayer meeting in the evening; but a shower nullified the plan. Such are the frequent obstacles to plans for good.

I tried at Washington to obtain a new supply of reading matter, to secure which was a main part of my errand there a week ago.' But I failed utterly. Now, I receive the welcome tidings that a box of well-selected publications is on its way. I am more than glad; I am grateful. A winter camp with no books, few papers, is a dull place. I have many calls for them, but no supply. A supply could have been accumulated, but no transportation could be afforded. So, small and frequent bundles are the only useful ones.

Still there are many men who read their Testaments, many with Prayer-books. I have seen this, in repeated cases, habitual. Some of these books are much worn. Many of them are gifts of mothers, whose prayers doubtless ascend continu- . ually. One which I yet use was a father's gift the night before leaving home for college. So well I remember the evening that I always think that every other gift Bible here has its vividly remembered time of parting. These Bibles ! what histories cluster around them. Here is *one* history. At the battle of Antietam, as our regiment was for the second time going into the conflict, a soldier staggered. It was from no wound, but in the group of dying and dead through which they were passing, he saw his *father*, of another regiment, lying dead. There too was a wounded man, who knew them both, who pointed to the father's corpse, and then upwards. Onward went the son, by his father's corpse, to do his duty in the line, which, with bayonets fixed, advanced upon the enemy. When the battle was over he came back, and with other help buried his father. From his person he took the one thing he had, a Bible, given to the father years before, when he was an apprentice.

Let me suggest that any friend can send to some soldier, by *mail*, a Testament, at very slight expense. If you do not know whether he has one, bid him, if he is already supplied, give it to some one who has none. Some of our Episcopalians can also send a little book, " Selections from the Book of Common Prayer," published by Dutton. I have seen these made the rule of daily Scripture reading, by some unused to regularity in this respect.

One seldom knows what he does. Last summer, at Little Washington, I gave a small book to an officer belonging to another brigade. Soon after he was taken prisoner. That little book chanced to be in his pocket. Meeting him recently, he said to me, " Do you remember giving me a copy of ——
——, last summer?" I did not at first. " Well, that little book," said he, " has been the greatest comfort to me. It was all I had to read in jail at Richmond, and it was a treasure to me daily." That book he will cherish always, with, I trust, the God and Saviour of whom it tells.

Singing books are useful. The temporary effect which sacred music has is so wonderful that, in the absence of other opportunities, it is well to foster its use. A few nights ago some singing was heard, and the first hymn was one in which occurs the verse —

" When we've been there ten thousand years "—

— sung to " Emmons " (I believe that is the name. I may be wrong as to the name, but I used to like the tune in prayer meetings at home) ; after one verse the camp became entirely quiet. Officers and men listened to the good old hymn, rolling up calmly in the dark woods. It seemed to tranquilize the whole. It is a remarkable fact that, amidst all singing, sacred words bear almost entire sway in camp. If I was a parishioner, I should dislike to vote to " call " a minister who could not sing. But don't take the hint, when I get home, for, alas! I cannot myself sing; yet there is beautiful singing in my home.

These few hints will serve to show that soldiers are impressible, for good or evil, easily. Men in hospital are particularly ready to converse. Indeed, there is no lack anywhere. There seems to be two reasons for this: one is, the circumstances in which we live — or die; the other, that the soldierly frankness, which is the rule in all intercourse, runs through everything. Yet it is a hard place for young men of no rough experience with temptation. There are wicked men, *very* wicked men, in every regiment.

In cases of wounds and death, it is remarkable to see the quickness with which men appreciate and understand Christian truth. God seems to show special grace. With former fears as to death-bed repentances, yet I have seen as good evidences of grace in such cases as I ever saw. I recall one case, where a wounded man said to the chaplain after a severe battle, " I want you to tell me the shortest and most direct road to Jesus Christ." " There is but one road: ' Believe on the Lord Jesus Christ, and thou *shalt be saved;*' commit your soul to him, with your whole heart." The next day the man joyfully said, " *I believe* on the Lord Jesus Christ." He lived for several days in great happiness, though about to leave his strongest tie in one whom he was never to make his wife; and he died in joy.

An old Christian is not injured. His faith is strengthened by army life. He dies in peace. One of ours died recently. He had been long absent, and when he returned the chaplain was sick and absent. He had been a great helper in prayer-meetings; a meek, consistent, faithful Christian. Entering the hospital, the chaplain looked around a moment, and then

saw him. " You have not forgotten me," said the dying man,
with a smile. " No, not you; nor has God, I fully believe."
" *No*," said he, "he is gracious." " Is there anything
you want, or want done?" asked the chaplain. " Nothing.
Christ has done all." True, Christ *has* done *all*. But how
weak our faith sometimes is.

In the Mud, Va., January 30, 1863.

Rain. Mud. Snow.

That is the history of the last week or two.

Orders had, for several days, kept our corps waiting in
readiness. On the 19th a movement forward, simultaneous
with the movement of the whole army. Our corps, General
Slocum's, is part of the grand division reserve of General
Sigel.

Our elegant camp, laid out in streets of uniform width,
with twelve log-houses of uniform size and position to a company, with its well-built chimneys, and its beautifully cleared
ground, had to be left. A day later — we should have remained for weeks. As it was, while the other corps (what
is plural of corps — corps-es?) returned to their huts, ours
had made thirty-five miles of " impossible" marching.

An effort has been made to advance, and it failed. There
is now demonstrated the wisdom of the quiet of a year ago,
in the sick men, the abandoned provisions, the disheartened
spirit. Nobody knows what Virginia winter mud is till he
tries it. And yet even Boston wisdom is still clamoring for
an advance. Suppose the movement had been made a few
days earlier, in dry weather. Then the army would have
been unable to get supplies, located immovably, in most dangerous circumstances. The delay was a blessing.

And now, another change of commanders. General Hooker takes command.

Who wonders that the army of the Potomac is not in the best condition, when its commanders are changed so often? I speak now of no merits or demerits in any one of them, for it is none of my business, nor of course am I qualified. I believe that any commander, whatever one's individual preferences are, has the right to the heartiest sustaining from any person in his command. If I were not in the army, I should try to do the same, without regard to personal predilections. How much more so in present circumstances?

Yet frequent changes do work badly. The men have no time to get confidence. There is a marvellous power in a hearty, enthusiastic faith towards the general. It is half our strength. But we have no time to gain such a faith. It is like a school which has a new teacher once a week.

That the army is in the best possible condition, is absurd.* It is not. The long delay in paying the soldiers their just dues, not only made them discontented — it exasperated them extremely. On their thirteen dollars in season, often depends whether a wife and child shall go cold and hungry, if not go to the poor-house. Such letters from homes, as came, would melt a heart of stone. Payment has been partially made now. Believe me, the long delay in payment, which every soldier firmly believes (whether right or wrong) was unnecessary, has left a bitter feeling not easily to be overcome.

Besides, there is a feeling that we are the football of political movements. Whoever they would like for a general —

---

* True. But it was surprising how rapidly General Hooker changed all this. He went to work quietly, and soon made most marvellous improvements. The army was never in better condition than after a few weeks of his command, — nor in better spirits.

they want somebody long enough to find out his good qualities.

But worse than this, it is felt that there are dissensions in high quarters; that some different leaders fail in a single-minded readiness to obey orders, do their duty, and serve only their country. In some corps, I presume, there is not the discipline there ought to be. I have heard (though I cannot vouch for it) that one specified regiment indulged itself in groaning for a certain general; but this must have been a single instance. In our corps such a thing could not take place.

But with all this, it is absurd to say, as a general thing, that the Potomac army is not perfectly reliable. Notwithstanding any and all grievances, in spite of all disappointed preferences, they will go readily wherever their generals will lead them. They will fight bravely under any general placed over them. They are patriotic, and ready to show their patriotism now, as they have on so many bloody fields. They detest traitors everywhere.

If there is one thing needful now, it is thorough discipline. I mean discipline which shall embrace all, high and low. The commander of this army ought to be an autocrat. Unless he can be so, he cannot succeed. If he is not to be trusted as such, he ought not to be trusted in command.

A little of the same discipline would not hurt all the way up. If a soldier gets drunk on duty, he is surely punished; if insulting, severely punished. The soldier must not speak in censure of Congress; yet that drunken rowdy from Delaware goes drunk into the Senate, refuses to obey orders, draws a pistol on his superior for the time; he goes in the next day still under the power of liquor; arrested, it is true, — but he makes an apology — and such an apology! "If".

he has done certain things, he regrets it. Instead of being
instantly kicked out of the Senate, with the readiness with
which a soldier would be punished, these men, who make
laws to punish soldiers, drop the whole matter. Verily, there
is no need of " speaking disrespectfully " of Congress.

What is to be done with the Potomac army is doubtful.
Rumors from high quarters intimate that it will be broken up
as such ; that a sufficient force will be left in front of Washington, and the remainder used elsewhere. At present, *mud*
embargoes everything, and citizens say that it is likely to do
so for weeks. Perhaps the weather may change. One thing
is certain, mud or no mud, this army will do what it is told
to do, if within the bounds of possibility. There is not one
word 'of truth in the reports of a mutinous spirit, or any
approach thereto, which some papers insist upon.

General Slocum's headquarters are at Stafford Court
House, and his corps are all near him.

An old friend touches me 'up in the *Journal* for growling
at the cheats of quartermasters in the matter of forage. His
hard work to get fodder for his horse he laughs at, and con-
trasts old soldiers and new. Now here is the principle : no
one ever heard me complain of any personal hardship, but no
old soldier will allow his helpless horse to suffer, when in the
immediate vicinity of a quartermaster, who has *ample means*
at hand to fulfil his duty. Just so, an officer who will bear
any hardship himself will growl if his men, who cannot help
themselves, are exposed to useless hunger on account of some
rascally commissary. On a march, unable to get supplies,
nobody complains. But when the means are at hand, and
some official neglects his duty, or swindles the men into hardships. " old " soldiers, and especially old army regular officers,
do feel it " unpatriotic not to find fault " in behalf of helpless

animals or helpless soldiers.   It is a *duty* to prefer compiaint.
" Your *first* duty," said our noble first colonel to his company
commanders long ago, " is *not* to see that *your* quarters are
ready, but your *men's ;* not to get *your* supper, but to see
that your men have *theirs*."   And he set us the example
that helpless dependents should not suffer, because some lazy
or scoundrelly official neglected his duty ; and with it the
example to bear every *personal* hardship with a cheerful face.
I wrote those statements because I knew they would meet
the eyes of men high in office, who would investigate.   When
we (and I include myself) have been eight days without taking
off a boot ; have slept on wet ground and in rain, shelterless ;
have been five days with but four meals ; have been four
nights with less than four hours sleep, and that on the
ground ; have lived on green corn as we plucked it ; have
drank water that an hour's quiet could not make transparent ; have been for weeks at a time without a tent or
other shelter, — with all our officers and men, — we only
smiled at the hardships.   But if a commissary or quartermaster needlessly starves a horse or starves the men, then
an officer who does not attack him is a fool or a knave.   Are
the distinctions plain ?

CHAPTER XI.

THE PREPARATION SPRING.

Stafford Court House, Va., March 6, 1863.

I have been trying a remittent fever. I tried a mild one last October ; and, for variety, a shake or so in December. I don't like them. Fortunately I have been in *the* city while ill ; fortunately, considering the sickness.

I don't like the " remittent." I have a vague recollection of considering one day that it was not myself who was sick, but a crockery image of John Wesley on the mantel ; but I was puzzled to understand how he could have nausea at the stomach, when he was only a bust ; and how his limbs could ache, when he had no limbs. But I am satisfied that the crockery John was right, as the real one was in head and heart. But as to this detestable climate — Virginia will always be as despicable to me as the mean trickery of its convention at secession time. I shall never think so highly of General Washington as I should if he had been born somewhere else — although, poor man, it wasn't his fault.

Government is kind to its sick. An officer sick in Washington may go to hospital (where he must pay his board, which is fair, because he takes cash instead of rations), or to the house of a friend or a hotel-keeper. He " reports " to a surgeon, who has the care of sick officers, if out of hospital.

The surgeon sends one to examine and prescribe. The sick man's name is entered as "under treatment," and is also reported to the provost marshal, who graciously gives a "pass" to the officer. Then the surgeon takes good care of the patient; mine was a most kind and skilful one, Dr. William R. Dewitt, whom I shall always remember with gratitude. Government furnishes medicines of the best quality — its quinine being outrageously bitter, its calomel, ipecac, and opium sufficiently disgusting; but its citrates taste too nicely to be good. Medicines, you know, should taste abominably, else will "children cry for them," which wouldn't do.

Getting out of doors, I heard a few debates at the Capitol. Some of the speeches were *too* disgusting for a sensitive stomach, too ipecac-like, — the vile frauds. Some excited the nervous system unduly, — the miserable treason. But some were a good, healthy tonic; manly, patriotic, noble. I tell you, in the senate-gallery, I felt proud of old Massachusetts and of my native New Hampshire. Senators Sumner and Wilson are *men*, whatever their imperfections. How some of the traitors did cringe under Senator Wilson's lash. You can't spare that man, nor can the country. He is too useful, too manly, too honest, too able, to be spared. Senator Clark had the true ring. So did some war-Democrats; in fact, I guess *I* am a "war Democrat;" I mean when I get home; now I don't know any distinctions but patriot and traitor. Unless the country comes to that same position, its speedy ruin is certain. I see you have a "Union League" in Boston. Good, but I belong to a better one; it numbers seven or eight hundred members, and it bears the splendid title of the "Massachusetts Second." There is room for a few more members in it now. It had more, but they are buried at

24

Winchester, at Cedar Mountain, at Antietam, and in many a wayside grave. Do not, O home friends, do not now yield to treason; else these men have died in vain.

To get back to camp requires some circumlocution. Tired of delay, six days before my sick leave was out I applied for the papers to return. The surgeon gives a paper releasing one from medical care, ordering him to his regiment, and sending him to the provost marshal. That functionary takes his " pass" and keeps it, and indorses on his paper from the surgeon " pass returned," and sends him to the " transportation officer," who gives him the paper entitling him to pass on government boat and railroad to his specified destination, good for the next day only. The man thus sent back had to sign a paper at the surgeon's office, stating his residence in Washington; which residence is visited next day to see if he has gone.

So, with several direful prognostications from medical authority,* I took the boat for Aquia Creek. For the first time, I went down the magnificent Potomac. I saw, for the first time, our sacred Mount Vernon. In a few hours, a small bay filled with vessels, showed the creek. Steam tugs were puffing around and across. Loaded and empty vessels were lying around. On shore, half a dozen locomotives were charging in various directions. A busy crowd was on the wharf. We showed our " passes," and went ashore; found a train of baggage cars, and speedily were at Brook's Station, a flourishing village of one house. Then such a road for three miles. I thought I had seen bad roads before, but I never had.

How pleasant it was to get into camp; to shake hands; to see the evening parade; to hear tattoo and taps; to sleep

* Unfortunately realized before long.

under canvas again ; in fact, to return to a place of order,
system, and true civilization.   It was a luxury, too, to see
real soldiers, instead of the poor fellows condemned to the
stupidities of Washington — that is, when one is well.   It was
a comfort to find that we had *five hundred* men fit for duty.
Never has ours seemed in better condition.   Drill, company
and battalion, and officers' recitations, have kept up the character of our regiment to its old standard.   Health, too, is
greatly improved.   The order of General Hooker has insured
good rations — fresh bread, vegetables, &c., in abundance ;
and the effect is most apparent.   Indeed, the new regime has
improved the army very greatly.   Merit is commended.
Inefficiency finds no mercy.   A healthy *tone* is perceptible.
Everybody feels that the army is on a fighting basis, and will
have work and success yet.

As to the recognition of merit — the first order I heard
read was one commending certain regiments for efficiency
and discipline.   Orders now allow a certain number of
absences to officers and men.   But many regiments are pronounced so deficient that no more " leaves " are to be granted,
and all absentees are recalled.   Others, medium, are allowed
their present privileges.   Only eleven in this army are
highly commended, and, as reward, are allowed an increase
of fifty per cent. of leaves of absence.   Among these is, of
course, ours, and, I was glad to hear also, the First and
Twentieth Massachusetts.   The language of General Hooker
is, — " have earned high commendation."   Only one Massachusetts regiment falls under absolute condemnation.

Our Colonel Quincy is expected back immediately.   Wounded while bravely engaged at Cedar Mountain, then long a
prisoner at Staunton, he has had a lingering recovery, even
if now thoroughly well.   He left us as a captain ; he returns

by regular promotion, our colonel, and will, without doubt, maintain the regiment in its steady excellence. I well remember, in the pursuit of Jackson last year, how, when sick, he sprang from the ambulance to put himself at the head of his men, while the shot and shell were briskly flying about.

Among other changes of officers, Dr. Stone, our highly successful surgeon, is absent, probably to occupy a position in another corps. Major Mudge, for some time in command, has been obliged to go home from sickness, temporarily. Captain Shaw * becomes colonel of the Fifty-fourth. General Gordon is again unable, after trial, to endure the hardships of camp, and is assigned to duty at Washington.

STAFFORD COURT HOUSE, VA., March 11, 1863.

DID I speak of Stafford Court House as being a village of one house? If I did I was wrong. Careful explorations have satisfied me that there are *two* houses, besides a jail and a court house. This large town is situated in a dreary waste of worn out lands, and is several miles from anywhere. Digging into the ground, one finds, a few feet down, vast quantities of shells. Does that imply that the land was once under the water? If so, it was a mistake, humanly speaking, ever to have raised this miserable tract to daylight. So far I have seen no aborigines, though a few scattered houses indicate the former presence of a partly civilized race. The main house is General Sigel's headquarters. Half a mile eastward, General Slocum, our own corps commander reigns. Five or six miles nearer the Rappahannock, General Hooker is to be found — whom I have never seen but once, and then I had only a glimpse in the tumult of Antietam.

* This was Robert G. Shaw, who fell at Wagner.

But while one may not have *seen* General Hooker, every one feels that General Hooker *commands*. It is really surprising to see the ease with which he has taken actual control of the Potomac army.. Every now and then appears some straightforward order, which shows that he knows exactly the condition of one or every corps. Merit is commended; sluggishness reproved. A soldier seems to feel that if he does something especially worthy of praise, General Hooker will understand it. There is, too, a returning confidence that when something is attempted it will be done. As to "demoralization," I suppose those stories are about ended. No "demoralized" individual would meet with any leniency, nor a traitorously inclined person with any mercy. There are no sympathies here, so far as I can discover, with the school of Connecticut or New Hampshire "copperheads," I say "copperheads," but "woodenheads" would be more appropriate — to think that peace is *possible*, even were a separation to be assented to.

When we consider the circumstances which have been dexterously taken hold of, I am not surprised at the growth of a peace party. But when we look at the real questions underlying all circumstances, it is perfectly astonishing that any person can advocate the South side. Are we prepared to yield to the demands of traitors? Can we assent to the establishment, out of ourselves, of a slave empire? Could we surrender the loyal citizens of Missouri, West Virginia, Tennessee, Kentucky, New Orleans, to the cruelties of brutes by birth, and tyrants by education? Can *Northern* men advocate the division of their country? Those infatuated persons who give "aid and comfort" to the enemy, by encouraging the South to persevere in their rebellious butcheries, the provost marshal's cord is their just due for mere treason.

24 *

But there can be no good reason to suppose the people of any party will follow such leaders. It must be that only a few men are so besotted. The masses will never follow men who would lead us to national ruin. The party which carried through the glorious war of 1812–15; which insisted upon and obtained redress from Mexico; which has always stood by the old flag; — it always will maintain the country's honor. I believe it. The signs show that it is so.

But men who are in favor of perseverance for the right, are liable to make mistakes when they separate too nicely the administration and the government. I heard this distinction dwelt upon in some speeches at Washington; but while the speakers attacked the errors of the administration ferociously, I did not hear them censure the rebels with any severity. I could not see them, in general, voting for measures indispensable to success. I listened in vain for any plans as substitutes they would stand by. Indeed, what substitute could be offered? Their grievance was that the present administration was in power. But that cannot be helped for two years. The government and the administration are distinguishable in theory; but the government can be carried on only by the administration. Doubtless there have been mistakes, many mistakes, in the conduct of the war. There have been measures that, as an individual, I intensely disliked.* But is that a reason why I, or anybody else, should withhold the allegiance due to our country? Is that a reason why I should try to weaken the hands that are lifted to strike down this infernal rebellion?

---

* Yet it is surprising that so few mistakes have been made. When the war is ended, and men look calmly at its history, they will admire the far-seeing plans and single-hearted honesty of our President. I wish I could say as much for all his subordinates. Some of them we heartily detest.

Men do not like arbitrary arrests. Do they any better like Jefferson Davis's arresting, hanging, scalping loyal men, without the shadow of even their own pretended laws?

They do not like the suspension of *habeas corpus*. Are our friends at the South enjoying that privilege?

They do not like the freeing of slaves. Do they like better the Southern custom of seizing our free negroes while under a flag of truce, and selling them into slavery — as at Manassas?

They do not like the arming of blacks. Do they like it better when their own soldiers are shot by blacks forced into the rebel armies — as in Jackson's army last year; in which (and the proof is ready) blacks and whites stood side by side in the ranks as soldiers?

They think it is a "cruel" war. Do they like better the decoying men by a flag of truce, and then shooting them, as at Harper's Ferry? the shooting unarmed negroes, as in Kentucky? the murder of women, as in Tennessee? the making of drinking cups of Yankee skulls, and spurs of jawbones, as at Bull Run?

So loyal, so meek, so humane, so liberal is Davis's rule — no violation of laws, no treason, no cruelty, no tyranny — is that the reason why our administration is assailed? Does anybody's *tastes* lead him to sympathize with this treason? If so, he is hopelessly corrupt. He is putrid. Even the southern buzzards would leave his carcass untouched.

We are *all* rejoiced at the conscription act. I have heard no dissenting voice. I argued vehemently for such an act last summer. It ought then to have passed. I had some little opprobrium for attacking the bounty system as outrageously costly, unjust to the old soldiers, and low in its appeals, and eventually to be abandoned. You know how comfortable

one feels when he can wisely nod his head and say, " I *told*
you so ! " I nod my head just so, and rejoice that Congress
came to the same conclusion. We are all hoping that there
will be the proper nerve shown in enforcing it. It is not
unjust. Every man owes his life to his country, if his country needs it. The humane exemptions in the act are
admirable. Others than those, rich or poor, ought not to
hesitate.

But it is not to be overlooked that before these levies can
come into the field most critical months will pass by. The
dawn of a suitable moment will start the armies. The South
is putting everything into the field ; boys and old men, as
well as the able-bodied. Evidently they have staked everything on the coming campaign. They must succeed now, or
fall. And does not everybody see that their *only* hope is in
Northern divisions? A united North can raise armies after
the Southern ones are destroyed. Sickness alone will ruin
the rebel forces in time, and they cannot afford to wait.
Will any patriot at such a time, when the superior resources
of the government are beginning to tell — will any one now
fail by word and deed to strengthen the cause of his country,
and of (what is more) the right? Let complaints be laid
aside now. We will settle them by and by at the ballot-box ;
and with them we will bury every Northern traitor in a political grave from which there is no resurrection.

The health of the army is still improving. Food is good
— thanks to a government always liberal, and to the general
at our head. Drill is had, with us, twice a day. and our officers study and recite to the regimental commander.

STAFFORD COURT HOUSE, VA., March 19, 1863.

No change yet. But there is drill in this corps three hours a day. In our regiment the officers recite daily to the colonel, and in turn have classes of non-commissioned officers, both in some military work. The men amuse themselves hugely with games of ball at all unoccupied hours. There are but three men in the regimental hospital, and they are not very sick. A good spirit prevails, with a remarkable unanimity in favor of the conscription law and of aversion to traitors. The commanding general continues to grow in confidence, and thorough order prevails. Each man keeps his supply of sixty cartridges, and expects to use them by and by. Yesterday we had a division review. It was a very pretty sight. The three brigades and three batteries made a fine appearance ; of course you know which regiment was the best. I never saw our men more statue-like in line, nor march better in column of companies or by flank.

This review was before General Slocum. Our regiment is one of six making up the brigade commanded by General Gordon ; the brigade is one of three making up General Williams's division ; the division is one of two forming General Slocum's corps ; and the corps is one of — several — composing the army of the Potomac. Formerly there were three grand divisions, each made up of several corps ; but General Hooker, on taking command, abolished them, and had each corps report directly to him, which seems to work capitally. To-day a review is expected before General Hooker.

Day before yesterday we heard cannonading at a distance, at intervals, all day, but nobody has enlightened us as to its whereabouts. There are no other special items, except that, after a careful and patient recconnoissance on Stafford Court House, I find that the village has *three* houses instead of two ; this is a final estimate.

.

———

WHILE the position of the army of the Potomac is unchanged, indications point to early movements. Not, perhaps, by any direct advance, for the roads are yet in execrable condition. Twenty-four hours rarely pass without either rain, snow, or hail. When the sun comes out, it dries up the ground very rapidly. The rains are soon over. But, like the master who told his servant, " I get angry quick, but then I am no sooner angry than I am over it again," and was replied to, " Yes, and no sooner over it than you are mad again," — so it is no sooner fair than it rains again. Last night it rained beautifully. Don't you remember how much you liked, when a boy, to go into an attic to hear the rain? Well, a tent is *all* attic. Doubtless the sentries did not enjoy it so much. Corduroy roads have been built in various directions (and I wish no worse penalty on the copperheads than to have to ride over a corduroy road, six hours a day for life), but even the corduroys are sometimes under water or under mud. Still, I think that after each rain the ground is a little harder than after the preceding.

Whether there will be a battle near Fredericksburg, is doubted. It is exceedingly questionable, good judges say, whether the rebels can risk one there. Of course this implies that their communications are threatened, in which case they must come out and fight, or retreat. It is suspected that they are now preparing to evacuate. Their pickets have commenced firing on ours, and they have a large cavalry force threatening us on the north, which looks like a retreat of their main army, as they are always very ferocious somewhere when about to draw back their armies.

If there should be a battle, there is every confidence of success. Never has this army been in better condition, if ever as good. It is in fine spirits. It is well fed. It is healthy. It is most thoroughly equipped. The general seems to know everything, everywhere. Officers everywhere understand that negligence is not to be winked at. Inspections of everything seem to be going on. Medical officers have been informed that the army has been long enough in service to presume them thoroughly acquainted with their duties. A fighting basis is the rule, and ability to move rapidly.

When the work is begun, there will be a tremendous campaign. The rebels are suffering. Their armies are as large as they can ever be. Their leaders are desperate. On the other hand, if our general's ability, as at present seen, is a guarantee of the future (and the army unitedly believes it), he will show a daring, a rapidity, and a skill, when he does move, which will make decisive battles. If the rebels fight fifty miles from Richmond, as they now are, and are defeated, their army will be annihilated.

The recent cavalry exploit has raised that branch in general estimation. They needed it bad enough. I remember a cavalry officer, who returned from a slight advance upon inferior forces, with the astonished remark, " General, they've got *guns* there !" Poor fellow — he is not in service now. General Hooker has been putting his cavalry into fine condition. In fact, he puts everything in that condition. He has, too, I believe, one element of success in this — that he has a thorough confidence in his *destiny*, and has had it since the war began. The army believes it too.

Mr. Alvord is still working away with good results. He is near Stoneman's Switch, on the railroad. The Christian Commission has four regular stations for supplies — Aquia Creek, Belle Plain, Stoneman's Switch, and Falmouth. One of their agents, Rev. Mr. Smith, of Pepperell, I had the pleasure of meeting a few days ago. That he is active and useful, his Massachusetts friends need not be told. The Commission is just now busily distributing Testaments to the soldiers, for which there is occasion. I have the promise of some from the Commission, for which I shall be grateful. And none the less grateful, but more, to various friends who send small packages by mail or otherwise, sometimes anonymously, but always welcome.

STAFFORD COURT HOUSE, VA., April 8, 1863.

SATURDAY evening we had a ferocious snow storm. Sunday was a wet and uncomfortable day. Nevertheless, in spite of the weather, the time passed cheerfully with me, in visiting many of the habitations of our little town, in distributing a good large supply of Sabbath reading, both in our camp and to our companies detached at General Slocum's headquarters, and in a couple of hours spent with that Christian gentleman, General Howard. In fact, it was as pleasant a Sunday as I have had for a long time. Part of this is doubtless due to improved tone of bodily system caused by long rides in the saddle. The best gymnasium in the world is a saddle — with a good horse under it. The next best is Dr. Dio Lewis's. But give me the saddle, with a rubber coat and cap cover strapped to it in case of rain, and some cavalry boots as the enemy of both rain and mud. You are on the road of health, always provided you have some errand, even it be only amusement. "Taking exercise" merely *for* exercise is of very little use. It is just as great a humbug as " early rising," which I am glad has been rooted out of the rules of our colleges and seminaries.

In various long trips I have taken quite extensive views of our army. Its vastness, its order, its equipment, its stores, its contentment, astonish me. Do not be anxious for the army of the Potomac. When the time comes it will do what it attempts.

On Monday, my brother chaplain of the Tenth Maine and myself took such a trip. We made a day of it. Starting in the morning, though rain was threatened, we took the road towards Falmouth. How pleasant is the saddle, with another saddle, and a genial and congenial companion in it, with nothing to do, and all day to do it in. The road was picturesque. A young river meandered down its centre, towards which sloped down beautiful banks of mud on either side, while the fields were delightfully variegated by alternate patches of snow and swamp. You have your choice of path ; whichever you take you will wish you had tried the other. Like the complaining toper, it is not the length of the road, but its width that troubles you, as you tack continually. Three or four miles, as measured by line, brought us to a by-road, which, turning towards the left, took us into the woods. All along we found tracks, which we recognized as those of Mr. Alvord's wagon. We followed them, and they led us correctly. Moral : It is safe to follow Mr. Alvord's tracks ! Two or three miles through the wood, — ten miles of swamp (ridiculously estimated at only half a mile !) — Potomac creek to ford, — a hill, — a long plain, delightful for a canter, — and we saw the Stoneman's Switch station, and, near it,

Mr. Alvord's meeting-tent. We heard singing as we dismounted. We found there quite a number of chaplains, with more soldiers. A two hours' meeting passed off rapidly, and the chaplains made mutual acquaintance. Several chaplains disclosed their difficulties. I had occasion to thank God inwardly that I had no acquaintance with many of their obstacles ; for Providence had cast my lot among gentlemen. I wish that some of our people at home, who give ear and tongue to disparagements of chaplains, had been there. They would be ashamed of themselves. I enter my protest against such insinuations. I assert, after nearly two years' observation, that the average of energy, ability, and uprightness among the chaplains is not surpassed by the average of those qualities among the ministry of even New England and New York. I cannot see why Christians should try to disparage this class. It is an outrage. It hurts their influence here, of course.

We learned that a review was to take place a mile off, and after the meeting we went thither. It was the review of a whole cavalry corps. Long lines of the cavalry stretched for vast distances, necessarily making various angles, on account of their great number. They were all motionless and silent when we first saw them, save their fluttering pennons. But in a few minutes, as the reviewing party rode rapidly up, every sabre flashed in the air, and the music burst forth, to salute a man at the head, who, amidst the golden ornaments of generals, wore the plain black dress of a civilian. He was the commander of all — the President of the United States — and these generals were only his creatures. That simply dressed man, riding bareheaded in courtesy, wielded a more imperial sway than any monarch in the world. An army of near a million was obedient to his word. Two millions more

were subject to his call to arms. Yet, God help the President
of the United States ! For he needs it. He had a careworn
face, while we knew he had an honest heart. Though a
mighty army lay there, yet plainly in sight were the hills
behind Fredericksburg, frowning with works and manned
with enemies, — a section of the thousand miles of frontier in
which our morning reveille is answered by rebel drums.

A natural curiosity took us to the brink of the river a mile
and a half off. The Lacy mansion stands near it, and from
the terraces of its garden, almost overhanging the narrow
stream, we looked down into Fredericksburg. An officer
kindly pointed out the memorable localities. Here was the
main crossing, just on our right. There the street by which
our forces advanced. Beyond, the basin into which they entered. And over all, the rebel earthworks which sent death
to our soldiery. Between us and these works lay the town,
less shattered than I had expected to find it, — and in some
of its streets rifle pits were visible. The path worn by the
rebel sentries one could almost throw a stone upon, and the
sentinels were walking their posts. Where we stood were
loyal watchmen. The owner of the deserted house is in the
rebel army ; most of his trees are cut down ; his shrubbery
is gone ; his garden is a waste ; but what moved me most,
a child's rocking-horse stood by a door, unharmed in all the
strife.

Half a mile back are the ruins of the Philipse mansion.
The walls remain standing in part, and show that the fire had
destroyed a beautiful edifice. It was of brick, nearly cruci-
form in shape, and of fine proportions. Standing on an
eminence, it commanded a view of miles of beauty. Desolate
now, a once happy home. Who can help pitying these
misguided men ?

Turning southward we came near the plain headquarters
of General Hooker, who lives in a tent, as a soldier ought.
A mile southeast, over roads fenceless, of course, and hard
to trace, we suddenly come upon the camp of the First
Massachusetts. For the first time I had the pleasure of
meeting my excellent brother Cudworth, whose hearty welcome was delightful. As long time as we dared remain soon
passed. Then a mile or more brought us to the Seventeenth
Maine, who are building an elegant camp of split white oak
— the best camp I ever saw. The good appearance of the
men, and the kind hospitality of the officers, made me respect
my father's native State more than ever.   .

It was near sunset, and we had six miles to go, a wide
creek to ford, a hard road to travel, obscure paths to track out.
Long before we were at home darkness settled down upon
us. Passing through lonely valleys, we heard the tattoo of
artillery bugle mellowed by distance, on the one side, and the
softened drum beat on the other. The robins and blackbirds
had ceased their day's music. Horses picked their way over
hard corduroy, whose only comfort was that you could not
sink far in their mud. The last mile was not even corduroy,
but swamp, and ditch, and brook, which led us to rejoice when
we came upon our lights just as tattoo was advising everybody
to go to bed.

We had stopped at only a few camps. But these we
selected. Everywhere are camps. For prominent lines of
travel, are miles upon miles of corduroy. It is a vast army.
As for roads, if the Virginian natives ever return, their high-
ways will undoubtedly be these Yankee built corduroys. This
State, if peopled by a decent race, would be a magnificent
State, after all. But their worn-out farms need Yankee culture. Their ignorant population need the Yankee school-

master.   The State needs, in fact, to change hands.   The
negroes themselves would, I am satisfied, be far better prop-
erty-holders than the late ones ; for so far as I have seen
Virginia, after taking out the few persons of high culture, the
average ability, sense, and thrift of the *white* Virginian is
decidedly below that of the *black* Virginian.

STAFFORD COURT HOUSE, VA., April 15, 1863.

ON Thursday last the Twelfth army corps was reviewed
by the President.   The review on a preceding day of several
corps together surpassed that of the Twelfth in point of numbers, of course, but not in soldierly characteristics.   The
Twelfth corps, General Banks's old command, — numbered as
the Eleventh till after Antietam, — is unsurpassed in this army.
At least, so declared the authority which all respect ; who
also stated that but one other would bear a comparison
with it.

The day of review was wonderfully beautiful.   The corps
was ready on the ground at noon precisely, as ordered.   Then
it waited.   The President was reviewing the Eleventh corps
in the morning, and it was half past three when he reached
ours.   I was where I saw him when he approached, and saw
his suite following.   He is a good rider.   Mounted on a
horse with a general's caparisons, he dashed on through
mud, swamp, and ditches, without the slightest hesitation,
evidently to the disadvantage of some of his followers.   The
twenty-one guns saluted him, and he rode very rapidly along
the lines (if " lines " they were), while the escort of lancers,
with their gayly fluttering red, formed three sides of a square
around the spot occupied by the President's wife and the

25 *

chief military dignities, and in which the President soon
stationed himself.   He was dressed in black, with a curious
article on his head, the upright part being cylindrical, very
much like a section of stove pipe, with a flat roof, and a horizontal and circular rim at the lower part.   It must be quite
stiff, and I should judge, painful to the head.   I have heard
it intimated, however, that such absurd things are quite common at the North.

When the President had taken his position, the corps prepared to pass in review.   The two divisions had been formed
in two parallel lines, each line consisting of the regiments
formed by divisions (two company front), and closed in well.
Suddenly the bugle gave the order, and at once each regiment, moving at double-quick, changed front.   The effect
was indescribably beautiful.   Then the marching ; each regiment still formed by divisions, moving at quick step around
the field.   The ground was rolling, and the sight of regiments
disappearing in the hollows, or emerging, was picturesque.
As the consolidated drum corps of each brigade reached the
President, they wheeled to the left, and there remained to
give the " ruffles " as the flag of each regiment was successively bowed in honor to the chief magistrate.   I need not
say that the beautiful neatness, the perfect lines, and the firm
and soldierly step of ours received commendation in high
quarters.   I never saw it look better.

As pageantry, such a review was wonderful.   As reality,
it was the exhibition of qualities for the field of blood.   Those
same regiments must march into deadly combat.   Those
lines will be thinned.   Alas ! for the necessity ! but who can
grudge our country its rights?   Perhaps, before this is printed, the great trial will have passed.   Indications, which I

better not mention, point to early operations. Movements already made are momentous — you will have learned then.

For movement, every soldier, officer, or private is to take eight days' rations upon his person. Each enlisted man has. his complement of sixty rounds of amunition, while near reserves will be at hand. No man can " straggle," no man can " fall out," without the surgeon's pass, and then only to an ambulance. Superfluous blankets, coats, and flannels are already sent away ; " throwing aside every weight." A falterer in battle is to be shot. Division hospitals are arranged for, under the care of men already selected, and the corps of operators already named. Other surgeons, mentioned by name, are to accompany their regiments, choosing sheltered places near their own. Men detailed to remove the wounded are to be distinguished by a green badge on the left breast. Never have I seen such perfect organization as this army now has. The men are in good spirits also. They know that there is a probability of great events, and they feel confident of success.

But to-day it *rains*, rains *hard*. I don't know what effect this may have on plans. It *may* affect them greatly. But only for a time. The army is ready.

CHAPTER XII.

TO CHANCELLORVILLE AND RETURN.

STAFFORD COURT HOUSE, May 7, 1863.

Some eight miles westward from Fredericksburg, and about three south of the Rappahannock, is — or was — one brick house, occupied by " V. Chancellor," which, with one other house, constituted " Chancellorville." The house stood by the " plank road " which runs from Fredericksburg to Orange Court House. V. Chancellor was postmaster, and his total receipts for a quarter of last year, as I found by his official report to the confederate postal authorities, were $10.75.

The birds were singing around Chancellorville. Violets were smiling in vast abundance. The pine-wood air was fragrant with spring.

The house is burned. The air is filled with sulphureous fire and with thunder. The flowers are wet with the blood of thousands. But the whippoorwills never stopped their mournful utterances in the conflict.

On Monday morning, April 27, our reveille sounded at half past three o'clock. The long waiting for movement was ended. Months of labor had put the army into the finest condition. Organization was perfect. The commissariat, as it proved, would not fail. The hospital department was admirably prepared. The pioneer corps was wonderfully efficient. The plans of the leader had been matured at leisure.

On that beautiful morning our Twelfth corps, General Slocum, took the road towards Warrenton, each man carrying eight days' rations and sixty cartridges. The Eleventh corps, General Howard, followed the Twelfth. Ten or twelve miles brought the corps to within a mile of Hartwood Church by half past three P. M., and there it bivouacked.

No drum beat the next morning, but all were quietly waked at half past three. Past six o'clock the column moved (our regiment at the rear of our division), the Eleventh corps in the advance, on the road toward Kelley's Ford, which crosses the Rappahannock some miles above the spot where that river receives the waters of its tributary Rapidan. It was a wet day, but the troops made seventeen miles. Two miles from Kelley's Ford our corps bivouacked; while the Eleventh, being in advance in its turn, crossed the river on pontoons, and our advance cavalry drove in or captured rebel pickets.

On Wednesday morning our corps, starting at daylight, moved on over the river, and passed the Eleventh,—the Second Massachusetts at the head in the road, flanked by the Twenty-seventh Indiana and the Third Wisconsin, on the right and left, as skirmishers. The Twenty-seventh Indiana and the Second Massachusetts by and by changed places. Through woods and underbrush ours went on, till close to Germanna Ford on the Rapidan. At this crossing the rebels were building a bridge. They had a small force on the other side, with rifle pits, and these were surprised. The Third Wisconsin moved straight to the ford, while the Second Massachusetts, wheeling to the left, came out on an open height. A few minutes' fire killing some, and our two regiments having a cross fire on the road by which the rebels must leave, white signals fluttered from the rifle pits, and a hundred and three surrendered, and were ordered to cross the river to our side. Our men then forded. The river was very high and very swift, and three men of the Twelfth corps were drowned. The pioneers of our division built a bridge for the remainder of our forces. Our corps bivouacked a mile and a half beyond the river; — that same stream, towards which we were moving last August, when we met the sad field by Cedar Mountain.

Thursday was a drizzling day. At eight o'clock the troops moved, General Geary, with our Second division in advance. Our regiment was the rear guard of our corps. Not far from the river the plank road was reached, on which a march of twelve miles towards Fredericksburg brought the corps to near Chancellorville, — where our brigade (at last), under General Rogers, turned to the right into the woods, and again to the right, and there bivouacked in line of battle, a little in advance of the plank road. This evening came an order from General Hooker congratulating the Fifth, Eleventh, and Twelfth corps on their operations for the three days, which he characterized as "a succession of brilliant achievements," and saying that the enemy must "ingloriously fly," or "come out from behind his defences and give us battle on our own ground, where certain destruction awaits him."

Friday, May 1, was a beautiful day. It being "muster day," that work was begun as usual. But when it was half done in our regiment orders came to move. The result was a march of two miles in the Fredericksburg direction. As I understand it, this was part of a demonstration which forced the enemy to retire from United States Ford, which I take to be about ten miles up from Fredericksburg. This movement was successful, and other troops were enabled to cross at that ford, over which three pontoon bridges were thrown, which afterwards became our main channel of communication with the north of the river. During the movement just alluded to there was sharp musketry on the left, and artillery fire was rapid overhead of our brigade from both sides. After a few hours the brigade returned to their old place. The shot here fell dangerously, but no active service was required. The troops were under arms all night.

On Saturday morning orders came to intrench. Logs were felled and built up breast high, and abatis constructed in front, — a work the whole army was engaged in. The line as now established was, perhaps, four miles long. The Eleventh corps had the right. Unfortunately its right rested on no position giving any natural advantages, — abruptly ending in accessible ground. The Twelfth corps joined the Eleventh on the left of the latter. Another corps, I do not know what, rested on the river below. Our line, therefore, commenced on the river (that was the left), below United States Ford, and ran in a rather irregular course so far as to show a convex front to the enemy. Its weak place proved to be the unprotected right flank.

About half past four P. M., while furious fighting was going on at the left, it was said that the enemy was retreating. A long line of wagons was visible, and some scattering forces. Whether this was a ruse or not it acted like one. Orders came to the Twelfth corps to advance on the wagons and troops. It left its intrenchments, therefore, a very small guard remaining with the knapsacks in the line of works, and advanced over a mile. Then the noise of battle was heard on the extreme right. The Twelfth corps was ordered back.

There was need of it. The rebels had massed heavy forces on the right flank, completely turning it. The cavalry outside had given no alarm, when suddenly Jackson opened a tremendous fire, enfilading the line of the Eleventh, and then poured in his columns. Taken in such way the Eleventh could not be relied upon. They gave way. Their general succeeded in rallying a small force, but his best brigade had been detached, and it was too late to save the line.

When the Twelfth corps got back to its line most of its works were already in the possession of the enemy. But crossing the intrenchments it took position at a right angle to them, facing westward. " Stand steady, old Third brigade ; stand firm, old Second Massachusetts ; " — was the address of the brigadier. Of course the Third brigade would, with such regiments as Colonel Colgrove's Twenty-seventh Indiana and Colonel Hawley's Third Wisconsin, and ours. So stood the whole line. The firm front and the tremendous artillery fire checked the enemy, while General Sickles's corps attacked in another direction. It was now dark. The imminent danger of the annihilation of the wing was past, and the rebels admitted that — with all the damage done — they had failed of their main object. A new line for the right was eventually established, — that wing swinging back and resting on the river above United States Ford, — infinitely stronger than the original one, and considerably shorter. The left remained in its original position. The hospital of our corps had been removed from Chancellorville, having been enveloped in a tornado of missiles, and was taken across the river — the last surgeon there being killed at the door of Chancellor house. All night firing was going on in every direction.

Sunday morning the fight grew into a tempest. The Third corps, I think, changed position. Some troops ran back over the Twelfth, and the enemy dashed up, but the Twelfth held its line and repulsed the enemy. The rebels attacked furiously, but were splendidly met. Of our own brigade, the Second Massachusetts and the Third Wisconsin, well mated on many a field, were together. The corps had so long a line to occupy that there were few reserves, and no second line. Coolly and orderly our brigade pressed back the enemy in front of it a quarter of a mile. Three rebel lines it broke successively in the several hours' steady fighting. In the last, ours came against a South Carolina regiment, said by prisoners to be the First. Three times the Palmetto flag was shot down, but was always gallantly raised again. Three times our flag changed hands. At last the Palmettoes sullenly yielded.

Our line was out of ammunition. It sent for more. In the mean time the officers took all the remaining ammunition from the fallen and distributed it. From the bodies of dead or wounded rebels in the ground gained, were cartridges taken and returned to the enemy. Then, with nothing left, bayonets were fixed, and at "order arms," our men quietly stood until the answer came back from high quarters, "I cannot make ammunition." The front line was then ordered to retire, which it did orderly and most bitterly, and ours fell back to Chancellorville, losing still by artillery fire, to replenish its cartridge-boxes. Thence it was ordered to the cross road running to United States Ford, while the right wing was swinging back on the river.

Then came news that General Sedgwick, with his separated corps, had, in the morning, brilliantly carried the Fredericksburg heights, which the enemy had greatly weakened when they had swung their line around on its right at the river, as on a pivot, to confront our main army. Tremendous firing was going on below, supposed to be an attack on

26

Sedgwick in the coming evening, he having been ordered to
move up and join General Hooker. The night was hideous
with the sound of battle. After dark, the Twelfth corps was
sent to the extreme left of the main army, and rested in
excellent intrenchments on the river.

On Monday there was no activity above, except at isolated
points, at which the rebels were easily repulsed. General
Sedgwick's fight still continued, and the query was whether
the enemy had not moved his force against that general, near
Banks's Ford. Whether so or not we lay idle ; and that general, who had obtained control of that ford, was obliged to
cross the river.

When the council of generals was held, I do not know.
Report said that a majority favored, at first, bold and vigorous
attack, but that it was finally decided to fall back. This was
indicated, when, on Tuesday morning, the trains were ordered
back, and did not stop until they were back to Falmouth, or
to Potomac Creek. The hospitals too were moved. Long
ambulance trains conveyed their loads to Aquia Creek. Our
Twelfth corps hospital, in its second position north of the river,
had already proved insecure. On Monday morning its
reveille was the landing of shot and shell in its midst. One
shot passed through three tents, and killed a wounded man.
Six or seven men were killed or maimed within a few minutes,
in its immediate vicinity. One shell killed a rebel prisoner
near by, and wounded five more.

Tuesday night orders came to the front to prepare to retire.
It was not until daylight that the left moved, after passing a
wet night in the trenches. Pickets were still kept out ;
artillery posted. No annoyance took place, and the troops
recrossed at United States Ford, where a tremendous rain
on the afternoon of Tuesday had already carried away one
of the three bridges.

There has been no better fighting in this war than in this battle by some regiments ; no worse than by some others.

To my knowledge, there has never been better hospital arrangements than those organized by our medical director, Surgeon McNulty ; no better hospital than that conducted by Surgeon Casey, of the Twentieth Connecticut. The chief operator of our brigade, Surgeon Tryford, of the Twenty-seventh Indiana, did his work admirably. Coolness, kindness, and skill did wonders. Our own surgeons, Heath and Wightman, answered the most sanguine desires.

A rainy day, Wednesday, brought us back to our old camp. The movement of the army had failed. Up to Saturday it was a great success. History records that this army, numbering, according to the official and published report of the medical director, one hundred and sixty thousand men, of which one hundred and twenty thousand must have been effective — magnificently equipped — taking its own time for movement — evidently surprising the enemy — with confidence in its commanding general — with splendid fighting qualities — was baffled. Not routed — only baffled. Where the fault lies, it is for others who know to say.

Very likely there are errors in this hastily written letter. But none in the fact that the army moved, failed, and returned.

STAFFORD COURT HOUSE, VA., May, 1863.

WE learn from the New York papers that the bulk of our army has crossed the Rappahannock, and is following up General Lee. Very likely ; but we have not heard it in our corps. We learn a good many other things from the papers. From one we should judge that only one particular corps appears to have engaged in the recent battle ; while from another, it was a wholly different corps. Now I insist that *our* corps did the best fighting; but as General Slocum does not carry a special reporter with him, as some others do, the glorification is less. I remember an account of the battle of Cedar Mountain, in which one brigade appeared to have done everything; but the *date*, " General ——'s headquarters" explained the mystery. The fact is, every corps engaged did well with the exception of the Eleventh; and for that there are some circumstances which palliate, though not really excuse their fault. To their excellent commander nobody attributes a fault. I presume that the corps would retrieve their laurels in another engagement.* Our Twelfth certainly fought magnificently. For hours its front was a perfect blaze of fire. Without reserves, with a thin line, yet it held at bay the choicest of Jackson's force. Our corps is an old friend of Jackson's. ♦ General Banks's old force, — it met him in the Valley repeatedly. Except near Richmond, our corps has been his regular opponent, — always left weaker by the powers that be, — who are ordained of God, and therefore God bless them.

The papers say that the enemy's loss was greater than ours. They always say so. But this time the rebels must have suffered greatly. The way in which it happened, was by their pursuing their usual course of bringing up heavy masses, trusting to their ability for a rapid deployment as needed. This time, our artillery got the range of their masses, and made terrible havoc.

Among their losses seems to be our old opponent, Jackson. I well remember the bugbear his name used to be. After Bull Run first, Jackson took charge of rebel matters in the Shenandoah. During the winter we lay at Frederick he

* It did. At Lookout Mountain it behaved magnificently.

was intensely active up and down the river. In the spring he attacked General Banks's force at Winchester, and was defeated. We followed up (that is southward) the valley, and drove Jackson beyond Harrisburg. From that point General Banks most reluctantly retraced his steps in obedience to a peremptory order from Washington. Jackson eventually followed up, heavily reënforced as he could be, when General McDowell was prevented from coöperating with the army before Richmond. With an overwhelming force, Jackson persuaded us to hurry into Maryland. Afterwards our corps met his attack at Cedar Mountain. In his last action we again encountered him. No man rejoices at his death. He was a good man, though strangely misled by this vagary of state rights; a man of much prayer and Christian experience. A brave, gallant, and chivalric soldier, —no stain of cruelty or even harshness rests upon him. May God pardon his one fault! I wish *we* had more generals like him.

The wounded left beyond the Rappahannock have been brought over under a flag of truce. Those on our right wing number about a thousand. Rebels there insist that they outnumbered us, having been very strongly reënforced. They say, too, that the cavalry raid cost them but a slight inconvenience, all damages being speedily repaired. They say, also, that on the night of our return they were moving large forces by our extreme right, into the wilderness, west of Chancellorville, to retake United States Ford, which, if successful, would have made hard work. Whether so or not, General Hooker undoubtedly understood what he was about.

The losses of our brigade number just about one third of all in action. This is paralleled only by our loss at Cedar Mountain.

26 *

Our regiment is now in its *third year* of service.   May 11, 1861, was its natal day, — our mustering in dating from that, although the field officers were not commissioned until later in the month.   Colonel Gordon had received direct authority from the war department at Washington to raise a three years' regiment, and was the first to undertake it.   Our date of muster as recorded probably gives us the priority of all the three years' regiments, — while some companies were full in April, even.

STAFFORD COURT HOUSE, VA., May 20, 1863.

CHLOROFORM is a blessed thing.   Not but that sulphuric ether is good.   But here they use chloroform, to the exclusion of ether.   At home, I believe it is the other way.   Divers fatal cases supposed to result from the use of chloroform were reported, I remember, and people were afraid of it. But I have repeatedly asked experienced surgeons about it, and have uniformly been told that they have neither seen nor heard of a single case of injury from the use of chloroform in the army.   It takes very much less bulk of chloroform than of ether to produce the requisite insensibility, and less time to secure the desired condition ; and the patient comes out of it much better.   So they use chloroform here.

But one cannot look, after a battle, on anæsthetics, without rejoicing.   They spare the terrible pain.   They disarm the fear of the knife.   They prevent the groans which would terrify those about to take their turn.   They place the part at the entire disposal of the surgeon, and enable him to perform a better operation, without haste, without disturbance from struggles ; and to venture on delicate but needful work, otherwise impossible.

I have thought of these things repeatedly, in witnessing terrible operations. I thought of them at Aquia Creek, the last time I was there, — whence these paragraphs. For they use a good deal of chloroform at the never idle tables there.

Aquia Creek landing is about eight miles from this place, or, vice versa, according to your estimate of local importance. Roads which are mixed, — part dirt, part corduroy, part stumps, part gullies, part nothing, take you there ; about a hundred of them go there, from which you can choose ; or you can make a new one. There is nothing special on the way except dead horses. Two or three miles from the landing you catch a glimpse of water, but lose it again. Farther on, you come in sight of several fortifications, between two of which you pass, and soon stand on the brow of a height, from which there is one of the prettiest views imaginable. The broad Potomac stretches up and down, dotted with white sail or the puff of steamer. The Maryland woods are dark on the far off shore. The wide creek is hardly separated from the lordlier river by a long, narrow, green point ; and down below you are the sombre-roofed government buildings hardly lifted from the water, with two causeways, one for wagon, one for rail, crossing the wet lands between upland heights and wharves. It is worthy of a painter. What a pity it is in Virginia !

Aquia Creek landing ought to be an important place. The terminus of a line of steamers from Washington, and the starting-point of railway to Richmond, — in time of peace it is a transition centre on the great line of Northern and Southern travel. It would be something, but it is in Virginia ! That eminent State, in which Wise said, the poor farmer chases a stump-tailed steer through a barren ten acre lot to get a tough beefsteak.

But my interest in Aquia centres, not in its little city of government shanties, nor its piles of supplies; but in some tents on the airy height half a mile back. They are the tents of the hospital of the Twelfth army corps. Hither were sent the sick prior to our recent movement. And hither, on return, flowed in the stream of wounded men. Hundreds upon hundreds have been sent from them northward, but still seven hundred remain. Dr. Goodman is at the head, with two surgeons and ten assistant surgeons. Our corps took into the field between nine and ten thousand men; it lost in killed and wounded three thousand one hundred and forty-three. Our division (the corps has two) lost one thousand six hundred and fifty-nine, — General Williams's hardened troops. Think of this when you read certain newspaper accounts which seem to make out that General Sickles's corps did the brunt of the fighting. When a corps loses one third in a fair, stand-up fight, without flinching, you may set that corps down as veteran, And when you want fighting done, call on General Williams's division, — the best, sturdiest, toughest division in the army. "Who are those devils with red stars on their caps?" asked some rebel prisoners. The red stars signify our division. Even *Carleton*, in his most admirable account of the battle, makes Captain Best to be chief of artillery to General Sickles; whereas, he is that same to *our* corps, General Slocum's; and it was *our* forty pieces, supported by our infantry, whose horrible fire made such havoc in Jackson's columns. Our corps breasted the wave of the fleeing Eleventh; ours made an impenetrable wall of fire on Sunday, and then stood with fixed bayonets and without a cartridge till regularly relieved, while the broken enemy dared not advance.

But, ah me, the hospital at Aquia shows the cost, besides

the nameless graves at Chancellorville. There is every kind
of wound, from simple flesh hurt to shattered limbs or pierced
trunk. The poor fellows are lying on beds made by filling
large new bed-sacks with the best of straw. Some have
frames above them, from which are cords running over pul-
leys to hold in easy position the hurt limbs. The tents are
well open to the air, and are not crowded. Cook tents are
at proper distances. Nurses take care each of a certain
number of patients. Government furnishes supplies liberally, and the stores of the invaluable Sanitary Commission
seem exhaustless.

Under an awning is the operating table. Experienced
men work unweariedly, quietly, and calmly. They are a
blessing from God. As to unnecessary operations, — none
can operate but men specially designated, whose characters
are above such suspicion.

As I arrived, there was a man upon the table etherized.
It was one of ours. A bad wound in the thigh required re-
section. He soon came out from the influence of the chloroform, and looking up, his first words were, " How do you
do, chaplain ? " He was a brave soldier.

It is lonesome for the men. Away from home, some never
to see home again, wearing out the tedious days and nights,
they are glad to see a friend's face. On Monday, there were
three of us to see our men, — our surgeon, a captain, and
myself. We made a day of it. As we were returning,
" This has been a good day," said the captain.

It is remarkable how cheerfully, all things considered, they
bear their lot. Here is one almost gone with consumption ;
he has but few days. Here, one shot through the lungs.
Here, one with the stump of a leg, and very far gone from
past hardship. Here, one with a bullet-hole through his

head. Yet they do not murmur. They are all ready for religious advice. The men seem generally more anxious about their friends' feelings than about themselves.

I was to write to the friends of one. He called me back. "Chaplain, be sure and tell mother not to worry!"

Another had been reported dead, but he had been found alive, a prisoner, and sent back to us.

" I wish they knew at home that I was living," said he.

" They do," I answered; " I telegraphed the very day it was known."

" Thank you, thank you," said he; " because mother must have been feeling so bad. "

On Monday there were marks of the labors of the Christian Commission the day before. I was very glad of them; glad for the sake of our men. There is room enough for the Commission; room in plenty. They find it, they tell me, not very practicable to go in action, where recognized officers can; but in such a place as our corps hospital, they are just the thing. I cannot be very often there to see our own men, nor other chaplains to see theirs; there are regiments represented there who have no chaplains; there is no hospital chaplain. I rejoice that good men *can* be there. Possibly not all the plans may be wise; perhaps not all the men are judicious; but the Commission *has* good men, trying to do good, I know. Mr. Alvord's work is different from theirs, and cannot be spared. The Tract Society at New York, also, has plenty of room. Bring on *all* the helpers.

One of our men told me, by the way, in detail of hardships, how one man ministered to them while in the hands of the rebels: how he spared no labor; cooked for them; got some slight shelter for them; comforted them. My informant thinks that lives were saved by that man, whom

he believed to be the chaplain of the Twelfth New Hampshire, reported a prisoner. I doubt not it was he, our brother
Ambrose. He has earned a gratitude never to be forgotten,
certainly by some of ours.

I was going to speak of an hour at the Landing. Of
the outrageous imposition of the newspaper sellers, who
charge ten cents for a daily, retailing for five in Washington,
from which place the scoundrels come in a few hours, and
free of expense. Of the lemonade you look at — but don't
drink if you are wise — at ten cents a glass, the net profit on
which I found by an arithmetical calculation to be exactly
nineteen hundred per cent. Of the soda-water — pah ! Of
the stationery stand, whose note-paper is fifty cents a quire,
worth literally eighteen. Of the trashy publications on the
counters. Of the eating house where you pay a dollar for a
mean dinner. (*We* dined with the surgeon, and had butter !
As soon as I saw it I knew it was butter, from impressions
indelibly made in childhood.) I began with alluding to chloroform. Chloroform has seized the consciences of the whole
villanous pack of traders there. They took the vapor easy.
They are completely under its influence. They stay under
it perfectly. I should like to be provost marshal there for
just half an hour, with charge of the rascally traders who
are cheating the crowd of soldiers thereabouts out of their
hard earnings. I would amputate their every stock in trade,
and then relieve the vagabonds of their anæsthetic slumber
by planting every fellow of them ten feet deep in dock mud.
— I was going to say all this, but as there is no room I will
not.

We are having good weather now, and of course our
usual religious worship.

STAFFORD COURT HOUSE, VA., June 5, 1863.

I HAVE omitted to write. But loss is slight. Little has occurred. Even now one gathers up only "odds and ends," of not much interest, save a tremendous cannonade going on all day in the direction of Fredericksburg, whose import we are yet ignorant of.

In common with probably most regiments we have changed camps. In common newspaper style of late, I should say that " We have moved towards the enemy ! " So we have — an eighth of a mile ! So did General Hooker move " nearer to Washington," as by the papers, — moving several rods ! At least one half of the current reports as to facts or feelings here are false. Old camps become unhealthy. The army has been in those about us at least six months. It was time to move.

We have not a man in our regimental hospital. A few are sick in quarters, but none severely.

The cannonading to-day may signify something. Yesterday morning we were called up at four A. M., to be ready to move immediately. Tents were struck. Goods and chattels all packed. Horses saddled. Then we waited for orders. And waited. They came in the forenoon, — " to water the horses, but not unharness them." Then we waited again. Orders came towards night, — permission to pitch again ! Very pleasant — to stay waiting in a hot sun all day, merely because somebody perverted a simple order to be " under arms " into " breaking up camp," before it reached us. However, three days' rations are kept constantly on hand, which is very judicious, as we are in the most exposed part of the line.

One matter I ought to refer to particularly. It is the

value of the Sanitary Commission. The good it does is perfectly marvellous. With its work thoroughly systematized, it seems omnipresent. In the recent operations I do not know what would have been done without the Commission. A few hours only, after the Sunday battle, nourishing food was cooking at our general hospital. "Where did this come from?" "The Sanitary." Delicacies, even, tempted the appetite. "Where from?" "The Sanitary." The Commission is really doing an immense work, often noiseless, but very effectual. Its agents and inspectors are everywhere.

———

SALEM, MASS., June 16, 1863.

I WROTE the above in an interval between two "intermittents." Since then — on the next afternoon, our regiment was selected as one of six or seven tried bodies to form part of General Pleasanton's expedition across the Rappahannock. I cannot tell about that movement, for I was helplessly sick when it left; and before it returned two or three surgeons agreed that the sooner I found my native State the better. So, for five days I was on the road home — of which journey I should like to write my impressions when stronger.

Nor can I record anything of the current movements. Lee's advance, expected before, has taken place. O, that I had health, to be with ours. It is terribly hard to be submissive to the lot of uselessness at such a time.

I doubt not that Lee will do some harm. But I cannot believe that he will permanently reap anything but disaster. I caution all not to be excited by newspaper reports. Last fall I was in Pope's army. When files of newspapers at last came, it was strange how rumors most untruthful had daily excited

the public mind.   Now, — trust !   We have a gallant army,
a noble cause — and God.

Dover, N. H., June 30, 1863.

Nothing could have induced me, I think, to write now,
but the desire to relieve the anxieties which the whirlwind of
attack on the *Ambulance System* of our army has created.

I was completely astonished on learning the condition of
our ambulance system.   I had occasion once or twice to crit-.
icise it myself, but the evils were minor ones, and have been
corrected.   I had the pleasure once of nearly choking a driver, besides well nigh shaking him out of his boots.   But that
the whole set needed a similar operation, I was unaware —
till now.   I thought Senators Wilson and Sumner to be really
humane men, and my idea was supported by various acts of
theirs — many of them private — which seemed to evince
ready and kind hearts.   Little did I think they needed to " be
shot through the chest and jolted over a corduroy road, with
a drunken driver," &c., &c., &c.   I imagined that our surgeons and generals — many of the former of whom I know,
and some of the latter — were the same kind-hearted, honorable, human beings they were at home.   But now they seem
to be brutes.   Ambulance drivers I should have considered
to be usually respectable people, especially as many of them
I could mention from Massachusetts are thought to be, in
their own towns, men of good character and often of Christian influence ; men venturing into the heavy fire ; men whom
I have seen quiet when the very horses in the vehicle were
struck by balls ; men whom I have seen lifting the wounded
as tenderly as you would handle a babe of days ; men with

whom I would have trusted myself implicitly until I found that they are " miserable, drunken wretches." I thought we had an ambulance system. But I find that " vain appeals have been made to the President" to establish one ; that " Congress, General Halleck, Stanton," have been uselessly begged " to do something, and all in vain ; " that both our Massachusetts senators are dumb, or in open opposition to all action in the premises ; I see that we — the people — are " to write to the authorities, and demand action : " to " cut this article from the paper . . . and send it ; " to " get the pamphlet and send that ; " to " call meetings, and circulate petitions : " to " overwhelm the powers that be with your importunity," &c.

What for ? Because " on the battle-field, and from battle-field to hospital they (our wounded) depend on chance comers." Because " there is no system, no provision worthy the name." And it is triumphantly asked if an ambulance corps " is practicable there (in Europe) why is it not practicable here ? "

I respect motives. I reverence a stricken father's anguish. But I have too much regard also for the thousands of suffering wives and mothers not to relieve their anxieties somewhat by saying emphatically that the statements quoted in this last paragraph are simply the *grossest errors.* I judge, it is true, from the working in one corps, but I am confident as to the others also, in the army of Virginia.

True, there was one occasion, last September, when certain barbarities were witnessed in an ambulance train sent from Washington to Manassas. I judge that every one of those drivers ought to have been shot. I know that, in our corps, if such men existed, they would have altered their conduct, or enough of them would have been shot on the spot to reduce the others to obedience. But in reference to that case,

remember the train was started under very peculiar circumstances; that its drivers were " men of the lowest character,
taken from the purlieus of Washington," which our regular
drivers never are ; that this was only *one* case, which I know,
personally, *not* to be a fair representation of the whole system ; and that since then an *entire modification* of the system
has taken place. The system has been improved. In our
corps, and I suppose in the Potomac army as a whole, it is
just what (as to plan) is asked for.

Let us look at our system.

At the head of the army of Virginia is a medical direct-
or, who is virtually a medical autocrat. To each corps there
is a medical director. To each division in a corps there is
a medical director. The senior surgeon in each brigade is
acting medical director of the brigade. And to each regiment there is, or should be, one surgeon and two assistant
surgeons. By the superior surgeons, the directors, there is
constant oversight and care.

Now besides, there is an AMBULANCE CORPS. It is under
the general charge of the medical director of the army
corps. All the ambulances were long ago taken from regiments and put under the charge — not of quartermasters —
but of the medical powers. Each ambulance has its driver,
not taken from " purlieus," but permanently detailed from the
various regiments, and these ambulances and their drivers
are under the control of military officers, who are also permanently detailed. I cannot tell just now accurately every
feature of the plan above brigades ; but to our brigade there
are (if I remember accurately) thirty (odd) ambulances —
six or seven averaging to a regiment. These are kept together in quiet times. There is in charge a lieutenant permanently assigned to that work, well instructed himself, and

rigid in his requirements. The brigadier himself cannot take one of those ambulances for a moment — so exclusively are they under the control of the medical authorities. I had occasion to need one lately. It had to be obtained by a requisition made by our surgeon, and approved by our brigade surgeon, when the lieutenant sent it instantly. Not an ambulance can be used except to carry sick or wounded. I have seen these ambulances "parked." They were in perfect order. On the road the other day, when being transported, in sickness, I needed water. It was immediately drawn — good water — from the well-filled keg. The men employed are under strict discipline, and would be punished for ill conduct. As they are assigned to the one duty, they understand their business. In addition to the lieutenant there are all the sergeants he needs ; and if a train moves either the lieutenant or a sergeant (according to its size) goes with it, with military authority. The medical director has entire control, and the ambulance corps is really just as distinct a body as the artillery.

Now, further. In case of expected movements, the corps medical director issues his plans, to which the corps commander orders obedience. One surgeon is named to remain till further orders, the superintendent of a corps general hospital, should one be established. Another, to be its clerk. One surgeon from each brigade is detached as chief operator, and four or five as assistant operators. Others are ordered to report for general duties. The hospital attendants of every regiment are to repair immediately to the corps hospital, in case of action. Certain surgeons are ordered to remain near their regiments. The ambulances are stationed by personal order of the corps medical director. And — mind this — ten men from each regiment, previously selected by the sur-

geon of the regiment, as suitable men — have the simple and
sole duty of removing the wounded from the field of battle
even during the engagement. These are *picked men ;* they
constitute a distinct corps ; they can do no other duty, and
each wears a conspicuous *green badge* on his breast. They
use the " stretchers " which go with every ambulance, and
convey the wounded to the ambulances stationed near.

Now, what more complete " ambulance corps " can exist, I
cannot see. The *only* variation would be to enlist men specially for this corps, instead of taking them from regiments.
but that would not necessarily be an improvement. They
now remain permanently detached, unless some special reason
should occur for dismissing a man. They camp together ;
they are under no regimental control whatever. And by
selecting from men already in service, there is opportunity
for choosing those who are known to be *specially adapted* to
the service wanted. Such men were taken from our regiment
— with a sergeant ; and to those men's care I would *trust my
life.* Possibly it might be better that the ten " stretcher-
bearers " should be removed from the regiments, but as for
the most of the time they would have nothing to do, it is
questionable.

Now, on a march, the ambulances, under charge of their
officer, follow the corps ; and *one* ambulance goes with the
regiment often, for special and sudden use. If the surgeon
of the regiment finds a man actually unable, from illness, to
go further, he gives him a certificate (printed blanks he keeps
with him) which entitles him to fall out till the ambulances
come up, and to a seat when they do come up.

But how this system works is the next point. It works
well. Not perfectly, for we have neither omnipotence, omni-
presence, nor infinite goodness, in either surgeon, ambulance

driver, or hospital attendant. But it works better and better. At any rate it is, in substance, the system used in " every army of Europe." It has no defects which I can see would be removed if all critics had *carte blanche* to devise a system ; for its defects are mainly the incidents of frailty in man, not in plan. At Chancellorville it worked finely. Men were left on the field ; but it was because the field passed into the enemy's hands. The battle of Sunday was not ended when our corps hospital was reëstablished north of the river (driven there by previous artillery fire), when tents were up — when cooks were at work — when operating surgeons were at their task — and *five hundred* men from our one corps were there, many lying on beds of boughs, each tent under a surgeon's watch and care — and the whole was as quiet, as calm, as neat, as systematic as though the enemy's balls were not to crash through its trees next morning, and require another move.

Possibly I have mistaken in thinking our well-regulated plan to be general. Possibly Dr. McNulty and Dr. Chappel, our corps and division medical directors, are exceptions in skill and sense. Possibly the splendid Twelfth corps, with its noble young general, is as much a model in hospital matters as it stands preëminent on the field of battle. But I do not believe that other corps are far behind. I tell you, anxious reader, that while your and our wounded *must* suffer, cases of peculiar neglect are extremely rare — at least in our corps. And I assure my friends that precisely the plan demanded was established months ago ; I cannot say that there will *always* be water in the ambulance kegs ; men are sometimes neglectful. Nor that ambulances will always be where the changing tide of battle makes them needful. But great care is exercised to insure what is wanted. I bear my testimony to the general skill and kindness of the surgeons. I have been with many of them in bivouac where the slumber was by moments only ; with them as they were tenderly handling the wounded ; with them to see their unselfish devotion to their duty. Of our regiment one of our surgeons received an enemy's ball ; and one has just laid down his life, a sacrifice to his unremitting labors. But surgeons cannot do everything. Be just to them. It may be that " three staff officers . . . . thought our wounded ought to be seen to, many of whom they believed were still lying on the field." But why append the exclamation point, when on referring to the pamphlet you find that what they " thought " was that " *a flag of truce* ought to be sent over the river to see to our wounded, many of whom," &c., that is, these wounded were in the *enemy's hands*, and these staff officers had no more power or right to " see " to them than they had to desert.

I say these things, not because our system answers every want, but because it is just what is asked for ; because it is *not* the system of the days of Manassas, when each regiment had, or pretended to have, its own ambulances, but the system in which we have a consolidated *corps*, as do the French ; and because I feel that the anxieties of numberless hearts need this reply. And as I write it in a state of suffering, with the certainty that I shall feel the labor for days, I ask that its motive be understood.

PARK BARRACKS, NEW YORK, August 24, 1863.

OF all the strange vicissitudes of the SECOND, it seems the queerest to find ourselves suddenly taken from the Rappahannock, and planted in the middle of New York town.

After a tedious illness and slow recovery, after losing the

historical days of Gettysburg, after restlessly mourning over the gallant sufferers whom I could not see, and the gallant dead none shall see here, — I seized the earliest feeling of elasticity as the occasion of return. Barring the friends at home, — the good father and mother, the patient wife, and (without the *slightest* prejudice) altogether the finest five-year-old girl who ever loved a papa dearly, or whose mischief a papa ever thought was the perfection of genius — home has fewer attractions in these times than the spots where history is made. How the able-bodied young men whom I saw could, endure the littleness of trade or profession, when their country's life or death is the question of the age, I could not, I cannot understand.

Not fully well when I left home, every day's journey made me stronger. The beautiful trip by the Fall River line, which I take to be the only decent way of going to New York, with its lovely evening quiet, and its charming morning approach to the city ; the horrible New Jersey passage ; the detestable horse-car jaunt through Philadelphia's spectral-looking, staring, white-shuttered streets ; the miserable course to Washington, through which I managed to sleep ; even the usual imposition of hack drivers in Washington — all added health and strength. And when the steam engine puffed away towards the Rappahannock, I found I was well again.

Down by Kelley's ford, on the Rappahannock river, was the Twelfth corps. I left it before its long and rapid marches to Pennsylvania ; before its invincible stand on the right at Gettysburg, where Ewell in vain hurled his masses against the star-marked veterans of Slocum. Now, after renewing its historic glory, the corps had got back to its old river. How pleasant it was to meet friends, and to hear words of welcome, and to have hearty handshakes, I need not say.

But on Saturday, August 15, came orders. And on the next morning various regiments were on the road. Picked troops were taken. From our brigade, the Second Massachusetts, the Third Wisconsin, and the Twenty-seventh Indiana, who, with eight others form another division, were placed under command of our own soldierly Brigadier General Ruger. All superfluous baggage was left behind. Five or six miles up the river is Rappahannock station. There the troops were placed on board of four or five long trains, and at night we found ourselves at Alexandria to take boats.

But the boats were not there. So we were turned into a field, or an empty square rather. That night I tried bivouac again, and with decided success. We waited there until Wednesday.

It is a duty to be resigned to the will of Providence. If Providence should cast my lot in the detestable city of Alexandria, I should try to be resigned ; but it would take *grace.* Nasty, shiftless, shabby is it for the most part, with here and there a decent street dropped in by accident, and evidently wondering how it got there, — that is Alexandria. While we were there, it seemed as if all the boys and women, and a good share of the men, had turned pedlers. The camps were inundated with them. Everything that a soldier could be tempted to buy, so far as Alexandria could furnish it, was offered. I will say for Alexandria that these women pedlers were generally very well behaved ; but some of the articles sold were mean enough to counterbalance. Shoeblacks were thick as bees ; and it was very amusing to see the dignity with which our privates would employ some of them in cleaning up equipments. Ice cream was abundant, and afforded the novel sight of being eaten by the *pint.* Bad whiskey showed itself to be in Alexandria, but, on the whole, made no great way.

We were heartily glad when we got out of the dirty spot
where we bivouacked. I do not think that we liked city life
at all. It may have charms, but we did not see them.
Wednesday evening we marched through town, and into vessels. The three regiments of our brigade, with the hundred
and something Ohio, (I never remember regimental numbers
so high), were put on board the *Merrimack.*

Remaining at the wharf that night, about six o'clock the
next morning the boat started. Rather crowded for accommodations, of course, but on deck it was delightful. The
trip down the Potomac needs to be tried, not described. The
Potomac is a beautiful river to steam down, though ugly to
live near. Fort Washington, Mount Vernon, Aquia Landing — showing only the blackened ruins of its former busy
haunts — were the only noticeable points, until, at the mouth
of the river, Point Lookout showed its hospital buildings and
its grove of green trees. Methinks the sweetest spot for a
hospital must be there. Then into the magnificent Chesapeake, and all the evening, to a late hour, the beautiful moonlight silvered the waves; the cool salt air refreshed the men
of the sultry Rappahannock; and snatches of music from
the band, or songs from the musical, enlivened the hours.
That is, on deck. Below it was hot and close.

I did not see the junction of the Bay and the Ocean. In
fact, I was asleep. It was in the middle of the night. But
the morning brought evidences that we were on the ocean.
No land was in sight. The waters had a peculiar smell.
Divers persons were intently looking over the sides into the
sea. They were not sick, O no! There were fewer at the
officers' breakfast than one would have imagined. Some left
the table rather suddenly. Cigars seemed neglected. Dinner was less attended to than was formerly the case in our

brigade. Some seemed quite indifferent to all considerations except those which let them lay quiet. But the *Merrimack* kept steadily ploughing on. The *Erricson* appeared, (a sister transport), but the *Merrimack* walked by. And so on until Saturday morning, when the breakfast table was crowded again, and boots were blacked, and white collars appeared once more. We were nearing New York — our destination which we had suspected while at Alexandria, but which government, for a rarity, had kept concealed until we were on board.

The entrance to New York harbor from the sea was new to me ; but how beautiful it seemed I cannot tell. Up between the forts, by lovely Staten Island, through fleets of white-winged vessels, and to the anchorage off Governor's island, the panorama was perfect. And after General Ruger had reported to General Canby, and orders came, then we landed at the foot of Canal Street, North River side, and left the *Merrimack*. A very comfortable vessel is that iron steamer, built by Harrison Loring, Boston, a year or two ago — of two thousand tons, or to be exact, one thousand nine hundred and ninety-one and one fifth ; with two low pressure engines, and seventy-four life preservers ; intended for the Boston and New Orleans line, but does not run there ; and commanded by a gentleman, viz., Captain Sampson, of Dedham, Massachusetts.

So we marched, without music, to Broadway, and into City Hall Park, by the same gate we entered over two years ago, and stacked arms on the same spot, and in the same line we did then. But the difference ! Then a thousand and one strong ; now a very few hundreds. But they are the men of Winchester, of Cedar Mountain, of Antietam, of Chancellorville, and of Gettysburg ; and if the good people of New

York want help in maintaining order, these men are as willing to fight their country's enemies North as South — but they fire bullets, not blank cartridges, as those battle-fields could testify.

But though we are in New York, and just opposite the Astor House, and a stone's throw from the City Hall, and oppressed by the horrible noises of this babel, we are in camp. That is, the men are in barracks ; the officers in tents. Guards are as strict as ever. We cannot run round the city. A battery, also, is our nearest neighbor ; and we are on a war footing. One New York paper says we have tents, each capable of containing forty men ; as each tent is but nine feet square, you will allow for a slight exaggeration.

Yesterday we had our usual Sunday services, and it seemed a luxury. Most of the city churches are closed, they say. Ergo, there is more religion in the army than in the town. Without pleasantry, I believe there *is*. In the afternoon I obtained permission to go to a very pleasant service at Colonel Howe's New England Rooms for soldiers. There, too, I saw some disabled and sick Massachusetts soldiers.

Now we are in a Northern city. But there are some things I want to write. Some work of our brigade and regiment at Gettysburg. I have picked up what ought to be chronicled ; for when a regiment loses a hundred and thirty odd out of less than three hundred, and presses on and fights on without a wavering, it ought to be recorded. Of some hospital doings and relief, I will write also. I want also to describe Colonel Howe's admirable relief rooms here. And perhaps long before I do either, we may be confronting General Lee again.

28

City Hall Park, New York, August 23, 1863.

Had there been any very active service for ours in this city, you would have heard of it. Guard duty, of course, goes on as usual. Drill has been recommenced. Evening parade has become quite an institution, gathering a huge crowd as anything will here. The crowd seems to admire the Second. A few nights ago, the perfect movement of our regiment extorted a sudden and general applause. They even said " that beats the Seventh," i. e., New York, which is considerable for New Yorkers. But another rather sulkily said, " they have spent all their time in drill." Correct — except a few little episodes like Gettysburg.

Yesterday we had public service. In the afternoon the chaplain conducted worship at the New England Relief Rooms. We also had for members a good supply of reading matter from the Tract Society, 150 Nassau Street, which liberally offers every help — and a bundle of papers from the *Evangelist* office — all of which were rapidly taken by our men and those of Wisconsin. The New York Bible Society has also re-supplied us with Testaments. Yesterday, indeed, we had extra evidence of the kindness of friends, in the sudden appearance of a minister to preach to us — especially mentioning that there were Massachusetts troops here. We were *very* grateful, but our Colonel happened to think that the regimental chaplain was sufficiently qualified for that duty. In another place, however, a chaplain informed me that he was superseded. The Third Wisconsin, brave comrades of ours in many a field, also preferred to attend our worship, rather than have an independent meeting. The presence of quite a number of wives and friends who had come to New York to see their beloved ones, added greatly to the interest. And there is always something peculiarly interesting in seeing the men present in full ranks, with officers all there, save when on duty, and with the colonel at the head, showing his regard by example, for the worship of God; and to think, too, that these are the men who have borne the brunt of battle with undaunted heroism. Show me the parish equal to this!

I hope it will not be out of place if I go back in time to record the movements of this regiment, and thus mainly of the corps, prior to Gettysburg; especially as I have seen no public statement of the marches of the troops while General Hooker was moving parallel with Lee. I do not doubt that when history is written, it will be found that General Hooker's movement from Falmouth to Gettysburg (or near), all the time watching Lee, interposed suitably between Washington and the enemy, yet ready to confront him whenever Lee should finally strike — will be written as most masterly.

Our regiment was one of a few picked bodies selected to accompany a cavalry expedition across the Rappahannock, leaving camp June 6, about evening. Seriously ill at that time, I was left behind. But I have procured a record of events. They marched that night about fifteen miles, arriving near Spott Tavern about two A. M., where it rested until nine A. M. Then turning southwest it reached Bealston Station about six P. M. — about sixteen miles — having made thirty-one miles in the twenty-four hours. Bivouacking there, — hid in the woods — for a day, — the regiment moved the next evening — artillery, cavalry, and infantry, meeting about ten miles north of Beverly Ford. At the gray of dawn, sharpshooters were selected to go forward to clear the Ford — but the enemy had no infantry there, and our cavalry crossing, was instantly followed by the Third Wisconsin and

Second Massachusetts. Colonel Davis, commanding the cavalry, charged up to and over a barricade where the enemy had dismounted as well as mounted cavalry. He drove them in fine style. At that barricade, the gallant Davis, one of the best and noblest officers in the army, received the wound of which he died in the afternoon. The infantry moved up, and its skirmishers drove the enemy, with sharp firing, out of a wood which the enemy held. Here the troops remained until about eleven A. M., — the enemy trying to turn first our right and left, in order to gain the Ford, but without success, and with a good deal of loss, —.both sides bringing artillery into play in addition to both infantry and cavalry.

About eleven A. M. the whistling of cars from the Culpepper direction indicated the coming up of rebel reënforcements. Artillery firing was soon heard in the rebel rear. General Gregg had crossed at Kelly's Ford, moved to Brandy Station, drove Stuart and captured his headquarters, finding papers which indicated Lee's intended movement. Gregg had thus forced their right backward. Our left (in which was ours) then advanced for about half a mile. Firing slackened on both sides. Gregg came in on our left. The object of the reconnoissance being accomplished, and the enemy being in motion in great force, our whole force began to retire about three P. M., and recrossed the river about six o'clock.*

The corps (rejoined by ours on the 16th) moved on the 17th, reaching Leesburg and Alexandria turnpike a few miles

* The importance of this operation at Beverly Ford is overshadowed by the battle of Gettysburg. But it ought to be recorded that the capture of papers in this expedition disclosed the enemy's plans, and that the discomfiture of the enemy's cavalry, already about to move, was the means of nullifying the value of that force there and all the way up to Gettysburg.

southeast of Drainsville about eleven A. M. On the 18th passed through Drainsville, forded Goose Creek (when there came up a heavy hail storm), passed through Leesburg, and camped under the wake of the old rebel Fort Johnston, above Leesburg, the work being occupied by artillery. Here the troops remained until the 26th, when they crossed the Potomac on pontoons at Edward's Ferry, encamping about four P. M. near the mouth of the Monocacy. The next day, on the banks of the canal, to a mile beyond Petersville; on the 28th back to Petersville, and through Jefferson, to Frederick, and camped a few miles west of that town. On the 29th through Waterville, to within a mile of Bruceville. On the 30th to half a mile beyond Littleston. On the 1st of July, four or five miles slowly to near "Two Taverns," and afterward, to the sound of artillery, to about two miles from Gettysburg, on the Baltimore turnpike. On Thursday, the 2d, the line moved forward a short distance, found the enemy in force, withdrew, and the whole corps made a detour by the left, to hills near Rock Creek, and threw up intrenchments; the brigade was, about four P. M., ordered to the left of the whole line, but was sent back directly, and found the enemy in the works which General Geary had erected.

It was in obedience to the order to retake these works, about seven the next morning, that our regiment lost one hundred and twenty-six, killed and wounded, out of two hundred and ninety-four enlisted men, and ten officers out of twenty-two officers. Three color bearers were killed, and two wounded. Passing down a straight slope, across an open meadow, up to the edge of the other hill, in the face of a terrible fire, the men found some shelter behind works, and a portion of the front of the curving breastworks, still continuing the fire. But troops which should have supported

28 *

on the right failed to do it, and the enemy were flanking the
regiment in that direction, and after holding the position for
some time, the general ordered it back to the place it had
left. Need I say that no man flinched in the deadliest
storm?

Then the corps moved southward; watched the enemy at
Williamsport; left for the southward by way of Harper's
Ferry, after the enemy had moved; and on the 31st were
again on the Rappahannock.

I have some accounts of the *hospital* work at Gettysburg,
which I reserve. In regard to the ambulance system, it is
said that General McClellan advocated the establishment of
an ambulance system *five months* after the time which I
specified as the date of the present one. And that Senator
Sumner affirms, in June, 1863, that he tried to get such a
system established, while in July, 1863, Senator Wilson declares we have an admirable one.

Now there is really *no* discrepancy. There are *two* points
to be considered: first, what a good ambulance system is;
and secondly, by what authority should it be established.

As to the first point, so far as my observation extends, we
have a thorough, efficient, satisfactory system. I am confirmed in this view by accounts I have received of Gettysburg. Last fall, the system being new, showed much
friction; it is now in good running order. Then, it had
some special defects, which showed themselves badly; now,
these are removed.

As to the second point, the present system is established
merely by military authority in the army itself. It *might*
be established by *act of Congress.* Senator Wilson is right
in saying (I have not seen his remarks) that our present
system works well — it does do all the work any system can.

But Senator Sumner may be equally right in desiring to have this system (or an equivalent one) *made obligatory by Congress.* The only real change in the system would be, that men employed in the ambulance corps, now detailed from the regiments, would then be enlisted for the corps ; or perhaps the present men would be transferred. The advantage of that would be that the men would be thoroughly taught, and would remain permanently ; but now it works with us in the same way, the men so detailed having been left undisturbed. And it is to be remembered that men now detailed *cannot* be recalled by regimental commanders ; they can only be *sent* back by the *medical* authorities. This affords some advantage over the separate corps system. Now, an unfit man can be returned ; then, he could not. General Mc-Clellan, indeed, prefers the totally separate plan. He wanted an act of Congress, by which the officers and men of the ambulance system should be specially enlisted for that purpose. And *this* is what his plan for action evidently meant.

Our present system is good. It secures the desired result. But it is not established by act of Congress. It rests simply on military orders. At the next session it would be perfectly easy to pass an act, declaring that the officers and men now employed in the ambulance corps shall constitute a distinct branch of the service, to be under control of the medical authorities, and that in future vacancies shall be filled by enlistments, instead of by detail. It would not change the present real work in the slightest degree. But it would, indeed, make uniform in the " army of the United States " what may be only partial.

The only point I have insisted upon is, that our soldiers are not neglected ; that, barring the usual human frailties, the care is as perfect as any plan can provide, — at least in the Twelfth corps.

If it were not so, we know Senator Wilson's * heart well enough to be assured that he would spare no pains to remedy evils. . We need only to look at his constant efforts to improve the condition of our soldiers. The country owes him a debt of gratitude, as well as to the other noble senator from Massachusetts.

CITY HALL PARK, NEW YORK, September 5, 1863.

A FEW days ago, one of our men (a faithful man too, one who is detailed for special duty, but always takes his gun, and shares the dangers of his comrades when there is a fight), was told that his wife and child were just outside of the guard, and went to bring them in. As soon as he was in sight, his little boy, who had not seen his father since the war opened, rushed past the guard and over the tent ropes, and climbed up to his father's neck and hung there, while his father could not help the tears of delight. Wasn't it soldierly? Well, some of the guard themselves put on a very soldierly air — but they wiped their eyes. They are no worse soldiers for the memory of the little boys and girls at home, and much better men for it.

Camp life has indeed been a good deal variegated (in the city) by the presence of wives and children. It is astonishing how much the dull mess-room, which has been made a kind of general parlor, has been brightened up by family groups. While I write, two active youngsters are daring to

* If I had to choose from all the public acts of this senator what should be the ground of honor, it would be his masterly exposure of the hideous Slave Code of the District of Columbia.

play marbles in the sacred precincts of camp; but the bayonet glistens still on the sentry posts.

The great feature which seems to distinguish this war from all others, is the great system of home help to the army. What other army ever had such benevolence poured out? What one, even, ever had such a mail-system as ours — so wise as it is in its effect on the men? What other ever had the sick, the wounded, and the dying so ministered·unto? The government has done wonderfully in this direction itself. But such outside helps were never before witnessed. They are good. They do the army good. Every child that helps sew on a garment for a soldier is doing what our Lord approves. Every stitch is a work of love. The old man who, poor, learned to knit so as to do something, in his chimney corner, for the soldiers, was a hero; that pair of stockings came to our regiment, and the men reverence the old man.

The chief among the links to home, as an agency for relief, is the Sanitary Commission. The more I see and hear of this institution, I am amazed at its wonderful efficiency. I regard it as chief, not as exclusive. But chief it is. I lately saw and heard more of its doings. Perhaps your readers do not know its plan beyond Washington, and you will allow me to outline it as it is in our army, — merely for furnishing supplies.

The central agency is, of course, at Washington. Here supplies are accumulated, and large deposits are necessary for any emergency.

In the army, each corps is supplied with a relief agent, who *lives in the corps.* He moves with it. He has a four-horse wagon, supplied with sanitary stores — articles additional to those furnished by government. These wagons are generally with the ambulance train, and the relief agent has discretionary power to dispose of his articles. He issues them to field hospitals on requisitions from the medical officers there. New supplies are constantly sent, so as to have plenty on hand.

The whole arrangement is under the care (I have asked for the names) of J. Warner Johnson (firm of Johnson and Brothers, law-book Publishers, Philadelphia), and Captain Ira Harris of New York. The relief agents are, — First corps, W. A. Hovey, of Boston; Second, N. Murray, Jr., of New York, and Rev. J. Anderson of California; Third, Colonel Clemens Soest, formerly commander of Twenty-ninth New York; Fifth, E. M. Barton, of Worcester, Massachusetts, — a son, I think, of Judge Barton; Sixth, D. S. Pope, of Baltimore; Twelfth, S. Hoag. And Dr. W. S. Swalm acts as inspector in the field. While Dr. Steiner, of Frederick, Maryland, has general charge at Washington for this army, — a man of ripe experience and qualities for the post. These names are a guarantee for efficiency. These men work for little or no pay, but they are *permanent* agents.

That this system insures success, there can be no doubt. I think I wrote you that at Chancellorville the hospitals were well supplied with even luxuries, by the Commission, while the battle was still in progress. I am now told, on most reliable authority (that of the surgeons), that on the Thursday and Friday, the great days of the Gettysburg battles, the Sanitary Commission were distributing their stores *under fire*. In two corps (one is ours), that this was done, clear evidence also exists in the receipts given by the surgeons at the battle-ground. I was somewhat astonished at this, as, while at home, I had read statements that some other agency was *three days in advance of all* others with supplies at Gettysburg. But as the Sanitary Commission was there while the battle was still in progress, this latter statement is evidently a mistake!

One great reason why the Sanitary Commission works so well is, that it works in and by means of the regular authorities. It does not set itself up as independent of the medical officers. It distributes through the surgeons. The wisdom of this plan is evident at a glance. The surgeons know what is needed, and how to use it. An indiscriminate administering of relief by independent helps is subversive of all order. A case just in point happened — no matter where, but I know. A soldier had turned the critical point of disease, and was doing well. A benevolent individual, distributing supplies out of a basket, gave this soldier some pickles, and I know not what else, which he ate. The kind visitor came next day. " Did you give pickles to that man? " asked the surgeon. " Yes." " Well, you meant right, but you insured his death." In fact it did, — within forty-eight hours.

The independent method is bad. The medical authorities are the only ones who ought to be in general intrusted with supplies. It is sometimes well to place the article in the hands of the soldier himself; but while this course could do good occasionally, as a system it would be bad. The surgeon knows what the sick man should eat, and what he should wear. And an institution which furnishes things at the time needed is invaluable.

It is of great importance to harmonize all outside management with the methods which government has established. The Sanitary Commission avoids all complications.

While the Commission was thus harmoniously acting with the authorities in relieving the suffering, several chaplains were, as I have learned from others, working night and day in corps hospital at Gettysburg. I am informed that they were invaluable. They ministered to the wounded and the dying like brothers. I know how it was, for I know these men. Such men are not praised in newspapers. But these men do the steady, every day, heavy work. When others at Chancellorville failed, these men risked shot and shell, and some found captivity in doing their duty. No letter writer tells about them, because it is the *regular business* of those men.

The Sanitary Commission has shown true wisdom, also, in its plan of employing regular and *permanent* agents. Sudden spasms of work do little. The Commission knows that. It takes time for men to learn their business. When taught, one man is worth twenty temporary volunteers. The work which the tract societies are doing in the army is more effective, because they employ permanent managers, and work in harmony with the recognized religious workers of the army. Mr. Alvord, for example (I refer to him because I know his work), accomplished wonders, because he used all existing facilities. Finding a chaplain, or (in case there were none) some other religious man, in each of (say) a hundred regiments, he had a hundred permanent agents all his own, for Christ's sake. Gathering them together, and thus exciting new fervor, holding meetings for prayer of those hundred laborers, each of whom had his own field, in which none could do the work that laborer could, a life was sent through the whole, when *outside* workers could only have made a slight impression on the circumference.

The Sanitary Commission works through the proper channels. There is, therefore, no outside work which, in the matter of supplies, can rival the Commission in cheapness, directness, or usefulness. It does a work which fathers, and mothers, and wives at home ought to be thankful for. It ministers to the helpless. It succors where suffering and death would often be the result of absence of succor.

CHAPTER XIII.

ON THE RAPIDAN.

ALEXANDRIA, VA., September 10, 1863.

MY last writing ended abruptly. Orders came to " be ready to move at a moment's notice," which required instant preparation. For, however expectant we may be of some movement, there is always something to pack, if it be only a blanket to roll up. It was Saturday afternoon then; and in a short time came orders that we were to move as soon after three P. M. as possible. We were ready, of course; but we were not actually sent towards the transport until evening. Then the line was formed in the Park. Wives were there to take leave of husbands. Children received a " good-by." A tear or two glistened. Our drum corps played, and we marched down Broadway to Battery Park, and then were conveyed on lighters (or whatever they are rightly called) to the steamer *Mississippi*, lying a mile away. All night baggage and rations were crossing, and horses were being swung on board for the three regiments — the Third Wisconsin, the Twenty-seventh Indiana, and our own. And so our fortnight's trip to New York city suddenly ended. So we left friends and acquaintances who had been very kind; left the din and hubbub of Broadway, and turned towards the army again.

29

I ought not to omit to mention here the kindness of Mr. Stetson of the Astor. He had offered the officers of ours the free hospitalities of his house at the beginning of our stay ; and at the last moment, after unvarying good offices, he came over to bid us good-by. He was always fond of the SECOND ; and doubtless he thought, also, of one of our young officers, born in his house, always a favorite of his, who, after a brave and gallant service, fell while leading our regiment at Gettysburg, and now sleeps in a soldier's honored grave. It was that commander who, on our last Sunday before the recent movement, in which he lost his life, in the sickness of the chaplain, called out the regiment at the usual hour, and himself conducted divine worship.

So we left New York harbor early on Sunday morning ; passed down by Staten Island, and in front of the magnificent fortifications erecting there ; by and by left Sandy Hook ; steamed on in sight of the long, low, silver-fringed Jersey coast, and by afternoon were out of sight of land again.

There was not a lively company on board that day. Bodily reasons had some influence. For myself I confess to decidedly uncomfortable sensations all day in that organ, which some ugly woman has said was the most direct avenue to a man's heart, viz., the stomach. *That* is a vile calumny. But then people must *eat;* though how one can do it when he is — not seasick ; O, no — but feeling somehow as if — well, not exactly as he did on dry land, is a puzzler.

Then the detachment felt a little blue. Not that we were leaving a city ; that is nothing. But the new partings from friends who had come on to see us ; the plans which one week more would have completed ; the friends who were just coming, some to see, perhaps, a son whose brother had just fallen, — these things left a sombre shade over us. For

myself, a wife and child had come the day before ; and in the
suddenness of departure it was rather hard to be unable to
inform them of the movement, to see them once again, to say
" good-by " before leaving for — how long? But such is the
life in war. It knows no ties but ties to country ; and no
rules, but instant obedience. God keep our wives and
children !

On the boat I thought of these things. I thought of the
likeness of this event to God's mode in providence. How
often does it happen, not only on the battle-field, but at home,
that the summons comes, with no delay for parting interviews,
for men to embark on the infinite eternity, for no return?
Even if circumstances allow, as they happened to for some of
our men, to take farewell interviews, yet it must make no
delay. " Forward ! " is inexorable when the moment comes.

If unprepared, there is no time to prepare. If the knapsack be unpacked, it remains unpacked. If plans are not
finished, they remain unfinished forever. " Forward ! "

If we felt this, we should be less unprepared for life.
What rule is there for any one but this army order, " Ready
to move at a moment's notice "? Let business be arranged,
and affairs of property settled. Let the heart be right
towards God, and eternal interests cared for. " In such an
hour as ye think not the Son of Man cometh." And happy
is that man in life, who is always " ready to move at a
moment's notice.

There is no need of lingering on our trip. The same waste
of waters, the same phosphorescent lights struck out at night
in the wake of our propeller, the sight of white sails, or of
puffing steamers, and the steady throbbing of our engines
carrying us on, until, when Tuesday's daylight appeared, we
saw Cape Charles, and in the forenoon Cape Henry, and then

we turn up into the lordly Chesapeake ; and at evening just pass the light at Point Lookout, which marks the entrance to the Potomac, and there, because the river is hard to navigate in the night, we anchor until daylight. By two o'clock the next afternoon, we are opposite Alexandria ; and before sunset we have occupied our old field just west of that miserable town.

The return trip was, on the whole, pleasant. It is easier journeying by sea than over dusty roads. Our steamer was the iron *Mississippi*, a twin of the *Merrimack*, which took us to New York ; made on the same plans by the same good builder, Harrison Loring, of Boston, finished nearer like that than any pea is like another ; but as twins differ, so this boat measured exactly seventeen tons and forty ninety-fifths more than the other ; and it had seventy-two cork jackets (probably not intended for three regiments), and six life-boats, and eighty buckets, and sixteen axes, and was fit to go " one thousand two hundred miles," which was more than enough for us. We had a capital captain, Captain Baxter, of Hyannis, who believed in his boat, as a colonel always believes in his regiment, and a very clever purser, Purser Sampson, of Dedham, who did his best, which was very good.

So we are on our return to the army. We have a delightful prospect of sixty miles march on hand, almost in " a land where no water is." And then, whatever Providence may have in store. Our episode is over. The good friends in New York — and I had for myself many kind callers at camp, and so did others — we shall remember. And our men will be no worse soldiers for seeing those dearest to them.

SEPTEMBER 15, 1863.

WE left Alexandria (our three regiments) about two P. M. on Thursday, September 10. Our expectations that transportation by rail would be furnished to us as it had been to other troops of our expedition, were frustrated; and we started over a road familiar to the army of Virginia, and in parts as much so to us as our native State. The present march was our first direct and entire one over the straight road, though we had before been over roads parallel for the same distance.

We made eight miles that day. What a waste that country is! Inhabitants gone, lines generally obliterated, houses destroyed. About seven miles from Alexandria is Annandale — called a "dale" doubtless from its being situated on an elevated plain, just as the South calls itself "chivalric" because it whips women and sells babies. Annandale was made up of half a dozen houses; now it comprises one or two houses, and the balance in chimneys. There was also one fence, a weak attempt — a kind of "poor but loyal" fence, probably. There is a small stream just south of this, on the south bank of which we camped.

At four A. M., reveille. At six A. M. we were on the road. And so was a long train of fresh horses going to the army under cavalry escort. The method of security was by attaching — say fifty — horses on each side of a long rope extending from a wagon in front to a wagon in the rear. It was amusing to see the starting after any halt; the horses' legs being on all sides of every rope at once. But it was not amusing to have the affair on the road. Despite all effort at peace, the cavalry managers tried to interfere with us continually. If we halted, they halted. When we started, they

29 *

would make every effort to break our line. At one place, they succeeded in driving a wagon of our detachment into a ditch, and breaking some part. As more trouble was likely to ensue, our commander wheeled a guard across the road. Thereupon a young lieutenant drew his pistol on the guard; but a dozen Indiana bayonets pointing instantly at his breast, he quickly concluded to postpone his funeral, which would certainly have been provided for the moment he had fired a shot. At a subsequent attempt of that train to make trouble, the butts of muskets were used with great success; the only mistake being in not using the steel, for we were clearly right. The dust, too, was a nuisance. Imagine a road covered with the dryest and finest powder — whole regiments passing over it — cavalry starting it up — and you can conceive of a road in which a decent breath was next to impossible. Add the want of water, and pity the troops. And then we met and passed an immense train of empty wagons of sutlers, coming on under escort, — it seemed unendurable. How many a soldier will recognize such a description!

But we had some relief, when, having passed through desolate Fairfax, we arrived within half a mile of Centreville, and halted. There we found the Second Massachusetts cavalry and met friends. Dr. DeWolf, their surgeon, took two men of ours in his hospital, for we had no accommodations, and showed us other kindnesses. Some old friends were there, — and I found the excellent chaplain whom I had met once before on a sad occasion, — and we should be old friends, I am persuaded, in a very short time. Here the men had their dinner, such as it was. And then, passing between the old earthworks, we went to Bull Run.

Having had a march of seventeen miles already, there being no need of haste, the men being footsore and tired,

there being plenty of water there, and none of any consequence for miles onward, after a rest, the order came, of
course, to fall in!" We did so, and went on three miles to
Manassas Junction, and got in camp after dark, and obtained
a little dirty water; to be roused up at four A. M. again.

Then to start, and to see no signs of life for miles, except
as the army gave them. Chimneys were plenty. Indeed, if
any enterprising man wants ready made chimneys, as being
handy in case of building, he could doubtless drive a good
trade, and lay in a large stock on this road. Four miles
brought us to Bristow Station — to accomplish which re-
versely last year cost us twenty miles of detour. At
Bristow we found friends, the Thirty-third Massachusetts,
whose splendid band played for us as we moved on. There
was the spot where, last year, we witnessed the burning of
half a mile of cars; the one building then standing being
now gone. A few miles further, on the edge of Kettle Run,
was the spot where we lay all day idle, in sound of the battle
of Manassas, — with as many troops, I think, as Fitz John
Porter was cashiered for the alleged reason of not bringing in, — the number which, it was stated, would have
secured victory. From that point the heat was intense.
There was literally no water. The men suffered accordingly.
But after occasional rests, we halted at Catlett's, where a
little moist dirt was tried to quench thirst; halted for two
hours within a mile of our destined camp, and so got wet,
but relieved, by a thunder shower.

The next morning we marched to Bealeton, every inch of
the road historical and familiar. The march was pleasanter
for the rain of the day before, and another that morning had
lain the dust. The evil of occasional muddy spots was more
than balanced by the absence of clouds of dust. All day the

sunshine and cloud strove for mastery. Sometimes it was intensely hot, but then a good-natured cloud would interpose its sun-shade, and relieve us. Miles more brought us to camp. How pleasant it seemed to get back. The Thirteenth New Jersey were drawn in line, and welcomed, with cheers, each of our regiments back to the stout old Third brigade ; and so we settled down.

We have moved since. We heard that day the noise of artillery as we were getting home again.

After all, New York is a humbug compared with the army. It is tattoo, as I write. What music it is, compared with the nuisance noises of those city streets ! Our candles are not brilliant ; but the sight of the lights of the camps all around is more pleasant than the glare of the city gas. The air is the pure air of heaven, not the choky stuff of the metropolis. The men are doing something noble, not dawdling away these glorious days in selling tape and ribbons. The soldier lives to some purpose, and if he dies, it is a hero's death. The silks of that wealthy mart may be coveted by some ; but what are the whole, to our bullet-riddled old flag, which passed from the stiffening hands of one colorbearer to another in the days of many a battle ?

NEAR THE RAPIDAN, VA., September 22, 1863.

IT is no news to you that the army has advanced from the Rappahannock to the line of the Rapidan, or, correctly, the Rapid Ann. This river is a branch of the Rappahannock, flowing into that stream some twenty miles above Fredericksburg. It runs easterly, below the base of Cedar Mountain, and some miles south of Culpepper.

The artillery firing which we heard as we approached the Rappahannock, on the 13th, was occasioned by the crossing mainly of cavalry. The Second corps followed. Some fighting accompanied the advance to Culpepper.

Our own corps left Kelly's Ford on the 15th. We were not sorry to leave that vicinity; for although the scenery was pleasant, the water was scarce and detestable. In dipping up a cupful, you were often successful in catching a few hundred squirming little rascals. As we advanced, we lost this opportunity, but the dead-cat-ish taste was equally strong.

Crossing at Kelly's Ford, over a pontoon bridge, we were at the same point at which our corps crossed in the Chancellorville movement. Mr. Kelly's mill and little village was the same — the rank, rich, old rebel. The old path was followed, in the misty morning, for several miles: then, instead of turning eastward to Germanna Ford, the road was taken to Stephensburg, a little village of the usual decayed order, which is about seven miles from Kelly's Ford, and four eastward of Brandy Station. The rain of the forenoon ceased, though at night the weather was unsettled. We camped there. On a little knoll of land just above Stephensburg I noticed the side of a distant hill. I could not mistake the outline; it was the memorable Cedar Mountain.

On the morning of the 16th we were early on the road. Turning at right angles, in Stephensburg, the southeasterly road was the one to Raccoon Ford. It was only a five mile march; but the last part was crooked into every point of the compass, for the sake of avoiding the observation of the enemy, who occupied, as a signal station, a hill on the other side of the Rapidan. The firing of our cavalry pickets near the river was quite frequent with that of the enemy; and but for keeping in the woods, and for a mist shrouding us, we would have been greatly exposed at short range, as the road led along near the river. Before finding what may be called a temporarily permanent stopping-place, we were repeatedly halted, in line of battle, where the woods were pleasant, and the fall flowers, of red, and yellow, and white, and blue, were growing.

At one of these halts there came up a savage thunder shower. As soon as thoroughly wet, orders came to go into camp, a few rods from where we then were. It rained savagely that night, and we suddenly awoke to the fact, when well wet and thoroughly cold, with but few and small fires allowable, that it was the equinoctial.

An equinoctial is a very pretty thing, when you are at home in a comfortable house, before a snug wood fire in an open fireplace. But an equinoctial in the woods, with scant shelter of cloth and a little smouldering fire, and, every now and then the thunder of a gun throwing grape at every group of pickets, as that evening, is not charming. Even the pickets at one point could be relieved, then and later, only after dark. But the men bore it patiently. How abominable it is that traitors at home should try to weaken the army and lengthen out its hardships.

On the 19th our regiment changed camp a short distance, to get out of the mud. And on the next day early came orders for the brigade to change again, with the object of getting a little farther from the range of divers ugly looking affairs on the other side of the river. So tents and shelters were taken down, and after waiting for nearly four hours, we were ordered to put them up again and stay where we were. Ours and the Third Wisconsin were to support the pickets; that is, be handy in case of a breach of the peace. We are on the extreme right of our army's line.

It became quiet, our corps commander forbade all picket firing, and when the rebels found that no reply was made, they stopped it too. But the low ground here is not the most comfortable place to live in.

On the opposite side an enemy, apparently in plenty. I went out to take a look at them. Take a walk through the woods, *so ;* then turn, *so ;* then cross a brook ; then turn, *so ;* then go up a little knoll, and you see a nice earthwork opposite, and rows of rifle pits constantly growing longer, and rebel soldiers on duty, or going after water, or smoking their pipes. As a small party of ours were looking, the other day, the rebels brought out a flag, and waved it back and forth, which was pleasanter than a shower of grape. Their position is strong, being on bluffs, and they have improved it.

Of course we will not stay here long. Events are already in progress, and when I write again, something will have been done. If we leave soon, — the grounds of the Kansas Stringfellow I am told, — we shall not object.

A painful episode, the first of the kind I have witnessed, took place last Friday. It was a military execution. The person thus punished belonged to the Third Maryland, which is in our division. His crime was *desertion.* It was his second offence. For the first, he had been sentenced only to three months' labor and loss of pay. For the second, death !

While the army was passing through Frederick, Maryland, in its recent movement, he had got out of camp. His regiment passed on, and he went to Baltimore. Arrested there, he was returned to the army ; was tried ; was convicted ; and was sentenced.

On Tuesday last his sentence was formally read to him. He was to be shot to death with musketry, on the next

Friday, between the hours of noon and four P. M.   But he
had learned the decision on the Sunday before.

There is no chaplain to the Third Maryland regiment.
But Chaplain Welsh of the Fifth Connecticut, in the same
brigade, ministered to him in spiritual matters faithfully, and
like himself, day by day.   At last it fell to me to see him,
and to be with him during most of his remaining hours.   But
what could be done, in the way of instruction, had been done
by Mr. Welsh, and for it the man was grateful.

The day of his execution was wet and gloomy.   That
morning, in the midst of the provost guard, he was sitting on
a bag of grain, leaning against a tree, while a sentry, with
fixed bayonet, stood behind, never turning away from him,
and never to turn away save as another took his place, until
the end.   Useless seemed the watch, for arms and feet had
been secured, though not painfully, since the sentence was
read.

The captain of the guard had humanely done all he could ;
and it was partly by his request that I was there.   A chaplain could minister where others could not be allowed.

The rain fell silently on him.   The hours of his life were
numbered — even the minutes.   He was to meet death, not
in the shock and excitement of battle, not as a martyr for
his country, not in disease, but in full health, and as a criminal.

I have seen many a man die, and have tried to perform
the sacred duties of my station.   I have never had so painful a task as that, because of these circumstances.   Willingly, gladly, he conversed, heard, and answered.   While
painful is such a work, it has its bright side, because of the
" exceeding great and precious promises " it is one's privilege
to tell.

When the time came for removal to the place of execution, he entered an ambulance, the chaplain accompanying him. Next, in another ambulance, was the coffin. Before, behind, and on either side a guard. Half a mile of this sad journey brought him to within a short distance of the spot. Then leaving the ambulance, he walked to the place selected. The rain had stopped. The sun was shining on the dark lines of the whole division, drawn up on three sides of a hollow square. With guard in front and rear, he passed with steady step through an opening left in the head of the square, still with the chaplain, and to the open side. There was a grave just dug, and in front of it was his coffin placed. He sat upon the coffin; his feet were reconfined, to allow of which he lifted them voluntarily, and his eyes were bandaged.

In front of him, the firing party of two from each regiment, were then drawn up, — half held as reserve, — during which there was still a little time for words with his chaplain. The general stood by, and the provost marshal read the sentence and shook hands with the condemned. Then a prayer was offered, amid uncovered heads and solemn faces. A last hand-shake with the chaplain, which he had twice requested; a few words from him to the chaplain — a lingering pressure by the hand of the condemned; his lips moving with a prayer-sentence which he had been taught, and on which his thoughts had dwelt before; and he was left alone.

The word of command was immediately given. One volley, and he fell over instantly, unconscious. A record of wounds was made by the surgeons, who immediately examined him. The troops filed by his grave on the banks of the swollen stream, and then passed off, under cover of the woods as they had come, to avoid being seen by the enemy. And so, twenty years old, and with only a mother and sister, he was left there. The sun was soon covered with clouds, and the rain poured down on his solitary grave.

Are these things necessary? The whole history of war says they are. However much we pity, it is a necessity. Had there been greater firmness in these things near two years ago, life would have been saved now.

Every man who deserts increases the dangers of his comrades. He weakens their hands. He becomes a traitor to his country. I wish I could reach the ear of every man now in desertion, and urge him to be a man again. Voluntarily returning, his punishment might be mitigated. Taken as a deserter, his fate is clear.

It is true, a man may be killed in battle. True. But how long is it to be before we learn that the country has a right to *every* man's service ? How long before objectors to conscription will remember that instead of taking a part only, the nation has a right to call upon all? That it has a right to even those not " able-bodied," and waives it only because they could not be made useful? How long will it be before the blush of shame will cover the cheek of every man who, for slight cause, has succeeded in obtaining " exemption "?

" Slight cause." Doubtless rigid rules would have " exempted " a third of all our old force, if they had made efforts. But they volunteered, and have made splendid soldiers.

Men have been encouraged by their friends to desert. You who helped it, helped kill this man shot last Friday, and every other man shot for desertion. If the one you helped desert is taken, you helped shoot him.

And scarcely less wicked and more despicable is the conduct of some at home who are earnest for war. I have in mind some men who wanted this war, and who now urge it on that slavery may be abolished ; who have been furious, because the army, too weak, has not done impossibilities; who have clamored against the soldier's wishes, and faith, and enthusiasm. Such men should have volunteered long ago. When the army was faint and weak, and help did not come, who but advocates for a great principle should have hurried to arms! Many have, very many. But they who cried for war and did not go, — able-bodied men, — let them keep silent forever.

CHAPTER XIV.

FROM THE RAPIDAN TO THE TENNESSEE.

DEPARTMENT OF THE CUMBERLAND, October 5, 1863.

WE were at Raccoon Ford on the Rapidan. Our regiment was supporting the pickets at that crossing, and lay in easy range of the guns which frowned from the constantly extending earthworks on the enemy's hills. We had, on Saturday, September 19, gathered around our first autumn fire, kept low for security. We were eating our hard bread discriminatingly, picking out the — well, don't mention it — but it was old "White House Landing" bread. Eight days' rations were constantly kept on hand, which really means that men must live eight days on four days' food. Everybody anticipated a movement; and there is reason to believe that one would have taken place within two days, when orders came, which resulted in what the Richmond papers announced as the movement of the Eleventh and Twelfth corps to reënforce General Rosecrans. At any rate those orders set us to travelling up and down the roads of Tennessee, with an occasional touch of Alabama.

On the 24th of September the orders came to move. Where, was none of a soldier's business. Like him who "went out, not knowing whither he went," the soldier starts on his journey of ten miles or a thousand, relying on the guidance and care of superiors. So, on a pleasant day, after a few hours of waiting, we wound our way circuitously under cover of the woods, which, for the time, hid our movement from the eyes of the enemy. The other division soon appeared ; so we found that the whole corps was in motion. A few miles out, there silently passed us another corps to take our place. So the Ford was not to be abandoned, nor was any forward movement probable. Passing through Stephensburg, we took the road to Brandy Station, which looked like railroad-ing. And we speculated more. We had heard of disasters to General Rosecrans, and the wild idea began to float in our minds that we might be going thither. When, after dark, we had reached the station, and orders came to turn in all "transportation" and extra supplies, we knew that we had a long journey before us ; and everybody's heart beat with new expectations. We studied the map, and settled down on the Baltimore and Ohio Railroad as our probable route. We were right. Our corps was to leave the army of the Potomac, although as is said, on sufficient authority, the commanding general asked to have it left, and some other taken.

We bivouacked at Brandy Station. There the paymaster appeared and worked all night. I was not so well pleased as some. For, by a recent outrageous decision, no chaplain can draw pay for time when sick or disabled. So, for the time of my recent illness, all pay was cut off. It is true that no other officer or man in the service is so 'treated ; but chaplains are under the ban in certain departments. It is true that, in my case the surgeon of the brigade had examined me when the army was to move, and decided that, as I was unable to sit up. I could not accompany the troops — as was

30 *

354 THE POTOMAC AND THE RAPIDAN.

done with other officers and men ; and, furthermore, certified
that my illness was caused by " exposure in the line of duty."
But who cares for chaplains? As it is, the government
really says to every chaplain, " Do not expose your health
in the slightest degree. Be sure never to go within range of
shot or shell to help a wounded man, or comfort the dying.
For if, by any chance, you get wounded or sick in dis-
charging your duty, you are selected for special insult ; your
pay shall instantly cease, although you are subject to orders
the same as ever." In my own case, as camp expenses went
on as usual, and as there were the added expenses of sickness
— the entire cessation of a pay insufficient, at any time, to
support my family and myself, offered me a temptation to
leave the service for a settlement, whose overtures had been
made — a temptation, the strongest I have ever felt to leave.

But it was only for a moment. I can now say, while
feeling the sense of personal injustice keenly, what I could
not before have said as well — that any man who would let
any personal wrong from officials weaken, in the least degree,
his loyalty to his government, or cause him to array himself
against the men who are the only authorized administrators
of the government, is unworthy of being in the army. The
time may come when my vote and my influence may
remember certain individuals ; but the time is not now.
Now, the national life is at stake. Now, the administration
is trying nobly and heartily to save the country. Private
injuries are the things of a day. The national life is
essential to the prosperity of millions. I can just as cheerfully support the administration as though I was of its party ;
and I shall do so, I must do so, as a patriot. And this is all
I shall say of the dishonest affair. I here mention it only
because I want to call the attention of law-makers to the fact

that this is but one of a class of wrongs systematically wrought upon chaplains by departments at Washington.

But I had something else to think of that evening. Late into the night I was sitting by the side of a man condemned to die. There was no chaplain to his regiment. It was his last night on earth. Our General Williams, as kind-hearted as brave, had requested me to see him. The man had scoffingly, abusively, repelled all attempts to do him good; and had, both at his trial and ever since, shammed half idiocy.

He was only twenty years old, but was experienced in crime.

The clouds were fitfully gliding across the face of the moon as I found him. The guards drew back as I came near. He was sitting on a piece of wood, in front of a low fire, at which he was heating some water in his dipper.

As I stood there a moment quietly, he looked up, but he had no suspicion of my office or object. When the guards drew back, he cast furtive glances at the wood in the rear, but there was no chance for escape, even after the guards had loosened his cords.

At the settling of a half-burnt stick his dipper was near falling. I replaced it, and asked, —

"What are you heating that for? Coffee?"

"Yes."

"It's almost boiling."

"Yes, I am just going to put the coffee in." And he did, and I helped him.

"What are you under guard for?"

Suspicious instantly that I had some errand, he put on a stupid look. "O, I'm to be discharged, and this is an escort. I'm going to New York to-morrow. I don't know much. I know that."

I answered in some casual way, which checked his suspicion, and talked about indifferent matters.

He became quite communicative; told me when he had enlisted, and how he ran away; how he reënlisted, and got the bounty, and ran away again.

" You were not very shrewd to get caught."

" No, I don't know much. I'm going home again," relapsing into his former stupid appearance.

" Do you know," said I, " that you have been tried for desertion, and your sentence read?"

" Sentence? They read my discharge the other day. I don't know much."

I tried to keep his attention to that point, but he would not admit the idea. But from his eye it was evident he was shamming.

I asked him about his early life. Gradually he became communicative. His face lighted up.

" I was a newsboy; took good care of myself, too. They couldn't match me for sharpness, I tell you. I could swindle the best of 'em." And so he told me of various exploits.

It was time to try determinedly to do him good. The night was passing. I asked him of his mother. Yes, he had a mother; but, for the first time, I found a man who was callous on that theme. " I don't know much," was his constant conclusion.

By and by I said to him, —

" You are going to be shot to-morrow. You know it. It is useless with me to sham stupid. You *know* you are going into the presence of God. It is time you were thinking of this matter."

He interrupted me with an attempt at violent remark; but I looked him steadily in the face, and he yielded.

I talked for some time. He made no reply, except occasional assent to a question. By and by he said "I don't know much," and seemed indifferent.

I was almost in despair. A new thought struck me. He had, in speaking of his mother, and of his boyhood, admitted that in very early childhood his mother attended Catholic worship, though for years abandoned. I recalled the indelible character of early impressions, and the regard of that church for the symbol of the cross. So, having a twig in my hand, I said, —

"Look here." He looked. I slowly made on the ground the sign of the cross, and asked, "What is that?"

Instantly, with an entire abandonment of all pretence of stupidity, he answered, almost reverently, "The cross!"

"What happened on that cross?"

"Jesus Christ was crucified."

"What for?"

"To save sinners."

I record these facts to show how, when the certainty of death on the morrow, and all recollection of home failed, this impression of childhood opened an avenue to his heart.

Then for some time he listened and spoke freely. But I cannot tell whether any good was done by word or prayer.

The guards closed around him again as I left, and bound him; and the sentry took his place again by his side.

Before noon next day the condemned man was brought out. I saw the division marching to the spot, and the prisoner with a chaplain. Then I sheltered myself out of sight. The murmur of the drums came across the hill, and a subdued and mournful melody. Then a volley; and I knew that he was dead, and beyond any more prayer.

Early on Saturday we marched ten miles to Bealeton, and

waited until Sunday morning. The cars came then, and we were soon on board — horses and baggage to come in other trains.

So we left. Left the State where, for more than two years, we had studied every road, and every hill, and every water-course. Left the graves of our dead heroes. Left the noble army of Virginia, whose heroism can never be surpassed ; — firm in battle ; patient under injuries ; abused for want of success, when success was made impossible ; insultingly compared with troops who never had to fight with such disciplined and picked men as we have — except, indeed, at Chickamauga, when the Longstreet men, against whom we had stood unbroken in battle after battle, brushed away some divisions like chaff, swept up prisoners at will, and carried off whole batteries.

Through Alexandria. Across the Potomac. A few minutes halt at Washington. Then away, away! The country wants men at Chattanooga, and it is a thousand miles off. We stop at Relay to rearrange trains. A man was killed near there, falling from our train. He had left his own, which was contrary to orders ; he had got drunk, which was contrary to orders ; and he climbed to the top of a car, which was contrary to orders.

It was night at Relay ; and those of us who had room, spread our blankets on the car floor, and laid down to broken sleep. The long trains sped onward, and daylight found us at Berlin. The river mists were partially hiding the scenery, but we remembered it well. Harper's Ferry reappeared, with a new iron bridge. Martinsburg, where the men stopped for free bread and coffee. At Hancock, we saw the first red leaves of the year, which grew thicker the farther we went. Often did we see red vines clinging all about the trunk of a green tree. They were like the parasite-climbers, who try to crawl to eminence up the Memory of a great leader, but whose frost-falling leaves show they are only parasites, while the giant Memory is still fresh and beautiful.

Then we crossed streams, and pierced tunnels, and clung to mountain sides, and wound through valleys. We were in a magnificent country, and the road, in its bold and solid engineering, was fitted for it. But as pleasant was the waving of handkerchiefs from loyal little houses, nestling among the hills. Especially at Cumberland, a town hidden delightfully among the coal mountains, which we reached after sunset, the loyal crowds were heartiest. On again, and in the evening shadows we watched the glorious mountains. When I lay down that night, it was to think of the glory of Him, who reared these vast hills, and cut paths for the waters, and who gave to man the mind, the plan, and the hand to make the great work on which we rode.

At sunrise, the hills were behind us, but hills were before us. At Altamont we were twenty-seven hundred feet above Baltimore. In Kingwood Tunnel, we rode nearly a mile. After Grafton, where we saw relics of rebel raids, and water from an artesian well, and tasted something which was called coffee, we plunged again into more hills. It was a wonderful change from insipid Eastern Virginia, and the people a vast improvement over the sly-looking, deceitful-acting inhabitants of that tract, of which it is said (in paraphrase of the Englishman's words), that God made Manassas Plain, and it should be added, that he made it for Virginians. It is not decent enough for any other race.

Our engine was a frisky fellow. He was a stalwart concern, rioting in strength. Sometimes he would travel as steadily as a deacon's horse. The next moment he would

be peeping over some huge precipice ; and then, as if he had
frightened us enough, he would dart away from the edge
with screams of delight.   Then he would scrape against the
mountain side ; or change his mind, and rush across some
river, or follow its current, as if that was the best way out
of these bewildering hills.   Sometimes he would twist our
train into curves like a snake, and straighten out again.   He
would determine to tie us into a double bow-knot, or would
wheel around and look us in the face.   Then, as if ashamed,
he would dart out of sight into some hole in the mountain,
and come out screaming on the other side.   If tired of climbing up some steep hill, he would wait for a neighboring engine
to come out of some side track, and help him up with half of
the load ; and then ours would scream out " Much 'bliged,"
and go on again.   But, as if he knew what a precious load
of loyal troops he carried, he was very careful of us.   He
was no copperhead.   Among a dozen like trains, he never
ran into one, nor let one run against him.   If he stopped for
fuel and drink, he always shouted before starting.   And at
last, a little before midnight, he dropped us safely at Ben-
wood, far above that Potomac, whose course we had followed, till we saw it little more than a rivulet.

We crossed the Ohio on a pontoon bridge ; on the river's
pebbly bank took coffee and hard bread — the Western hard
bread, which is better than the Eastern ; were packed into
cars, and started about two A. M. of Wednesday, on the
Central Ohio Railroad.   Morning found us near Cambridge ;
and daylight showed us thrifty farms and respectable houses,
in a country more broken than I had expected.   At Zanesville, we had to delay ; and so took breakfast, after washing
off considerable dirt into the waters of the Muskingum.
Zanesville is remarkable for having an eating-room con-

nected with a railway in which you can get a good breakfast, the only instance of the kind in all my travelling
experience.

We were a couple of hours at Columbus, which we left at
three P. M. As our rambles were restricted to the limits
of the railway grounds, I have no very comprehensive view
of the capital of Ohio. To reach the capital of Indiana, we
took the Columbus and Xenia Railway to Xenia; then the
Xenia and Dayton and Western Railway to Richmond; then
the Indiana Central Railway to Indianapolis. We should
never have favored all this line, but our paternal government
put us along without change of cars from the Ohio River
at Bellaire to Indianapolis.

But linger at Xenia. For when we stopped there, in the
evening, a woman appeared with milk. And when asked the
price, "nothing!" And then there suddenly appeared a whole
swarm of women and girls, with huge quantities of meat,
potatoes, eggs, pies, cakes, fruit, and milk, which they proceeded to deal out to the soldiers most lavishly. "What is
to pay?" asked the astonished men. "Nothing. We are
not *Vallandigham* people; we take no pay of *soldiers!*" I
wish you could have heard the intense scorn with which
the word *Vallandigham* was spoken. The tone was that in
which men say Judas Iscariot or Benedict Arnold. The
soldiers ate till they could eat no more. It was not merely
the good nice food which rejoiced us; it was the frank,
hearty, warm-heartedness of these Ohio girls, who ministered
so freely to the wants of strangers, while their fathers, husbands, and ——, &c. — held the lanterns. We have never
been treated so before. As the hand-shakings ended, and
" good-byes were said, and the cars rolled off amid the
cheers of our men, everybody felt more brave, more patriotic,

more happy for that kindness.   I speak the wishes of the men
recording thanks.   They say, " God bless the Xenia girls ! "

_____

TENNESSEE, October 15, 1863.

THEN we hurried on, stopping briefly at Dayton, and at the
dawn of the next morning following, found ourselves in Indiana.   I liked the country there even better than Ohio,
as we passed through fine farms and walnut groves.   At
noon, we were in Indianapolis, a place which I remember
principally from the fact that dealers asked me nine dollars
and a half for. a rubber article, whose exact mate I had
bought in Washington for five dollars, and Washington is
not noted for low prices.   I have also a vague idea of a fine
city, and of an infinite number of railways centring in a very
fine station-house.   We left at six P. M. on the Jeffersonville
Railway, and at half past five A. M. were at Jeffersonville,
on the Ohio.   We crossed on the funniest ferry-boat I ever
saw, venerable for age, as its engine was also, — to Louis-
ville, a city which seemed to me one of the best built and
most charming I have ever passed through.   At the " Soldier's Rest," where the Sanitary Commission is to be felt, we
had bread, meat, and coffee ; and then hurried through Kentucky, a delightful State, and to Nashville, Tennessee, which
we reached on Saturday morning, half an hour after midnight.   My impressions of Nashville are only those acquired
in passing round its edge, and so around a great white marble building, staring in the moonlight, surrounded by a good
many fenceless houses lower than its foundations.   It took a
couple of hours to change trains ; and then we started off.
At morn we were near the Stone River battle-field.   At half
after midnight. Sunday morning. we reached Stevenson : we

were tumbled out of the cars on a plain between the mountains, and, our railway journey of eleven hundred miles from
Bealeton, Virginia, being ended, we bivouacked on the soil
of Alabama.

Let nobody think that seven days' and nights' journey by
railway is a delightful trip to soldiers.   Crowded into uncomfortable cars ; unable to preserve cleanliness ; with no
satisfying sleep ; often doubtful as to the next breakfast, dinner, or supper ; restricted at every stopping place by military
authority ; — I prefer a good wagon, a nice horse, an agree-
able companion, plenty of money, and lots of leisure.

On the Sunday when we waked up at Stevenson, a busy
depot for supplies, in the morning mists of the Tennessee
River, I almost hoped to hold public worship.   But as sing-
ing-books were all in our baggage, which, with horses came
in another train (only the horses have not yet come), I went
to the station of the Christian Commission to get a supply.
The agent there, Mr. Lawrence, kindly offered me every
facility, but it proved useless.   I got back to camp only to
find the men under orders to move again.

I was much pleased with the appearance of things at the
Commission's station, under the care of Mr. Lawrence.   And,
indeed, from still later observation and information, I am
satisfied the Commission is doing a most excellent work here.
Rev. E. P. Smith of Pepperell, is at the head, whose abilities
and judgment are themselves a guarantee of success.   There
exists (I learn and believe) entire harmony between the
various benevolent and Christian workers.   I anticipate
great pleasure in the help of the Commission.   If the Commission ever meets with friction, I am persuaded it is due
to a *violation* of instructions by delegates, and not to the instructions themselves.   These instructions seem here to be

adhered to. But the work suffers somewhat from the inex-
perience of "delegates." I wish that the Commission would
venture on the employment of a greater number of permanent agents; for a few weeks do not suffice to teach a "delegate" his business. "Delegates" and managers have
repeatedly told me this. The Commission can raise money
easily enough. Let it employ permanent laborers more
freely, at a living salary, and it will increase its efficiency
enormously.

We were ordered to move, by rail, back to Decherd. Such
a railway as we travelled on is a curiosity. Leading through
a range of hills, necessitating deep cuts, and one tunnel of
two thousand two hundred and twenty-eight feet, the road
seems built at as little expense as possible. Its cuts are
exceedingly narrow, as well as long and frequent. The blue
limestone up the sides of these passages seems inclined to
tumble down in masses. Great cracks are plenty; and I am
told that such occurrences are by no means infrequent. The
grade is enormous; often, for long distances, you climb at
the rate of one hundred and seventeen feet to the mile. Often,
too, all ideas of level seem to be disregarded. You go up
hill and down hill to save a moderate levelling process.
There were two trains of us that day, and at the worst rise
a third engine came out to help. But it took half an hour to
get the trains by the siding, to enable the third engine to get
on to the main track. Then it took time to get the three to
work together. One engine would scream twice, which is to
say, "start up." The second responds, the third agrees.
But when one pulled, the other two were lazy, and so *vice
versa*. And so they mixed up things, until one thought, like
the man who "worked his passage" on a canal by driving
the horses on the tow-path, that if it was not for the name

of riding, one might as well go afoot. But when we had passed the tunnel, and came down hill again, things whizzed!

But, while in the long and dark tunnel, where in some places there were but a few inches extra room, I heard a remark which hit my thoughts. It was, "Never mind. There's daylight ahead!" True. And how often, in darkest hours, by watching, we should see "daylight ahead!"

How often, when watching does no good, yet by faith we might *know* that "there's daylight ahead!" In darkness, we are tried. We are in trouble. We see no light. But God reigns. Have no fear, therefore. Keep on the path marked out. A powerful hand will take you through. "There's daylight ahead!"

We were sent to Decherd because a body of rebel cavalry were afloat on the east of the road, and it was not known where they would strike. They had come up through some gap in the mountains, having crossed the Tennessee. A long line of road like this is hard to hold, of course; but it must be held, because the army must be fed. We learned at Decherd, that the rebels had occupied McMinnville, a little town at the end of a branch railway, perhaps ten miles off. It seems that this was true, and that they made some captures. We learned that the rebels were about ten thousand strong! On Monday afternoon we were moved northward by rail four miles to Elk River, or Alisonia. Then we learned that the railway was cut above. Here we found most hospitable friends, and the genial Western kindness — of which, by and by. This day we learned that the rebels were only eighteen hundred strong! On Tuesday, we had orders to move. Cars did not come as ordered, and we *travelled* eight miles, to Tullahoma. I confess I did not prefer walking, but as we had no horses, that was our only resource. I came to the conclusion, on the road, that every commander charged with conducting the march of troops, ought to go on foot. Tullahoma, our two regiments had settled down, when about ten P. M., trains came along, and as there was room for half a regiment, some general ordered half of ours into cars. He hurried us with a promptness which entitles him to promotion. The cars were crowded, and it came on to rain. We were on board at half past ten P. M., ; fancy my astonishment, when conductor, brakemen, &c., went into their car-room, and went to bed! They waked up, however, at half past four A. M., and we started, and went to near a burnt bridge, on a branch of Duck River, where we abandoned cars. Then we learned that the rebels numbered fifteen thousand, with eighteen pieces of artillery.

In the middle of the forenoon we were marched. The plan was, I suppose, to clear out everything both sides of the railway so as to re-open. We, with other troops, were to do part. We were moved first to Shelbyville to the left of the railway, to help catch the rebel cavalry who had left that town ten hours before we started to march the ten miles. We got there. The road lay through most noble groves of beech, oak, cedar, and walnut. Shelbyville is a very pretty, well built, enterprising town, strongly Union. The chivalric rebels had robbed the citizens of clothing, money, and anything else they fancied. From Shelbyville we took a partly built pike road. I never saw a worse yet — saving mud. Three miles of it we traversed after dark — partly old, with pebbles rounded up; partly swamp; partly with broken stone, not yet covered with earth; varied occasionally by heaps of rock not yet levelled; but the climax was reached when, in utter darkness and wet we tumbled off a perpendicular descent of four feet, where they mean to build a bridge some day. We staggered on till it seemed useless to go further; and the troops were turned into a wood where, after candles were lighted, the companies stacked arms. We had marched eighteen miles that day, and after I had walked that distance with my overcoat and blankets, I rejoiced to learn from good Surgeon Heath that there are *three* layers of skin, as we had worn off two thicknesses certain. However, though wet and dark, huge fires dried and refreshed us, though unfortunately no water could be found short of a mile. That day I came to the conclusion that the general conducting a march ought not only to go on foot; he ought also to carry fifteen pounds on his back.

At five A. M. we were again on foot. Two miles to Bellbuckle, a railway station, and ten more to Christiana. At Bellbuckle, we drew part rations — cut down by order of General Rosecrans, as a measure of precaution on account of interrupted communications. And that day, I concluded that the general conducting a march ought to go on foot, and to carry twenty-five pounds on his back instead of fifteen.

At Christiana we learned facts. The rebels had really about four thousand men and six or seven pieces of artillery. They had cut the road in three places — one near Murfreesboro' — one at Christiana — and one at Grierson's Creek, a mile below Wartrace. At one place the commander loaded his men on a train, and started off his six hundred we are told; while thirty rebels came in and burnt the bridge. But if so, that commander will catch his deserts. "No bridge guards are to surrender!" Our pursuing cavalry had captured two guns, and a couple hundred prisoners.

We were at Christiana two nights. On Friday evening, the road broken on Monday had been repaired, three bridges built, and rails replaced; and the trains came through amidst

cheers. The mails, stopped since the Sunday before, were
to go again. As yet we have no mails, however. Early
Saturday morning we started, on foot, towards Tullahoma.
At evening we were tangled up with a brook called Crooked
Run. After crossing it eleven times, to the great distress of
artillery, the commander thought it foolish to go farther.
We had marched twenty-three miles; and were turned into
a sorghum field. *Mem. Thirty-five* pounds instead of *twenty-
five* for a leader!

We started before daylight. We crossed Crooked Run
(that is, walked through it) sixteen times before sunrise.
At the *fifteenth*, my *boots* began to feel damp. It is due to
the public to know that boots which kept feet dry in eleven
crossings at night, and fourteen in the morning, came from
Foster & Peabody, Boston. We wound up out of the cold
valley at last, into sunshine. Then we could see the mists
below. Even so the spirit, climbing up into the highlands of
God's free love, looks down upon the mists which had so
chilled him in his low estate.

To Tullahoma; and then to Alisonia the same day. To
get ready for as industrious rains as ever tried to wet us
through.

ELK RIVER, TENNESSEE, October 22, 1863.

I HAPPENED to be in Nashville (sent there by orders for a
day) the evening when General Grant arrived, and was at
the hotel where the coach brought him. A man by no
means tall, with a frank, honest face, dressed in a brigadier's
coat, though with major-general's shoulder-straps, came in
on crutches. That was the general. He was accompanied

by the usual staff. In the evening a military band and a crowd drew him out. The crowd wanted a speech, but couldn't get a word, until somebody felicitously insisted "Unconditional surrender!" The general good naturedly submitted so far as to thank them for their good wishes, to tell them he never could talk, and he was now too old to begin, and to say good night. This hero needs not to talk; his acts speak. Governor Andrew Johnson addressed the multitude, however, and his clear voice was ringing a square or two off, as — I confess it — I yielded to appetite, and went off in search of beefsteak, rare done, and fried potatoes.

To conjecture what will take place here would be useless.

We cannot help wishing that we had here some of the troops scattered in separate pieces hundreds of miles away; or, at least, that all worked at the same time. I saw a mule team the other day — of which, when one pulled, the other three didn't. It seemed to my inexperienced judgment that the wagon could not start until the whole four pulled at once. And in fact that was the result. But it is hard, doubtless, to time every mountain on a line of a thousand miles; and probably when the real history of the war is written, we shall wonder at the skill which planned, and the energy which executed. In the mean time let us have faith.

The battle at Chickamauga seemed to excite diverse accounts. I have inquired as widely as possible; and I cannot help believing this: That Bragg largely outnumbered our forces; that some troops of ours did break, very badly, and in a way that well-disciplined men never do, by which we lost guns and supplies; but that the partial success of the enemy was stopped by the skill of General Thomas and the bravery of some of the divisions; and that Bragg entirely failed of his great object, which was to reoccupy Chattanooga.

Our army holds its own. But the rebels occupy Lookout Mountain. A glance at a good map will show you that this commands part of the railroad, if not a more important point also, and that the enemy cannot be allowed to remain there. It is to be remembered that it was not by battle, but strategy, that the enemy were forced to leave Chattanooga; is it at all certain that the enemy may not attempt the same process? The importance of this key point to the insurgents cannot be over-estimated. But we have no fears of the result.

While matters are quiet, we are rejoicing over the election returns from Ohio and Pennsylvania. These are victories which will discourage the rebels worse than Gettysburg. Southern papers were gloating over hoped-for "Peace" successes. They are disappointed. I am convinced that the bulk of the Opposition have no idea of the sympathy they had in the South; nor of the terrible discouragement it would have been to the army had they succeeded. Their good men will yet thank God for failure. As for the real Vallandigham stripe — any such hope is foolish.

Nearly two years ago I wrote that I was convinced, from observation in a slave State, that there could be no national peace until the whole social — that is, slave — system of the South was overturned. I have never doubted it since. The ruling oligarchy must be utterly overthrown, and their power for evil taken away. I do not say that no peace *ought* to be made without the overthrow of slavery; but that no real peace, without that, *can* be made. It would be a mere farce. New men, new systems of industry, new ideas, the South needs.

There is much loyalty in Tennessee. But so far as I have now seen it, it is not what is called " Border State " loyalty. It is not the loyalty which regards slavery as of more consequence than the Union. It is becoming more and more disgusted with this hateful ulcer on civilization. Not that this latter feeling is universal; but it is steadily growing.

The rebellion in which we are engaged is recognized to be one based simply on the determination of a few to continue the authority of a caste — the rule of a few educated men over a mass of whites and blacks, purposely kept ignorant and poor. That rule was growing weak before the progress of free thought. Therefore the oligarchy tried to seclude themselves in a distinct confederacy. That is the way the Union men here look at it. Tennessee is more loyal than Virginia, because in Tennessee there is a better state of society. In Virginia, the few are educated and luxurious; the many are ignorant and shiftless. In Tennessee there is far more uniform intelligence and equalized comfort; and a far nobler race of people. But of this, more by and by.

In one of the papers which is "loyal," with a strong smell of " if" about it, I find plenty of carping complaints of the administration. I find also in the same paper, —

" For sale. A No. 1 negro man; sold for no fault."

And next following, —

" Horses and mules for sale."

How significant it is of the character of this contest, military and civil, that those who oppose the administration, whether North or South, you may be sure include those who, while trading in horses or mules, also sell No. 1 negro men " for no fault ! "

CHRISTIANA, TENN., November 4, 1863.

WE have been beech-nutting down to Anderson.

We were camped at the bridge over Elk River, where a

suitable fortification attests somebody's labors, and where we were beside the First Tennessee, colored. A mile north is the station of Estell Springs. The name of that place is derived from some springs there, and from Dr. Estell of that county, who owns the springs. Once it was quite a watering-place. Wealthy people came from further South. Dr. Estell laid out streets, and sold lots of a quarter acre each, for a hundred dollars each. On these lots the purchasers erected board shanties. And in the shanties, the builders who brought their " servants " and force with them, managed to get rid of July, August, and September. " They purtended it was for their health," said a lonely resident; " but it was to git over the time; and they didn't else know how to git shet o' ther money." He had seen as many as three hundred visitors at this picnicking kind of watering-place at once. But now, the boards of the shanties have travelled to loyal camps, and a few whites, a few blacks, and several pigs and chickens, are the sole denizens of this Tennessean Saratoga. Its silence is broken only by the trains which stop here to water the engines. The springs remain. I tested them the other day. One is what the citizens called " kollee-by-it," — the warm flatirons of Mr. Sam. Weller. A little distance off are three more; one is sulphur, one lime, and one pure water from sandstone, — all three welling out from the hill-side, *less than two feet apart*. The taste from the sulphur was — I confess it — my first in life. It was also — I assert it — my last forever. Ditto with *buttermilk*, which I unwittingly put to my lips a few weeks ago, and never shall again.

Our men had built comfortable huts, but we had to leave them. We were to go to Bridgeport, on the Tennessee River, where the new railway bridge was suffered to be finished.

It would be necessary to open the road to Chattanooga. The fact was, that as the rebels commanded the road from Bridgeport to Chattanooga, all supplies had to be wagoned round over a horrible mountain-road, fifty or sixty miles. It was impossible to keep a large army supplied in this way. The only question was, between driving the rebels away from Lookout Mountain and that neighborhood, and trying how long men could live on half rations. We expected, rather, to help drive the rebels off, and it was in that expectation that our brigade marched to Anderson, — only to march back again.

Anderson lies in a valley. The scenery of the Big Crow Creek valley is delightful — home-like, except that in New Hampshire we have *real* rock, and here only limestone. Beautiful bottom lands were showing rich crops — of which, in the shape of corn, our hungry horses ventured to partake. Tobacco, cotton, and corn grew side by side. Lands there will bear a hundred bushels of corn to the acre, and the cotton would have given an immense profit, but that the frosts were too early.

Anderson is no town. Mr. Anderson lives there, and owns nearly the whole valley back to Tantallon, with several mountains, and a few rivers. His land is reckoned by miles. We camped in a beautiful beech wood, whose nuts were good and inexhaustible.

At Anderson there are wonderful springs. One pours out from under the mountain a torrent; and, some hundred yards off, is an opening six feet high, into which we walked upright, until, deep into the hill, we reached the brook. Stalactites hung from the roof. The brook was coming out of the hill still deeper, but we could go no further. There are also in the valley extensive Indian mounds, out of which

they plough relics. This was the old Cherokee country, and
Crow was a "big Indian," from which was named "Big
Crow Creek."

A variety of orders is understood to have mixed matters
with us there. In fact, they varied the day before. But it
was settled at last that we *return*. The Second division
went on, and took their part in the battle. So, on the 26th,
we left Anderson. We recrossed the abominable mountain
by the road which a native told me had been disused since
the railway was opened. We camped at Cowan — for twenty
minutes. Because, just then, came orders by telegraph that
we take the coming train, and go somewhere north. We
took it, and our promptness here served it a good turn ; for
just after we started orders came for us *not* to take the train,
but to *march*. Too late, luckily. But at Bellbuckle the
engine gave out. It was then about two A. M. We left the
train, and made coffee, and laid down and went to sleep,
knowing by experience that it was hardly worth while to
keep awake for the engine that was "just coming." And
when we waked up the train was still there, waiting for that
other engine. So it was when we marched, and we left it
there. Our horses were at Cowan, and nine miles of equal-
ity tried our boots.

ELK RIVER, TENN. November 18, 1863.

I WROTE how we went down to Anderson, beech-nutting,
and what fine success we had, — heaps of nuts, — and how
we went back to Christiana.

There, the men worked like beavers. They tore down old
huts, — for what Massachusetts regiment could occupy the
slovenly edifices that the departing troops had left. They

built warm houses. One chimney still lingers mournfully in my memory. It was a beautiful chimney. It did not smoke. It threw out the heat delightfully. I shall never be so proud of another chimney, never. "I never had a dear gazelle," &c.

That chimney had been finished two days, when orders came to move. They shifted the troops guarding different points on the road, much like the child-play of "kitchen furniture change places." A, B, C, and D rushed round into each other's posts. They said it was done to bring into juxtaposition the scattered parts of some brigade. I wish they had thought of the need of concentrating that brigade, when they located us a fortnight before, and so saving us seventy miles of marching.

The chief feeling we had in leaving Christiana consisted in the unpleasantness of relinquishing our new-built camp to the particular set which came. A party of them came in advance, and commenced service by the refusal of three officers (all the commissioned ones present) to march, when ordered, a few miles to relieve an outpost of ours, and so expedite our departure. It seemed very strange to us, as we had always been taught that orders were to be obeyed. The enlisted men seemed good material, although it seemed funny to hear their first sergeant, when orders were sent for them at reveille to "fall in," answer, 'Why, captain, the boys ain't *up* yet!" But with good officers, the men would, doubtless, make capital soldiers. There is no difference, that I see, between Eastern and Western men as to fighting qualities. The only distinction between different regiments in general, consists in the character of the officers, and, therefore, in the discipline. I do think that the *officers* of the Potomac army (embracing both Eastern and Western troops), were better taught than any others I have seen; I mean, as a whole. Not but that orders have been strict enough. We have a pile of old ones, and they are comprehensive and decided. But they remind one, in their repetitions, of the girl, who said her brother Jack wouldn't lie. "Jack won't lie," said she; "he's afraid to lie, for mother has scolded him fifty times for it."

In the recent affair, the Potomac men met their old Virginia foe, and showed what they could do. The Eleventh corps, which has had reflections cast upon it, acquitted itself nobly. Massachusetts blood flowed there, — in the Thirty-third. That Colonel Underwood, formerly a captain in the Second, was mortally wounded, his old comrades were pained to hear. He is too true a man, too excellent a soldier, to be spared. Glad were we to learn later, that hopes existed of his recovery. Passing by us since, he was as cheerful as ever.

Matters are conducted here rather different from the Virginia method, as to guerillas. They have a short shrift. For instance, a commander reported, a while ago, that he had met twenty guerillas; he had killed eight, and captured twelve; but, unfortunately, in bringing his prisoners into camp, they all fell off a log, and broke their necks. It is hardly to be wondered at that such accidents occur. Tennessee soldiers are men whose houses have been burned, their families abused, their relatives murdered in cold blood, a price set on their heads. It is no wonder they are implacable. Nor can one pity the murderous guerilla taken in the act.

There is really much Union feeling hereabouts. And some of it is very strong, though some is evidently merely from self-interest. There is a theory which will go with the winning side. But, at present, I hope that government will not *trust* them. The " radical " policy, I cannot help feeling, is the only one for Tennessee, and all the South. Precisely that feeling do the real sturdy Union men have. I have heard the strongest desires expressed that slavery be got rid of. Men speak of it as the cause of the whole trouble, and the future disease, if not now removed. Even repentant secessionists say the same thing. As for an *election* being held here — anywhere near us men could not go to the polls with the slightest security.

How gloriously Massachusetts has maintained itself in the recent election ! There was a little danger that the dominant party would not feel the necessity of a large vote ; but such fears are not realized. I have heard many a glad mention of the result, and not one expression to the contrary. It is astonishing how soon soldiers see where the wicked cause of the rebellion is. The army is abolitionized.

The result in Massachusetts is wonderful, in that, by *both* platforms, the State is *unanimous* for the prosecution of the war. The majority, however, is anti-slavery. Do you ever think how a man must feel, a few years hence, when liberty exists all over the land, to think that he had no part in the glorious work, or worse, that he sided with slavery? For myself, I look for the only true policy — that which declares slavery in *any* State is contrary to natural right, and therefore unlawful. Let us get rid of the wickedness everywhere. The time is coming, for the Lord reigneth.

As to this railway, — the line of road from Nashville to Bridgeport, is one hundred and twenty-three miles long. It is the only avenue of supplies. Its importance is readily seen. Distances in this country are enormous. I have been figuring up some of them, and sum up the results :

32 *

If from Chattanooga one could go to Charleston, he would travel four hundred and forty-six miles: to Savannah, four hundred and thirty-one.

The rebels from their capital are distant, by the old railway, six hundred and two; by a circuitous route, eight hundred and eighty-four. We from ours, sixteen hundred and sixty-two, or by the road, in rebel hands, six hundred and twenty-one.

In reënforcing our army from Virginia, we had twelve hundred and sixteen miles; the rebels from their position, five hundred and thirty-five miles, — of which, however, a part had to be made by marching, unless they preferred to go by railway, over a route of eight hundred and nineteen. At worst for them, their distance was but two thirds of ours.

If from Chattanooga one wished to go to Boston, he could choose one of several routes:

By way of the rebel roads, now badly obstructed, he would travel ten hundred and eighty-two miles, unless he stopped in Richmond.

By way of Indianapolis, Crestline line, and Buffalo, fifteen hundred and twenty-one miles.

By way of Indianapolis, Pittsburg, Harrisburg, Allentown, and New York, fifteen hundred and nine miles.

By way of Indianapolis, Pittsburg, and Philadelphia, fifteen hundred and twenty-one miles.

By way of Cincinnati, Pittsburg, and Philadelphia, fourteen hundred and ninety-two miles.

By way of Cincinnati, Pittsburg, and New York, fourteen hundred and eighty miles.

By way of Washington, sixteen hundred and twenty-three miles.

Any way, it is uncomfortably far from home! Home! But over the fifteen hundred miles the heart goes in an instant.

CHAPTER XV.

LIFE IN TENNESSEE.

ELK RIVER (ALISONA), TENN., November 27, 1863.

YESTER^AY was Thanksgiving Day. Nobody needs to be told how our hearts turned homeward. It was with no unworthy or unmanly motives that every one thought how pleasant it would be to enjoy the festival with families and friends.

Our day was beautiful. After a cold night, the sun rose beautifully lear, and soon melted away the frost. It was quite warm long before noon. We had, of course, our usual religious service at eleven o'clock — gathering beside the formid ble fortification which frowns from the top of the hill, and under the flag which there was wind enough to float. It was our "storm" flag, not our battle flag; *that* is guarded as tenderly as a saint's relics, and only used when, although t bear it is almost a sentence of death, it waves defiance to the enemy, and when each man of our color-guard springs to catch it from the hands of the dying. But the storm 'ag waved near us. We were but a handful. Three tim ^ have we celebrated Thanksgiving Day, and each since the first with rapidly diminishing numbers. The dead sleep on e^ ry battle-field.

The men played ball, of course. And they had their dinner. It was impossible, in preparing, to get any supplies from Nashville, because the capacity of the railway is tried severely to carry the necessaries of life. So a large party had been sent out, well armed, into the country to make provision. They were gone two days, and found, at a distance of some fifteen miles, plenty of geese, chickens, and the like, which the people were very ready to sell. It would seem queer to friends at home, in doing their Thanksgiving marketing, to have to go fifteen miles, and take fifty well armed men as a matter of safety.

I have "figured up" a little; and to show that there was enough to eat, report that the ratio of supply was this: to every hundred men, fourteen geese, four turkeys, and forty chickens; besides a few quails, a pig, and some plum puddings. And plenty of geese still quack, reserved for subsequent eating.

In the evening, the officers came together, inviting also the officers of the excellent Second Kentucky battery. Singing and social pleasantry made the hours pass rapidly. Some of our officers came back: they love the old homestead. And the brigade band, some of whose members used to belong to our old regimental band, came on foot for eight miles (they would have come by rail, but that no trains ran, and they waited till impatient), and discoursed most beautiful music.

———

ELK RIVER (ALISONA), TENN., November 27, 1863.

WHEN we first came down this railway, we saw at Wartrace a squad of colored men; we learned that they had just come in to enlist; and we found that parties came daily for that purpose. At Elk River we passed the camp of a whole regiment, the First Tennessee, and on our return we were camped just beside them. They were commanded by Colonel Thompson, an active, energetic son of Maine, recently on General Rosecrans's staff, and numbered about eight hundred. Their camp was clean and orderly. No regiment could be better behaved. We witnessed one dress parade; and, considering that they had been but few weeks in service, it was the decision of our men that it was excellent: and if the men of ours say so it *is* so.

They were doing considerable picket duty; and no men could be more faithful. There was a shiftless white regiment near, which would not associate with these blacks as soldiers. But those whites would sit down while on picket duty; no black was known to do such a thing. Keen, alert, and faithful —their main fault was an excess of care — as they would fire at everything that looked doubtful.

They were uneducated. Most could not read; so that a pass was of very little use. And they made havoc of names. Thus, when "Ticonderoga" was one day the countersign, the nearest that one of them got it was "Ticonsternation!" But who is responsible for this ignorance? What are the stories good for, that Southerners did teach their slaves to read, when hardly one out of eight hundred Alabama and Tennessee slaves knew a letter?

But they were faithful. They obeyed orders. They did their duty One day there were four men on picket together — all black — a corporal and three privates. Just enlisted these three, it happened, did not know how to load their pieces. Guerillas fired on them and killed one. The corporal and the other two stood to their places, and while the corporal loaded the pieces, the two privates stood and fired deliberately, each waiting his turn, and neither stirred·

until relieved by a party sent to the sound of the guns. I
doubt if white soldiers would show better pluck.

There was, really, a manliness about these black soldiers
which inspired respect. Make a soldier of a slave, and he
feels he is a man. Slavery restored would be a nice thing if
a hundred thousand of them had learned to use the musket!
Almost all these men were fugitives. They had been
oppressed. But the moment they became soldiers, they
seemed to change. They felt that they were in a holy cause.
Why not? If it was right for Moses to lead those slaves —
the children of Israel — out of Egypt, it is right for any
new instrument of God to lead these people out of their
accursed bondage. The Red Sea has parted. Woe to the
pursuers. Foolish and hardened, they do not see that the
walls are only of water. The roar of the returning waves is
already heard. Do the idiotic oppressors think they can
roll back the wrath of the Almighty?

I was informed, also, by a man whose face grew sternly
sad as he told me, that these men's backs are almost all
hideously scarred by the lash. The accounts of Southern
brutality were sickening. Of the deaths in that regiment,
almost every one, the surgeon said, was due to the past brutal treatment, which had broken their constitutions. Kind,
patriarchal system! A lovely system for Christian men to
say of, " We have nothing to do with it!" But, alas! for
our blindness.

I have read in a Tennessee paper — opposed to the administration of course — an advertisement of a woman whose
" servant had run away." She says he " calls himself a
preacher," and that he is of good manners, &c. ; and if anybody will put him into a certain " jail," she will pay a suitable " reward." Well, I call myself " a preacher," and I

feel for that preacher. Paul says *he* was "a preacher" also.
Paul was put in jail, too, as this woman wants to put this
man. This preacher is accused of no crime, but she wants
to put him in jail, nevertheless. The matter puzzled me.
Do they put preachers in jail down here. If so, it is unsafe
to venture out of camp. In thinking it over, I have come
to *this* conclusion : It is the duty of government to protect
all its citizens, and guarantee their safety from "jail," except
for crime. Every citizen has a right to demand this. This
man is a citizen, or, being native born, ought to be declared
so by act of Congress. Government ought to protect him
in his rights. It ought to punish anybody that puts him in
jail ; and ought to take him out of jail, if anybody puts him
in, " anything in the laws of any State to the contrary notwithstanding." That's my doctrine, square.

By the way, it is, perhaps, worth mentioning, that when
some prisoners, coming in (Longstreet's men), were jeered a
little, being asked, " How did you get caught ? " they replied,
" You had to get men from the army of the *Potomac* to do
it ; we should have walked over *you* easy enough." There
has been a great change in feeling towards the Potomac men
since that affair. At first they were called " fancy soldiers,"
because both men and officers had never been taught that it
was the sign of an especially good soldier to be remarkably
dirty and slovenly. But they are now seen to be as eminent
in valor as in everything else. The western army never had
such foes as they do now.

ELK RIVER, TENN., December 24, 1863.

WHO can help rejoicing at the President's proclamation?
It holds out the olive branch, but on terms that preserve our

principles. It makes no treaty with rebels, but demands unconditional submission. It retains justice, but tempers it with mercy. It restores forfeited privileges, but secures the public safety. It assumes that the rebel State governments are extinct, but it provides for new loyal ones. Above all, it demands submission on the very point of issue — slavery. Slavery must end — I wish I could say everywhere — in every rebel State. Thank God that the plain, honest, manly common sense of our President has taken this course. He stands by the proclamation ; and so does the army ; and so do the people. Of course copperheads will hiss. But who cares !

As to slavery in the excepted States, it is not worth disputing about. With constant enlistments from the slaves, with the independent feeling spread where the army goes, and with a resolute abolition party increasing, the case reminds one of a black who once had purchased *half* of himself. His boat overset one day, and he was with difficulty saved from drowning. Being asked what his thoughts were while in danger, he replied, " I thought what a fool I was to lay out my money on sich onsarten property as niggers ! "

And yet I wish, for the moral wholeness of the thing, that slavery could be declared outlawed *everywhere*. It is time to be done with the humbug that the general government cannot protect the inalienable rights of every person who lives under the stars and stripes.

But I believe, on the whole, in " compensated emancipation." The masters have robbed and abused the slaves for a great many years. It is not fair to turn these blacks out into the world without paying them for past labor. Besides, if, as the masters say, the blacks cannot take care of themselves, the freedmen will need their wages, now long overdue. Therefore. compensate them for their past labor.

CHATTANOOGA, TENN., January 5, 1864.

How I happened to go to Chattanooga was on this wise : One day there came into camp the Rev. Thomas B. Fox, whom Governor Andrew had sent as a special agent to see Massachusetts regiments and Massachusetts soldiers in hospital, in this division. Governor Andrew is always send- ing agents, or writing letters, or making speeches, or coaxing officials, for the benefit of our soldiers. The soldiers will always remember their large-hearted governor. So Mr. Fox was sent, and he came to our regiment. His visit did us good. If the governor is as wise in all his selections, he is a wise governor. The visit occurred at a time of particular interest. The plan of reënlistment was before us. Mr. Fox helped it on finely. Apart from this, his address, conveying to us the assurance of the interest felt at home — was, for beauty, completeness, and heartiness, never surpassed by anything I ever heard.

Many men have reënlisted. In writing before, I had not faith enough. As it is, the bounties utterly failed of any effect on the men who enlisted on eleven dollars a month and no bounty. The only effective appeal proved to be that which led them to say, " We can't leave that old flag to strangers."

The agent kindly asked me to accompany him to Chat- tanooga, and addressed a request to that effect to our corps commander, which was agreed to. I had to apply, myself, for the formal pass ; let me tell you just how much formality was requisite in getting it.

First, you write out an application, and you place it in the hands of the adjutant, who is the colonel's prime minister. The colonel signs his approval. You want to take the paper

33

yourself to higher quarters, instead of waiting for the slow routine. So the colonel signs a special permission for you to do so. The higher quarters are at Tullahoma, and to get there, the adjutant furnishes you, by the colonel's direction, with a written document to that effect; and for transportation, the quartermaster gives you another paper, also by the colonel's order. And thus you are empowered to go seven miles!

At the railway you catch a train. The military conductor examines your military pass, and keeps it when used. The civilian conductor takes your transportation paper. You get to Tullahoma, and go to brigade headquarters, and, if you are as fortunate as I was, find our good Brigadier-General Ruger, just ready for breakfast, and he invites you to breakfast (not officially, you know, but friendly), and you get a capital breakfast. You don't hint anything about business at meal time; it "isn't the thing, you know." But after breakfast you give your application to the general's assistant adjutant-general, with your written permission to come yourself; and he asks the general, and the general signs it, and the clerk makes a minute of it, and the A. A. G. gives you a written permission to take it to the general of division. You go there and hand over both papers, and the A. A. G. gets the approval, and his clerk records it, and the A. A. G. gives you a new written permission to take it to corps headquarters. There the A. A. G. goes through similar processes, — clerk and all, — and you get a new document empowering you to go as you asked. And our gallant major-general drops into the office and has a friendly chat — perhaps. Then you go to the post quartermaster's, to get a transportation paper; he is gone to Nashville, and his clerk is gone to dinner; but when he comes back you have to go to the colonel commanding the post, and he approves (after seeing your last paper), and you go back and the clerk writes out the transportation pass, and you hurry to the cars while it is raining furiously. That is, that was my experience.

Is all this routine really needful? Yes. If I had room to explain it you would be satisfied that to omit any step would put things into a "muddle." Nevertheless it is a bore. Try it some day, when you want to take a little trip.

We tried to go on Tuesday, December 29, but the train did not stop ; but we succeeded on Wednesday. The train stops at Decherd for dinner. If anybody invites you to do so, don't you do it. Be warned in time. On the train, the civilian conductor examines your transportation paper, and the military one your military pass. The civil was not military, but the military man was civil. Nevertheless, he insisted on keeping my pass, because, he argued, that it was not good as far as Stevenson, on the ground that it covered ten miles beyond? I afterwards recovered it, however, by arguments effective and honest, but potent. Mr. Fox had no trouble, for he was loaded with all manner of authority from General Grant and a crowd of others.

It was after dark when Stevenson was reached, and it was raining. No passenger car runs further, and one hunts around until he guesses which baggage car (not of the train just arrived) is likely to go. We luckily discovered, at the last moment, the right car. Ten miles on is Bridgeport — a town without a house in it. Darkness, rain, and mud were uncomfortable to total ˙ strangers. But we found the SANITARY COMMISSION, God bless it. It was in tents. But what a change ! Out of the cold and driving storm into warm quarters, with a cup of excellent tea speedily made for the writer's racking headache — excellent blankets to sleep

in, on a hay stuffed bed, and with good Dr. Coates as the
presiding genius. And other travellers, and suffering soldiers
— all taken care of — fed, clothed, wounds dressed, beds
furnished at the Home. I tell you, people at the North,
pile up your supplies, give your money, strengthen the Commission every way. That Commission *saves life.*

From Bridgeport to Chattanooga, as yet, we go by boat
— the boat was " in " the next morning, but it came late in
the afternoon. It would leave in *three* hours. Transportation papers must be had ; and at the office, far away from
the boat, they said it would leave in *five* hours. We go with
others to the boat ; now it will leave in the night *some time.*
The Sanitary has a Home there (not the headquarters), and
we go in to wait. Before midnight we find the boat will go
in the *morning.* In the various tents of the Commission are
two hundred and fifty sheltered. The night becomes savagely
cold. It is *impossible* to keep warm or sleep. In our tent
are men, women, and children — white refugees from
Southern tyranny, included. For the fun of the thing, I
went to chopping wood at half past two A. M., with the ther-
mometer down out of sight of freezing. But in the group
was a pretty little girl of two years, with parents escaping
with only life from their burning house, fired by Southern
brutality.

In the morning the boat will leave at eleven. So we walk
back to Sanitary headquarters. It was a bitterly cold day.
There is a crowd. Here a soldier to go North, his arm is
dressed, he is fed ; thinly clothed — a warm woollen sack is
buttoned on him, and the armless sleeve pinned over, and he
goes off happy. Another is on crutches, his wound is cared
for, he is supplied as the other, and is helped to the cars.
Here, a lone woman, all the way from New Jersey, to find

her sick husband — mild, patient, grateful, careless of fatigue, with miles yet to go, and she is sheltered, fed, and directed; a good woman, she says she has "found only Christian people all the way." A mother, who has come to see her wounded son, an officer. Alas! his corpse has passed her on the road, and she is to return. And so with the multitude. But perhaps as near to the heart as anybody — a little girl of five years, who, with others, had sat in baggage cars all the cold night (in which time three soldiers had perished of cold), the managers had carelessly unfastened that car, and left it. The little girl, half frozen and crying, had come up with the others to the Sanitary. And now, warmed and fed, the child was happy, and I showed her the picture of another little girl, and we were friends, and when she left they wrapped warm things around her, and pulled socks over her shoes, and a strong helper carried her in his arms to the train. The Sanitary cared for the little girl; it was somebody's child; and so for the love of a blue-eyed girl at home, I owe just as much debt as anybody, and say again, God bless the Sanitary!

On the boat. It is to leave at twelve. To leave at two. To leave at five. It *did* leave at *seven*. It was the Paint-Rock, — a floor, with a funny old two-story barn on it, and a wheezy tea-kettle arrangement for running it. The weather was horribly cold. The "cabin" was a canvas box on top of the aforesaid barn. A few inches of it was warmed by an ancient cooking-stove, one door of which had departed. It is sixty-two miles to Chattanooga by river, it is twenty-eight by rail.

As to scenery, I remember that the rushing river looked like quicksilver as we entered the boat. The night was too cold for peeping out again till morning, and then only to see that men were cutting the ice off the stern wheel, and that huge icicles fringed the cliffs which bordered the river. Within, one could study human nature. Decency required that persons should give way to others in turn near the stove. Many did, some did not. I was interested in studying one man. He had a warm corner, and there he staid. He was a major of infantry, by his dress, — dressed showily, — with very dark eyes, and black mustache, etc., in regular dress uniform, felt hat and braid cord, and dark blue trowsers. He would have looked handsome, but for his insufferable hoggishness. Hints and open requests were useless; but his hours of sitting ended, I think, by his getting into the captain's room; anyhow, he disappeared till morning. He came to Chattanooga. I don't know his regiment. I wish I did. However, if anybody knows a major (not the one of the Tenth Kentucky) who was on the Paint-Rock on its trip to Chattanooga, January 1–2, 1864, he will inform that major that, in the unanimous opinion of the passengers, he is the most despicable hog that injures the reputation of that comparatively respectable animal.

On the boat were some delegates of the Christian Commission. They had some private stores of food; but they, in the dearth, shared with all. They made tea, they furnished bread. They did all the good possible. The passengers became their warm friends, from the conduct of these delegates, which was truly Christian. I was glad to meet Rev. Calvin Holman, of New Hampshire, and it was pleasant to pass much of the night together in common topics. The Commission opened its doors here to shelter to its utmost capacity; and there the soldier's wife found friends to help her to her husband.

Pulled up the rapids by ropes, or worked up by steam far

higher than the government allowance of pressure ; sighting bold Lookout, the scene of gallant combat, around its base — and so, about nine P. M., we reached Chattanooga. Hospitable doors are open, and friends are found.

I intended, at Chattanooga, to write out notes on several matters there. They were about Lookout Mountain and Mission Ridge ; the Sanitary Commission, and Dr. Reed in charge ; the Christian Commission, and Mr. Lawrence in charge ; the chaplain's meeting ; the National Cemetery, already planned, and the Mortuary Record ; the recruiting office for colored troops, under Mr. John A. Spooner, of Old Plymouth ; and Sergeant Johnny Clem, the youngest soldier in the army, being twelve years of age. The world will never know what it has lost, which is my chief consolation in so distressing a trial as that of consigning one's pages to the fireplace. But I will save one section. It is concerning Sergeant Johnny Clem.

Johnny is a boy of twelve, and was born in Newark, Ohio. He measures four feet and one inch in height. He has a frank, pleasant, firm face, with light eyes and hair. He dresses neatly, sports his sergeant's chevrons and a pistol. Johnny has been in service, off and on, for two years. At present he belongs to the Twenty-second Michigan, in which he enlisted as drummer. At the battle of Chickamauga he was a marker ; and there he showed courage. I met an account of that affair of his some time since ; but I thought it worth while to get his own statement. Here it is in his own exact language : —

" We were making a charge. As I was rallying, the rebel colonel rode up to me, and said, ' Halt, surrender, you [swearing] – – – '. I had my gun at right shoulder shift. I fetched it to a shoulder, and just at that he struck at me with

his sword, and I knocked off his guard, and cocked my
piece (which I could easily do, being so short, without his
noticing my cocking it) ; fetched it to a charge bayonet. He
rode right up in front of my gun, and was just going to
knock it out of the way and cut my head off; and just at that
I pulled it off, and the bullet went right through his breast."

So Sergeant Johnny got his promotion. He had, when I
saw him, his " descriptive list" with him — being just on
his way back as a returned prisoner from Wheeler's raid.
Johnny is really a manly looking little fellow ; is self-pos-
sessed, but modest ; talks freely, but not about his affair
unless others ask him. It is a wonder he has not been
spoiled, but no trace of such a result appears. He used to
drink whiskey and swear, but he has been taught better, he
says.

Some few items regarding the condition of rebeldom I
think worth recording.

The destitutions which are said to prevail, undoubtedly do
exist in some sections. For instance, the large tracts of
country which lie near, but outside our lines, are filled with
suffering people. These people are in a particularly unfortunate position, because really enjoying no advantage which
those have who belong somewhere definite. Their means of
support are in a great measure cut off. The men are to a
very great extent in the rebel army, having either gone voluntarily or been forced there by conscription. The farms
are ravaged by roving bands of guerillas, who are nearly as
terrible to friend as foe. What crops have been gathered
are apt to be seized for public service, excepting enough for
bare subsistence. South of Duck River, Tennessee (some
forty miles, I believe, south of Nashville), no trade is allowed.
The army itself cannot sell provisions, nor is any method

adopted of issuing food. There is an exception to this effect : that, as owners of slaves are obliged to furnish a certain amount of cut wood for railway purposes, those men can receive a certain allowance of provisions ; and all others, indeed, to whom the railway gives employment. Then there are some families which have managed to secure " protections," and are in near neighborhood to our posts. Close by our last camp were two women, whose husbands were in the rebel army, as officers, I believe, who had a "safeguard" from general Rosecrans. Why it was given to the property of these rank rebels I do not know, but it was, of course, religiously observed. These women used to charge us twenty cents a quart for the meanest milk I ever saw, while one of them was carried through a fever gratuitously by our good surgeon, medicines included in the gratuity. Another family used to bake bread (of our flour) for us, at the reasonable rate of five or six times the value of the article.

But many families have no such resource. Some of our men, while out on duty one day, found a family whose *sole* support for seven days had been corn meal purchased by a single dollar given by a soldier, for a family of father (a cripple), mother, and five children. For two or three days more our men shared their hard bread with them. Utterly helpless as they were, our colonel saw they did not suffer, until they could be brought in and sent northward. Before we left, one train (a sample) was loaded to its utmost with families of this starving population, who were being taken where they could be fed. It was, of course, out of the question to take supplies to such, over a road severely taxed to feed our armies. Thus it is that our government feeds the suffering, while many are the wives and children of rebels. But even such must not be left to starve. Christian charity forbids.

I was much interested in the families I casually met. They were refugees. A husband and wife, and a husband, wife, and sweet little child. The men had been in the rebel army. They had joined it not willingly, but yielding to a necessity. One had been a druggist, and was a man of few words but of fair intelligence. The other, I think, a farmer. Both men had escaped from the army in Longstreet's movement on Knoxville. They had got back to their homes, in the north part of Georgia, and had hid in the woods. I asked them if their friends did not know of their being there. "Yes," they said, " but we had no fear, except from two families Nobody else would betray us." They said that all others there were Union in feeling. Rebels had hunted for them in vain. Though in danger, they would not leave without their families ; and, at last, when these families had had their houses burned, and the women left shelterless, they made a determined effort, and succeeded in escaping. The little clothing they had was all they could save. But they were happy to be within our lines, and on their way North. They intended to go to Ohio, and endeavor to earn a living.

I asked them if the President's proclamation of amnesty had been circulated. They said it had, to some extent, and was fast spreading. Its effect, they said, was good. "We have always been told," said the elder, " that our property would be all taken away ; and, indeed, some acts at Washington made us think so. But now we know we can save our property, most everybody wants to submit."

" But you have abandoned your property."

" Yes, but the *land* we own is there. They can't move that ; and when the war is over, we can get its value."

" But," said I, " you cannot keep your slaves under this proclamation."

The wife of one, an intelligent and pleasant woman, instantly answered, " *We* have no slaves, nor do most of the people ; and so it is nothing to us. Let the men who own the slaves, and got up the war on that account, lose them. They ought to."

" Is that a widespread feeling? "

" Yes. There are but a few hundred thousand slaveholders, and we began to think that they used us to keep their power."

I cannot, of course, tell how much such feelings have spread. But they do evidently have considerable sway. Very large numbers of refugees have come into our lines, and all tell the same story.

Among other facts, one of these men told me that he had to pay for the ordinary felt hat he wore, two hundred and fifty dollars in confederate money. He had had considerable, but gave it all away to friends, as of no further use to him. A lawyer whom I knew, who was taken prisoner at Chickamauga, and sent to Richmond, had to pay (and it was only the usual price), eighteen dollars for having his boots half-soled ; and each half sole was made of three pieces of leather ; this was in confederate money ; in greenbacks, it would have been only a fraction of that.

The number of deserters coming in is quite large. All agree that the woods and hills are full of such. All said that rebel soldiers were constantly searching for them ; and so closely that, after making a little fire, they always moved away quickly to another spot.

My own impressions were that these accounts were true. And hence I am inclined to give credence to the other accounts we receive. But I think that the sufferings are only local, not universal. There must be much difficulty in obtaining the necessaries of life, merely on account of high prices — where wages are fixed as those of soldiers are, and yet whose families must be sustained.

But it is not likely that any such want is universal. Doubtless many persons have made fortunes in the South out of the war. They sell high for confederate money, it is true, but confederate money will buy lands there. Very large sections in the South are still cultivated by slaves, which enables the whites to fill up the armies. There is no reason in imagining we are to reduce the revolted territory to obedience, by their necessities, because such a land is not to be starved out. A military despotism, too, stifles the cries of the actual sufferers. We must fight it out.

Nor is it good judgment to suppose that the rebel armies are to crumble by desertions. Doubtless, the bulk of their soldiery is under strict discipline, and will remain in arms until the leaders are overthrown. We must not calculate on anything but overpowering force on our part. If we depend on anything else, we shall wake to the delusion in terrible disasters. If they are weaker, now is the time to overwhelm them with armies it would be madness to resist.

Just now everything indicates that the rebel leaders are preparing for a desperate spring campaign. They are putting every available man into the ranks. They are straining every nerve to equip their forces. That they will make a tremendous effort, is clear. If they succeed in that effort, they will protract the war. If they fail, we may safely believe that the disintegrating causes at work will speedily end the strife. Shall they fail? At the South, *every* man possible is made a soldier. Their farms, their cities, are almost bare of men. Here. I cannot tell, from the crowded streets of Boston, that a single man has gone. It rests with the people to say whether this war shall virtually end the next campaign. Do not leave the old soldiers alone. Join them, young men, and take to yourselves part of the crowning glory.

It took much less time to get from Chattanooga to camp, than from camp to Chattanooga. For, the sixty-two miles of river was down stream; and a boat kept in the current would slide down faster than steam could push it up. Six hours brought us to Bridgeport. The train which runs to Stevenson we discovered after a long search. There is no station house, and the train starts from anywhere in a range of two miles, and any time in a range of three hours. It was ten miles to Stevenson, and the train worked hard to get there. I saw it come in at last — having concluded with a few others to leave the train, after three hours of terribly cold travelling in freight cars unwarmed, and walk to Stevenson. It was occasionally doubtful which would beat; but eventually we came in a few lengths ahead of the train, at twenty-five minutes past one o'clock A. M. No station house there; but we found two passenger cars locked up, from whose windows streamed a bright light. A colonel in our party kicked the door in, and we found seats and snoring sleepers. If the government could afford at Stevenson a warm room, or even any room in which wounded, or even well soldiers, could find shelter prior to the departure of a train (which is at three A. M.), it would lessen the amount of profanity cold winter nights. Profanity is wicked; but the officials deserve the curses. At eight A. M. I was eating breakfast in our own camp.

I left Chattanooga suddenly, on learning that the official sanction was ready for our return HOME. I could not risk losing one of the most supreme pleasures of which I could

34

conceive. To go home with the regiment which had earned for itself an imperishable record, — it was a day of a lifetime.

To return with two hundred men, toughened by near three years of hardships, trained by the hardest battle fields, purchased by the best blood of Massachusetts ; —

To show the OLD FLAG, never carried but in battle, riddled by bullets, often falling from the stiffening hand, but never to the earth, always making the men about it invincible ; —

To see the tearful faces of friends, brave friends, brave mothers, remembering heroically the dead children, who went with us when the war was young ; —

To be welcomed as those who have done their duty ; for of our dead, none died but as heroes die ; —

And then, when the few days of furlough end, to rejoin the armies of the Union, and witness the final glory of the FLAG !

INDEX.

(399)

Heath, Alice, her gift to the soldiers, 266.
Heath, Surgeon, 303, 367.
Hedgeman's River, 179.
Heintzelman, Gen., 108.
Hicks, Camp, 62, 69.
Hillsborough, 250.
Hoag, J., 334.
Holman, Rev. Calvin, 390.
Hooker, Gen., drives enemy from Manassas Junction, 200; at South Mountain, 214; at Antietam, 218, 219; commands Army of the Potomac, 272; qualities as commander, 281; masterly movement from Falmouth to Gettysburg, 327.
Hovey, W. A., 334.
Howard, Gen., 288.
Howe, Col. Frank, 325.
Hyattstown, 56.
Ijamsville, 211.
Indianapolis, 362.
Jackson, Stonewall, at battle of Kernstown, 115; campaigns with Gen. Pope, 195–209; his lack of fighting qualities, 230; beaten by Gen. Lander, 230; his death, 304; resumé of his operations, 305.
Jamaica Plain, gift of books from, 266.
Jefferson, 329.
Jeffersonville, 362.
Johnson, J. Warner, 334.
Johnson, Gen. Andrew, addresses a crowd at Nashville, 369.
Johnston, Gen., his campaign with Patterson, 15–19.
Keedysville, Md., 216.

Kelly's Ford, 297, 321.
Kendall, Surgeon, killed at Antietam, 220.
Kenly, Col., guards Front Royal, 151; routed, 151.
Kernstown, battle of, 115.
Kettle Run, 343.
Kimball, Col., at battle of Kernstown, 116.
Kimball, Brig. Gen., drives Stonewall Jackson, 230.
King, Dr., medical director in Gen. Reynolds's corps, brutal actions of, 221.
Kingwood Tunnel, 359.
Lacy Mansion, the, 291.
Lander, Gen., skirmish by, 91; foils Stonewall Jackson, 230.
Lasher, Chaplain, 27.
Lawrence, Rev. Mr., agent of Christian Commission, 363.
Lee, Col. W. R., at Ball's Bluff, 39.
Lee, Gen., at Manassas, 231.
Leesburg, 38, 51, 251.
Leland, Surgeon, in charge of hospital at Winchester, 160.
Lewis, Dr. Dio, his gymnasium, 288.
Little Washington, Va., 179.
Littleston, 329.
Lookout Mountain, 370.
Loring, Harrison, steamboat builder, 323, 340.
Loudon Heights, 249.
Luray, 181.
Mansfield, Gen., commands in place of Gen. Banks, 215; at Antietam, 217.
Martinsburg, 76, 155.
Masanutten Range, 159.

www.ingramcontent.com/pod-product-compliance
Lightning Source LLC
Chambersburg PA
CBHW031350290326
41932CB00044B/866